One-Hit Wonders of Texas High School Football

SWAIM-PAUP SPORTS SERIES

Sponsored by James C. '74 & Debra Parchman Swaim and T. Edgar '74 & Nancy Paup

One-Hit Wonders
of Texas High School Football

ROBERT D. JACOBUS

TEXAS A&M UNIVERSITY PRESS
College Station

First edition

This paper meets the requirements of ANSI/NISO Z39.48-1992 (Permanence of Paper). Binding materials have been chosen for durability.
Manufactured in the United States of America.

LIBRARY OF CONGRESS CATALOGING-IN-PUBLICATION DATA

Names: Jacobus, Robert author
Title: One-hit wonders of Texas high school football / Robert D. Jacobus.
Other titles: Swaim-Paup sports series
Description: First edition. | College Station: Texas A&M University Press, [2026] | Series: Swaim-Paup sports series, sponsored by James C. '74 & Debra Parchman Swaim and T. Edgar '74 & Nancy Paup | Includes bibliographical references and index.
Identifiers: LCCN 2026006674 (print) | LCCN 2026006675 (ebook) | ISBN 9781648434044 paperback | ISBN 9781648434051 ebook
Subjects: LCSH: Football—Texas—History | School sports—Texas—History | High school athletes—Texas | Football teams—Texas
Classification: LCC GV959.52.T4 J335 2026 (print) | LCC GV959.52.T4 (ebook)
LC record available at https://lccn.loc.gov/2026006674
LC ebook record available at https://lccn.loc.gov/2026006675

Published by Texas A&M University Press
John H. Lindsey Building, Lewis Street
College Station, TX 77843
www.tamupress.com

This book complies with the EU General Product Safety Regulation (GPSR) (Regulation (EU) 2023/988). For regulatory inquiries and product safety matters within the EU, contact our authorized representative:
Mare Nostrum Group B.V.
Doelen 72
4831 GR Breda
The Netherlands
Email: gpsr@mare-nostrum.co.uk Website: https://mngbookshop.co.uk/

This publication has undergone a risk assessment and meets applicable safety standards. Traceability identifiers: ISBN, batch number, and publisher contact details are provided for compliance. No hazardous materials or components are included in this product.

In memory of my mentor and friend,

University of Houston History Professor Emeritus

Dr. James Kirby Martin

and

my wife, Eva, for her unwavering support

Contents

Preface ix

KINGSVILLE:
The Brahmas' Historic Run to the 1958 State 3A Finals 1

ARCHER CITY:
The McMurtry-esque Saga of the 1964 Class A Champion Wildcats 18

DEL VALLE AND KOUNTZE:
Underdog Versus Underdog in an Unlikely Playoff Showdown, 1967 37

RULE:
The Triumph and Tragedy of the 13–1 Class B State Runner-Up Bobcats, 1973 59

FABENS:
The Pride of El Paso, 1979 2A Quarterfinalist Wildcats 78

BEAUMONT:
Steve Shaver Leads the Underdog 1984 French Buffs to the 5A State Co-Championship 96

LADONIA:
The Friday Night Lights of the 1988 Class A Semifinalist Fannindel Falcons 117

CONTENTS

GROESBECK:
The 1991 Goats Grasp the 3A State Championship 136

ROCKPORT-FULTON:
Coach Autry's Texas Football Debut and the 2000 4A Pirates 156

FORT WORTH:
"The Most Unlikely State Champions in Texas History"—
The 2003 4A Division I North Crowley Panthers 176

Sources 197
Index 201

Preface

WHEN I MOVED IN 1972 as an almost fifteen-year-old from Minnesota to Texas, I went from one sport-crazed state to another. In Minnesota, high school hockey was and is still king, with the state tournament being broadcast statewide and even tiny northern Minnesota mining towns having their own plush indoor rinks for their local heroes' games. When I arrived in Texas, I quickly discovered that high school football is equal to and, in many cases, surpasses hockey in Minnesota as a religion, with plush football stadiums taking the place of hockey rinks.

Minnesota has had its share of hockey dynasties through the years. Northern Minnesota Iron Range towns like the Roseau Rams and Warroad Warriors, and Eveleth Golden Bears dominated the early years of high school hockey in the state and won twenty of the first twenty-four state titles. From the 1940s to the 1960s, what would have been my high school if I hadn't moved, the St. Paul Johnson High School Governors (alma mater of Herb Brooks, gold medal–winning coach of the Miracle on Ice in the 1980 Olympics) won four state titles and had thirteen other trips to the state tournament. Later, suburban teams of the Twin Cities of Minneapolis and St. Paul began to dominate, teams like the Edina East Hornets, with thirteen state titles since 1969, and the Bloomington Jefferson Jaguars capturing five titles between 1981 and 1994.

Like Minnesota with high school hockey, when fans reminisce about the history of high school football in the state of Texas, they usually think of the dominant programs through the years, starting with Coach Paul Tyson's Waco Lions in the 1920s, Joe Golden's Wichita Falls teams from the late 1940s to the early 1960s, Gordon Wood's Brownwood squads capturing seven state titles between 1960 and 1981, and the rise of Odessa Permian and MOJO from 1965 to 1991, which was chronicled in the book-turned-movie *Friday Night Lights*. Younger fans might identify with the more recent dynasties at Katy, Southlake Carroll, and North Shore High Schools.

Sometimes, however, in Minnesota and Texas, an underdog team would find playoff glory. With the Minnesota state hockey tournament, the most notable example was when Rochester John Marshall High School in 1977 won southern Minnesota's only state title by upsetting heavily favored Edina East 4–2 in the final.

As far as Texas high school football, there are several examples of teams—both large and small, from all corners of the state—that had that one special season, where lightning struck for one glorious fall, never to be approached or matched in the program's history. That is where this book comes in.

The idea for *One-Hit Wonders of Texas High School Football* came from a newspaper story I wrote for the *Tyler County Booster* in 2018 as part of their football preview issue. I wrote about the four high schools in Tyler County—Warren, Woodville, Chester, and Colmesneil—that play football and their lack of success through the years. For each of these schools, however, they had one special season in their respective school's history that stood out from all the others. For the article, I re-created each school's banner season by looking through old newspaper articles and yearbooks, plus interviewing players from those teams.

After completing the article, I started thinking about how many schools statewide had a similar story: a history of bad-to-mediocre football, then one memorable season, and then back to football obscurity. I once again scoured newspaper articles and yearbooks and in addition interviewed players, coaches, and fans from the respective schools. Another tremendous help was a website created and maintained by Joe Lee Smith called Texas High School Football History. For over fifty years, Smith has been compiling individual players, coaches, and school records for each high school through the years. The website was invaluable as I searched for schools that had that one banner season.

After much research, I narrowed the list of one-hit-wonder teams to about thirty-five. The thirty-five teams were whittled down to about fifteen to twenty schools and from there down to the eleven that are profiled in the book. The schools that made it into the book had to do with availability of game scores and write-ups from newspapers, access to former players and coaches and the quality of their interviews, and schools where I thought their story was compelling. Some schools that barely missed the cut were 1964 Vidor, 1967 Houston Bellaire, 1968 Sheridan, 1983 Morton, and 1990 Kingwood, among others.

Readers are invited to witness the rise and fall of eleven Cinderella teams, beginning with the Class 3A Kingsville Brahmas in 1958. The teams profiled vary in size, from what was before 1980 Class B, all the way up to Class 5A. Readers will take a tour through the Lone Star high school grandstands, all across Texas, visiting two teams each from West Texas, Southeast Texas, Central Texas, and the Coastal Bend, and one each from the Dallas–Fort Worth metroplex, East Texas, and North Texas. Our journey ends with the 2003 North Crowley Panthers, who up until that year had never claimed any title in their school's short history but captured the Class 4A Division I state championship despite a 0–3 start to their season.

This book mainly focuses on teams from the late 1950s to the early 2000s—a time when the playoffs showcased only the best of the best. Through 1981, only district champions advanced to the postseason in Texas, so the road to a state title was far more treacherous, with only elite teams making the cut. Starting in 1982, district second-place teams also advanced to the playoffs, which effectively doubled the number of teams in the postseason contest. Although some might argue that this effectively watered down the playoffs, the trade-off was that there were now some worthy schools that could still qualify for the postseason despite having stumbled a bit during the regular season. In fact, three teams documented in the book—1984 Beaumont French, 1991 Groesbeck, and 2003 North Crowley—won state titles as the runner-up teams in their respective districts.

Eventually, Class 5A went to three playoff teams per district in 1990, followed by the other classifications in 1996. The push for four playoff teams per district and dividing each classification into two divisions went into effect in Class 5A in 2007, Class 4A in 2008, and other classifications in 2013, which some say further watered down the playoffs. Times had changed, and the prospect of winning at least a couple of postseason games or going three to four rounds deep in the playoffs became more accessible than ever before. Because of this shift, no teams after North Crowley in 2003 are profiled in this book—since, in this new era, it is easier to qualify for the playoffs and advance several rounds without being challenged. *One-Hit Wonders of Texas High School Football* offers readers a glimpse into a time when postseason wins meant more, took more, and for these teams, changed everything.

What did these teams that were selected for the book have in common? Mostly, it was a new coaching regime that arrived at a school. Most took a few seasons for their program culture to take effect. In addition, there was usually a group of good athletes that coincided with the coaching change. For some of the schools, integration was a key factor for three of the teams covered: 1958 Kingsville and the 1967 duo of Del Valle and Kountze.

The exception to all the commonalities was North Crowley High School in 2003, the last school profiled in the book. They basically had the same players and coaches that had won just nine games the previous three seasons. In total, North Crowley had won just thirteen games and lost thirty-seven in the five years since it opened in 1998. The Panthers literally came out of nowhere to win a state 4A (now 5A) title.

The expectation of *One-Hit Wonders of Texas High School Football* is that readers will learn all about the scores and statistics that paved these teams' respective roads to victory, then go beyond to witness the drama, intensity, and human story behind the scrimmage line—both on and off the field. Players, coaches, fans, administrators, and more offer readers their first-hand accounts of games, plays, and key moments of these one-hit wonders' special seasons in candid detail. Readers can go inside the minds and learn about the lives of the coaches who inspired great plays and upped the ante via the book's in-depth profiles of these key individuals.

Finally, it is hopeful that these eleven underdog schools that are profiled in *One-Hit Wonders of Texas High School Football* will be remembered alongside the high school football dynasties in the prolific history of football in the Lone Star State.

One-Hit Wonders of Texas High School Football

Kingsville

The Brahmas' Historic Run to the 1958 State 3A Finals

KINGSVILLE, TEXAS, just over forty miles southwest of Corpus Christi on US Highway 77, was and is home to the famed King Ranch (the largest in Texas, surpassing a million acres) and Texas A&M University–Kingsville (formerly Texas A&I), home of the Javelinas. The Javelinas boast an impressive record as a seven-time National Association of Intercollegiate Athletics (NAIA) national champion football team. But historically, the town's high school team, the Richard King High School Brahmas, were not nearly as famous for their prowess on the gridiron.

That all changed in 1958. The Brahmas ran off a 12–2 record and reached the Class 3A state finals, which back in 1958 was the second largest classification of schools in Texas. In addition, that year the Kingsville underdogs became the southernmost team in Texas school-league history to reach the championship game.

Prior to 1951, football for the Kingsville high school had been an exercise in mediocrity. At that point, they had compiled a pedestrian 124–121–19 overall record since they started playing football in 1909. The Brahmas won only one district title during that forty-year span, in 1929, and promptly lost in the first round of the playoffs to Harlingen High School, 19–2. The following year, in 1930, Kingsville had lost 7–6 to Beeville in the game that decided the district title, but the Kingsville team still qualified for the playoffs when it was discovered that Beeville had used an ineligible player. Kingsville proceeded to lose their opening-round playoff game to Harlingen again, this time by a count of 61–0.

After 1930, more unexceptional football followed until the Brahmas' fortune started turning in 1951, when they hired Russ Holland as their head coach. Holland started his high school coaching career as an assistant at Brady High School in Central Texas, rising to head coach from 1938 to 1942. A civil service stint in World War II followed, and he returned to Brady and coached there from 1945 to 1950. In addition, Holland was also

Kingsville head coach Russ Holland. Courtesy of Kingsville Independent School District

an excellent track coach, as his teams won several Class A state titles during his time at Brady. In the spring of 1951, the Brady school board tried to end his contract, but they had to renege when more than fifty parents, players, and fans showed up to complain. Brady tried to hire Holland back, but he already had his sights set on Kingsville. He went on to compile an impressive 43–25–2 record with the Brahmas from 1951 to 1957, his first seven seasons as coach, but had no playoff appearances to show for it.

Several players on the 1958 Kingsville team reminisced on the high-quality character of Coach Holland and his staff. Doug Harvey was the fullback in Kingsville's single wing offense during their 1958 playoff run. According to the *Corsicana Daily Sun*, he was known as Kingsville's "bread and butter man." With a promising career ahead of him, he went on to play at Rice and later transferred to Texas A&I. Harvey was inducted into the Javelina Hall of Fame in 1978. He recalled, "Coach Holland had a great staff. He was kind of quiet. He meant business, though. He expected a lot from you and he got it. Coach Jay, his main assistant, was kind of like Coach Holland. Coach Richards and Coach Smith, a couple of the other assistants, were both Texas A&I guys. Coach Holland's hatchet man was Coach Spinks. He was much more intense than the other coaches. I think he went to Sam Houston State. Overall, we had really good coaches, plus some really good players. It led to a memorable season."

Kingsville defensive tackle Jack Burchers said, "Coach Holland was very quiet, very low key. Coaches Jay, Richards, Smith, they were kind of like Coach Holland. The other assistant coach, Coach Spinks, now, he could get a little excited. In addition to the coaches, though, we had great leaders on the team. Doug Harvey was *the* leader of the team. Heck, he even used to like to go out to practice every day. We had other leaders too: Preacher, Ronnie Johnson, Dean Bass. It was a great time."

Fred Hobrecht was a sophomore reserve end on the Kingsville squad, who only got into games "if we were way ahead." "Coach Holland was easy, really smooth," Hobrecht recalled. "He was very laid-back. He didn't do any jumping up and down and hollering. He did make it very clear as to what he expected, though. Coach Donald Jay, his main assistant, was a lot like him. Now, Coach Spinks, one of the other assistants, he was much more excitable and fiery."

Russ Holland and his coaching staff certainly added to the 1958 Brahmas' formula for success. Another crucial component that facilitated the team's rise was integration. The 1954 *Brown v. Board of Education* decision handed down by the US Supreme Court ended segregation in public schools. The Coastal Bend area of Texas, which the Brahmas called home, was one of the first regions in Texas and the southern United States to integrate. In District 15–3A, Kingsville was not alone in fielding an integrated team. Some other African American players in the district included Willie Jones at Robstown, Willie Reed at Beeville, and Moses Clay, Von Fore, and later Floyd Robinson at Port Lavaca.

Compared to other institutions, Kingsville dealt somewhat smoothly with the transition to full integration, though not without a few bumps in the road. Starting in 1955, Black players played a key role in the success of Brahmas football. The young man who integrated the Kingsville athletic program was Sherwood Thompson, who attended Kingsville High School from 1955 to 1958.

Thompson recalled his days in Kingsville: "I was the first Black player at Kingsville King High School in 1955 when I was a sophomore. Kingsville was a little town. Most of the Blacks lived in the same neighborhood. We all went to Frederick Douglass High School in Kingsville. Even after integration, the school stayed open until 1969. Some of the kids came over to King High School from Douglass, but most of those kids didn't make it. There was a lot of attrition. Just about everyone dropped out and joined the military.

"Growing up in Kingsville, the races were absolutely separate. As a Black, you knew your place. You knew better than to cause trouble. You didn't make demands anywhere. At restaurants, we had to eat in the kitchen; at movie theaters, we had to sit in the balcony. We had four soda fountains in drugstores in Kingsville. We couldn't go to any of them to sit down and have a snack. You could go in, order, pick it up, and leave.

"We had a football team at Douglass, but we would only play about five games a year. When we did integrate, there was a large number at first who went out for the Brahmas team. But like I said, there was a lot of attrition.

One problem arose when they started trying to verify the ages of the Black players. A lot of them were too old. Even though a large number went out, things went well for the most part. There was some preplanning before the schools integrated, and the new changes were met with an open mind.

"One thing that really helped the situation happened a couple of years before integration. It was a preparatory thing. In 1953, the Lions Club brought Little League baseball to Kingsville. The league was integrated right off the bat. It did more than anything to help with the integration of King High School a couple of years later. All the students knew each other from playing baseball together. I think it also helped make the decision easier for the school district to integrate pretty quickly after *Brown v. Board* in 1954."

"In football, I started as a sophomore," Thompson continued. "I made my reputation as a defensive back. By the time I was a senior, I was a running back. In 1956 and 1957, we had good teams. I thought we had the chance to go to state both years.

"I really didn't run into too much in the way of problems from opponents and fans. There was nothing major. Some things you came to expect, though. It was manageable. The UIL [University Interscholastic League] handled things pretty well. I thought the officials at the games didn't let things get out of hand either. I remember we did go into one town to play and there was some name-calling before and after the game. But all in all, it was mostly a positive experience."

Thompson made first team all-district in 1957 as a senior but graduated the year before the Brahmas made their run to the state finals. However, he helped pave the way for other African Americans in Kingsville, including the legendary running back James "Preacher" Pilot, who, along with Doug Harvey, were the offensive stars of the 1958 Kingsville team. Pilot had played alongside Sherwood Thompson in 1956 and 1957, scoring fourteen touchdowns each season to lead Kingsville in scoring.

By his senior season of 1958, Pilot led Kingsville to the Class 3A state finals. He was recruited by almost every major college in the North and West (but couldn't attend Southern colleges because they were still segregated). He chose to enroll in Kansas his freshman year, before transferring to New Mexico State. Pilot led the National Collegiate Athletic Association (NCAA) in rushing in 1961 with 1,278 yards and in 1962 with 1,247 yards. He was drafted by the 49ers of the National Football League (NFL) and the Chiefs of the American Football League (AFL). However, because of injuries suffered as a senior at New Mexico State in 1963, Pilot never played professional football. He passed away in 1991, and several of his former teammates recall him fondly.

Sherwood Thompson said, "Preacher Pilot was my friend. He was a wonderful player. It didn't matter the time period; Preacher would have been great in any era. He ran a 9.8 hundred-yard dash at the state meet as a sophomore in 1957."

One of Preacher Pilot's 1958 teammates, defensive tackle Jack Burchers, said, "I started playing Little League baseball with Preacher when I was twelve. He was always the stud. He pitched. Everybody liked Preacher. In football, he played both ways—running back and defensive back. He was a pretty big kid, about two hundred pounds. Preacher could run a 9.8 hundred-yard dash, though. He did pretty well in school, too. He was no dummy. We really didn't have any problems with Preacher or any of the other Black players on the team."

Doug Harvey said, "Preacher was a great guy. We really had no problems integrating. I played Little League and Pony League with Preacher, so I knew him already. What an athlete. He was about 5' 10" and 210 pounds and could run about a 9.7 hundred-yard dash. We had a great time the year we went to the finals in 1958. I never heard about or saw any type of problems regarding his race. We played the single wing. We were Class 3A back then; 4A was the top classification.

"We got along fine in Kingsville. We were one of the first schools to integrate in Texas. We did it in 1955. Preacher was still going to the Black school, Fredrick Douglass, but he ended up playing for the Calves, the Kingsville freshman B team. It helped because he became acclimated to the single wing. In tenth grade, Preacher started going to Kingsville High.

"Before we got to high school, we played Pony League together. We even went and got our haircuts together at the King Barber Shop—Preacher, Woody Houston, and Sherwood Thompson, who graduated the year before us. I remember one time the NAACP [National Association for the Advancement of Colored People] came to Kingsville and tried to meet with the owner of the King Barber Shop, Mr. Andrews, and its Black barber, James Mosely. They wanted them to stage some kind of protest. They basically told the NAACP to get their ass out of Kingsville. Nothing really came of it because we had everything just the way we wanted it. I didn't know this had happened until about ten years after the event. By then, I was principal at a school in Premont, and James Moseley came by one day selling some cleaning products and told me about the event. Besides Pony League, we played a lot of sandlot baseball with all the kids in town—white, Black, and Mexican."

Jack Burchers added the following about Woody Houston, another Black player on the 1958 team: "Woody Houston, who was a junior, was another good Black player on the team. You know, we were one of the first schools in Texas to have Black players. Woody was a real good guy, just like Preacher was. I first met Woody when I was twelve, playing Pony League baseball. That's where a lot of us first met and became teammates with the Black kids. Woody was ten, and he was a great shortstop. I remember one time, Woody came to my house. My mother was shocked. She had never had a Black boy in her house. She had been raised in East Texas and Blacks to her were like slaves when she was growing up. It was a bit of an adjustment for her."

Going into the 1958 season, it appeared both the Brahmas coaches and players knew that they could have a special season. Jack Burchers said, "Actually, there were stories out there that the coaches were grooming us for 1958. They knew we were going to be good. We had had a couple of good years in 1956 and 1957 where we just missed the playoffs. I think sometimes as players, we didn't realize we were that good. We figured it out during the season that we were, though."

Doug Harvey added, "I think both the players and the coaches knew we were going to be pretty good in 1958. We had two junior highs in Kingsville back then, and they both went undefeated in football for two years until they played each other at the end of the season. On top of that, my junior high didn't lose a track meet, so we did have some speed. In 1956 and 1957, we had a couple of good teams, but we got tripped up both seasons. Back then, you couldn't hardly afford to have a bad game because only the district champion went to the playoffs. Nowadays, they take four teams per district. One of the keys to our success in 1958 was that everyone stayed healthy and no one moved away.

"On offense, we ran the single wing. We had a great backfield. Preacher Pilot was the tailback, Woody Houston was the wingback, Ronnie Johnson was the blocking back, and I was the fullback. In the single wing, the fullback would call the plays, and I would be the one who would throw the ball when we had to. We didn't have to throw much—our running game was so effective. Why do it? The saying back then was, 'Three things can happen when you pass the ball, and two of them are bad.'

All-State Kingsville quarterback Doug Harvey. Courtesy of Kingsville Independent School District

"You know, Woody Houston was a great back, too. He was a year behind us, and he went on to New Mexico State after high school. Obviously, Preacher was super, too. Besides staying healthy, we always got along as a team. There was never any jealousy among us, especially with the Black players. Everyone pulled for everyone else. It was just a great time in my life. I loved it."

Fred Hobrecht added, "It was fun playing at Kingsville, and we had some good players. Of course, we had Preacher Pilot and our quarterback was Doug Harvey, but we had some other great players, too, like Dean Bass, Arturo Flores, and others. We wouldn't have gotten to where we were without Preacher, though. You know, we were one of the first schools in Texas to integrate. We had another really good Black player in Woody Houston. Our team chemistry was really incredible."

Thanks to solid coaching and the advantages of being one of the first schools in Texas to integrate, by 1956 Russ Holland was turning Kingsville into a powerhouse. In 1956 and 1957, Kingsville was favored to win the district, but upset losses both seasons derailed their playoff hopes. The 1956 Brahmas went 8–2. They lost their season opener to Alice 34–20 on September 15 but then proceeded to win their next eight games to set up a regular season-ending showdown for the district title against the Robstown Cotton Pickers—another school that had integrated early on with, among others, their star African American fullback Willie Jones. Kingsville lost the season finale on November 23 at Robstown 19–0. Because back then, only the district champion went to the playoffs, Kingsville stayed home.

Kingsville entered the 1957 season as heavy district favorites over Port Lavaca and Beeville. The Brahmas lost a nondistrict game to Edinburg 28–13 on September 27 and the following week tied McAllen 0–0. During these contests, the Brahmas had six players out with the flu. They went 4–1–1 in nondistrict and blasted 5–0–1 Port Lavaca Calhoun 27–12 as Preacher Pilot scored three touchdowns. They then lost to Beeville 26–25 on November 8 on a missed extra point. Cuero ended up taking the district crown, with a 9–0–1 record. The next week, the Brahmas lost to Cuero 20–6 to fall from contention.

At the start of the 1958 season, with all of the pieces seemingly in place, the Brahmas left no doubt they would be the team to beat in District 15–3A. They started off their season on September 13 by defeating their rival the Alice Coyotes 36–20 in their home opener. Junior second-string tailback Bill Whitaker was the star of the night, as he entered the game in the second quarter and scored three touchdowns on runs of five, fourteen, and sixty-five yards. Doug Harvey added a forty-five-yard touchdown on a keeper.

On September 20, Kingsville beat the San Antonio Tech Buffaloes at home 14–6, although Kingsville lost the statistical battle, with fifteen first downs and 274 yards for Tech and ten first downs and just 168 yards for the winners. Preacher Pilot capped a sixty-five-yard drive with a one-yard touchdown run in the first quarter, and the Brahmas added a second-quarter score on a John Morgan five-yard run. Pilot passed to Dean Bass for the two-point conversion. Woody Houston intercepted two San Antonio passes late in the game to seal the win. The Brahmas were now 2–0 for the season.

Edinburg was the Kingsville opponent on September 27 for the Brahmas' third-straight home game. The Brahmas needed a twenty-point fourth quarter to grind out a 36–6 win over the Bobcats. Preacher Pilot opened the scoring for the Brahmas with a sixty-seven-yard first-quarter scoring jaunt. Doug Harvey scampered fifty yards on a keeper for another Brahmas touchdown as Kingsville led but 16–6 heading into the last three minutes of the game. From there, Pilot broke loose for touchdown runs of fifteen, seventy-one, and ten yards and added a two-point conversion, to total twenty-six of Kingsville's thirty-six points.

Kingsville took to the road for the first time against the McAllen Bulldogs on October 3. The Brahmas improved their record to 4–0 with a 30–6 win. Kingsville shredded the McAllen defense for 384 yards rushing, and Preacher Pilot scored three touchdowns for the victors on runs of fifty-one, ten, and twenty-four yards. Jack Burchers added, "One of my highlights was getting to score a touchdown off of a fumble in a game against McAllen. I was a defensive tackle, and another one of our linemen, Ronnie Johnson, hit the ballcarrier and the ball popped up in the air; I ran about forty yards with it. I was probably the slowest guy on the field. I weighed 185 or so, which was decent size for a lineman back then. I just had great memories of that year."

After four games, the Brahmas appeared unstoppable. Their first four opponents were all Class 4A clubs, one classification higher than Kingsville, with the Brahmas outscoring them 116–38. Kingsville moved up to number four in the state Class 3A rankings.

In week five, the Brahmas traveled northwest 225 miles to Kerrville in the Texas Hill Country on October 10 to battle the always tough Tivy Antlers. Kerrville was led by Coach Tom Daniel and their star running back Tommy Daniels. The Antlers were 3–1 coming into the game and were favored to win their district. Unfortunately for Kingsville, the injury and flu bug hit the team, leaving eight starters unable to play. That was combined with Tivy's Tommy Daniels scoring three touchdowns on sixteen- and twenty-seven-yard passes from quarterback Alton Rhoden, to go with a forty-five-yard punt return. Rhoden added two touchdown runs of his own of eight and sixty-four yards as the Antlers rolled to a 50–6 win. Kerrville dominated the statistical battle with a 380–185 advantage in total yardage. Preacher Pilot was the only Kingsville leading player to enter the contest, so the Antlers' tough defense keyed on him and bottled him up for most of the evening.

Jack Burchers recalled the trip to Kerrville: "I think we eventually got up to being the fourth-ranked team in Class 3A. Then we got whipped by Kerrville in week five, 50–6. We had about eight players out because of injuries and the flu. We had about six really good players, and five of them were out, including our leader on offense, Doug Harvey. He was hurt. I think only Preacher Pilot played out of our stars."

Doug Harvey added, "We did have eight starters out for the Kerrville game. I had hurt my ankle and couldn't play. Add that to the fact that Kerrville was pretty good—that's why the score was so lopsided. Even though we lost badly to them, we knew there was a chance we could see them again in the playoffs."

The Brahmas got back on the winning track after their loss at Kerrville with a 44–0 shellacking of the Corpus Christi College Academy Cavaliers on October 17 in Kingsville. Jimmy Luker raced thirty-eight and eighty-six yards for touchdowns, Doug Harvey scored from twelve yards out, and fullback Jean Walshe scampered seventy-nine yards for another score. Sophomore lineman Fred Hobrecht got into the scoring act when he picked off a pass in the Cavalier backfield and raced twelve yards for a score. "Wow, I really don't remember that," said Hobrecht years later. "Are you sure that wasn't a typo?"

After a 5–1 start to the season, the Brahmas took on the Port Lavaca Calhoun Sandcrabs in Port Lavaca in their district opener on October 24. The Brahmas had won the previous two meetings between the schools, 51–27 at Port Lavaca in 1956 and 27–12 at home in 1957. Although they had been underdogs in five of their first six 1958 contests, the Sandcrabs had fashioned a respectable 3–3 nondistrict record. Kingsville had a distinct size advantage over Port Lavaca—close to twenty pounds per player.

The Brahmas made quick work of the Sandcrabs as they took a 46–18 decision. Kingsville spotted Port Lavaca a 6–0 lead but came back in the second quarter to take a 14–6 halftime lead. Preacher Pilot broke the game open in the third quarter with an eighty-six-yard sprint to the end zone. The Sandcrabs were outmatched as Kingsville rolled up 447 rushing yards on the evening. Doug Harvey ran for two touchdowns and passed for two others in the rout.

After a week off, on November 7, Kingsville beat the Beeville Trojans at home 14–6 for their second district win. The victory moved Kingsville to 7–1 on the season and 2–0 in District 15–3A play. Doug Harvey scored on a one-yard plunge in the first quarter to cap a fifty-six-yard, ten-play drive. Preacher Pilot broke a six-all tie in the third quarter on a seven-yard run. Pilot then added a two-point conversion on a run.

Jack Burchers said, "We knew going into the season that in our district, Beeville was good. Even though it was only our second district game, we knew we had to beat them to win district. It was a tough game, but we beat them 14–6. We did end up winning district, and it was the first time in twenty-nine years we had won it."

All that remained in the regular season for Kingsville were the two teams bringing up the rear in District 15–3A: Cuero and Robstown. On November 14, the Brahmas blasted Cuero 60–14 to avenge the previous year's loss. The Gobblers helped matters by losing six fumbles to the Brahmas, with Kingsville converting four of them into touchdowns. Kingsville clinched the District 15–3A crown, even though they still had to play Robstown the following week. Kingsville jumped to a 30–0 first-quarter lead and didn't look back. Preacher Pilot scored on runs of sixteen and forty-two yards, while Doug Harvey passed for one score of sixty-two yards to Woody Houston and ran for another and scored four two-point conversions. James Luker also scored on an eighty-seven-yard run for Kingsville. The Brahmas now moved to 3–0 in district and 8–1 for the season.

Kingsville wrapped up their regular season with an undisputed district championship on November 21 by punishing the Robstown Cotton Pickers 62–18 to complete a 9–1 regular season and a spot in the Class 3A playoffs. Kingsville broke out to a 32–12 first-half lead with Doug Harvey scoring three touchdowns. Harvey ran for his fourth touchdown in the third quarter, and Preacher Pilot scored on runs of thirty-five and forty-six yards.

Kingsville now prepared for their first playoff game in twenty-eight years, as they were to play the Falfurrias Bulls on November 28 in Kingsville. Falfurrias, from District 16–3A, were 7–3 on the season, outscoring their opponents 194–125 in the process. Falfurrias, like Kingsville, started playing football in 1909 and had not had much success on the gridiron either. The Bulls had won only two playoff games in school history prior to 1958.

On the evening after Thanksgiving in 1958, the Falfurrias Bulls were no match for Kingsville as the Brahmas rolled to a 26–0 victory. Kingsville stopped Falfurrias three times inside the twenty-yard line during the game. They got the scoring started in the first quarter on a bobbled snap in the end zone on a Falfurrias punt. The Brahmas rolled 323 yards rushing that night. Dean Bass rolled sixty-two yards on an end-around in the second quarter down to the Falfurrias twenty-three, and from there, Preacher Pilot scored on the next play. Pilot later added another touchdown on a ninety-yard sprint, while Doug Harvey added a thirty-two-yard touchdown.

From here on out, the Brahmas' playoff opponents would be decidedly tougher. Kingsville's next playoff contest was against San Antonio Sam Houston. Unbeaten in eleven games, the Cherokees had mauled their opposition by outscoring them 254–36. They shut out the San Marcos Rattlers in their opening playoff game 12–0. Sam Houston was an overwhelming favorite over Kingsville.

Before the Brahmas faced Sam Houston in the 3A quarterfinals, Jim McKone, a sportswriter and columnist with the *Corpus Christi Caller Times*, wrote on November 30 after the Falfurrias playoff game what Kingsville fans thought was a very unflattering column before the Brahmas played the Cherokees, claiming somewhat tongue in cheek that Kingsville should be a seventy-six-point underdog to Sam Houston. He came to the seventy-six-point underdog conclusion by comparing the scoring margins of similar opponents. Kerrville beat Kingsville by forty-four, San Marcos beat Kerrville by twenty, and Sam Houston beat San Marcos by twelve, which added up to a seventy-six-point differential. McKone said, however, "This sports writer doesn't actually believe Kingsville will lose by 76 points this week. Comparative scores aren't that accurate. Maybe the Brahmas will be beaten by 40 to 50 points, but not by 76. That seems a little high. A little more 'reasonable' prediction: Sam Houston, 48–16."

What followed was a backlash from Kingsville fans. McKone received a deluge of calls and letters from irate Brahmas supporters. Doug Harvey said, "That column by Jim McKone got us motivated. We had one nondistrict game against Kerrville where we had eight players out with injuries and the flu. I didn't play because of a bad ankle, and they killed us 50–6. We thought we might see them again in the playoffs, but they lost the district title to San Marcos. San Marcos then lost to San Antonio Sam Houston. We beat Falfurrias 26–0 in bi-district to set up a showdown with Sam Houston in the quarterfinals.

"Although he said he was somewhat joking, McKone said we should be a seventy-six-point underdog to Sam Houston because we lost to Kerrville by forty-four, San Marcos beat Kerrville by twenty, and Sam Houston beat San Marcos by twelve. He did predict Sam Houston would beat us by 48–16. And after the season was over, McKone said he wrote that column to try and keep us upbeat and to motivate us. We felt he was being anti-Brahmas."

Despite what Jim McKone had said in his column, there was hope for Kingsville if one used comparative scores from common opponents. Sam Houston and Kingsville had two teams each school had played during the season. Sam Houston beat Kingsville's district foe Port Lavaca 24–0 on September 19 in Port Lavaca, while the Brahmas beat them 46–18 on October 24. Sam Houston and Kingsville both shut out Falfurrias, with Sam Houston beating the Bulls 32–0 on October 10, while the Brahmas had just wrapped their first playoff win in school history the week before against the Bulls 26–0. Judging from the comparative scores of those games, it appeared the game between the Brahmas and Cherokees would be close.

However, the game on December 6 was anything but close. The unexpected happened as Kingsville dominated San Antonio Sam Houston 34–6 at San Antonio's historic Alamo Stadium before 4,361 fans. Doug Harvey carried twenty-three times for 168 yards while Preacher Pilot chipped in 108 yards rushing. Harvey also connected with Pilot for a twenty-six-yard opening-quarter touchdown. Pilot then added a touchdown jaunt of forty-three yards in the second quarter. He then scored three touchdowns on a pair of three-yard runs and a forty-eight-yard fourth-quarter run.

The Brahmas led 22–0 at halftime and never looked back. The Kingsville defense held Sam Houston to just forty-eight first half yards and only 105 yards for the game, all on the ground. Kingsville picked up twenty-eight first downs to Sam Houston's eight, and the Brahmas had 313 yards rushing and fifty-three passing to dominate the statistics.

Jack Burchers recalled, "It was cold in San Antonio that night. We thought the game against Sam Houston would be close. We played really well, though. Our defense stopped them cold. On offense, Preacher and Doug led the way as usual. When we got back to Kingsville, things started getting crazy. We were in the semifinals!"

After the Brahmas' rout of Sam Houston, Jim McKone apologized in his December 14 column. "The criticism from Kingsville was justified," McKone said. "This columnist 'rode' the Brahmas too hard (notably by picking them to lose, 48–16. They won, 34–6).

"The Brahmas have had several sportswriters eat crow. However, as the worst offender, this sniveling scribe apologizes."

This now set up a semifinal encounter with the always tough Cleburne Yellow Jackets. Cleburne, which is thirty miles south of Fort Worth, was in the middle of a three-year roll where they at least made the state semifinals each year. In 1957, Cleburne had made it to the semifinals, where they lost to Sweetwater 26–0. In 1959, the Yellow Jackets made it to the state championship game, where they tied Breckenridge 20–20 to share the Class 3A state title.

Jack Burchers said, "We played Cleburne in the semifinals in Kingsville. They were really good, too. It was about twelve degrees. Man, it was cold. I don't think it's ever gotten that cold in Kingsville before or since."

Cleburne, out of District 9-3A, were led by future University of Texas stars Pat Culpepper and David McWilliams. Like San Antonio Sam Houston, Cleburne entered the game as a heavy favorite over Kingsville. The Yellow Jackets' record stood at 10–0–2, and they had scored 355 points on the season and had given up but 18 points over ten games. The Yellow Jackets had recorded ten shutouts. The only blemishes on their record were back-to-back ties in nondistrict play in weeks two and three of the season against Garland 0–0 and Fort Worth Paschal 12–12. Cleburne had shut out its two playoff opponents, Aldine 34–0 and Alvin 22–0. No opponent had scored a rushing touchdown on the Yellow Jackets all season.

Although Cleburne was favored over the Brahmas, one lone sportswriter, Jim McLemore of the *Austin American*, predicted a 16–7 Brahmas victory, saying, "Kingsville is possibly the most underrated team in the state. Cleburne . . . hasn't met anyone with the striking power of the Kingsville club. Gonna pick the upset." McLemore was almost spot-on with his prediction.

Playing on an unusually chilly night in Kingsville, the Brahmas scored a 12–2 upset win over the Yellow Jackets before seven thousand frozen spectators. Preacher Pilot led the way for Kingsville with seventy-four yards on thirteen carries, while Doug Harvey contributed fifty-three yards on twenty-three totes. Kingsville had two first-half goal-line stands and went into halftime with a 6–0 lead. A turning point in the second quarter was when Kingsville went ninety-three yards in fifteen plays after Ronnie Johnson recovered a Cleburne fumble at the Kingsville seven-yard line. Harvey scored from one yard out to cap the scoring drive. After a scoreless third quarter, Kingsville capitalized on a blocked punt by Dean Bass at the Yellow Jackets ten-yard line. Kingsville recovered at the one, and two plays later Harvey punched it in for a 12–0 lead. Yardage was tough to come by for both squads during the evening, but in the end, Kingsville rang up 167 total yards to 149 for Cleburne.

Doug Harvey recalled the Cleburne game: "Against Cleburne in Kingsville, it was cold. The wind was coming out of the north. I scored all twelve points for us. Actually, I scored Cleburne's two points for them on an intentional safety. It was crazy. We had pulled off an upset for the second week in a row. I didn't really think of the Sam Houston and Cleburne games as upsets, though. We were good and we played well in both of those wins. Sportswriters and fans, people outside of our team, may have thought we had no chance, but we knew better. Like I said before, we were very close, and we had great team chemistry."

The Brahmas now headed to the State 3A title game once again as huge underdogs to one of the state powers of the 1950s, the Breckenridge Buccaneers. An oil town one hundred miles west of Fort Worth, Breckenridge had built a formidable reputation through the years as a football program. A town of just 6,700 back in the day, they would fill their seven-thousand-seat stadium on Friday nights and would defeat schools that were much larger than they were. Earlier in that 1958 season, Breckenridge defeated eventual Class 4A state champion Wichita Falls, a town with 68,000 residents, 26–22. Dressing in green helmets and uniforms, Breckenridge intimidated their opponents before they ever took the field.

The Buckaroos historically had good coaching, starting with Pete Shotwell in the 1920s and continuing with Joe Kerbel and Emory Bellard through the 1950s. However, some claimed that Breckinridge's reputation was built on buying players. According to Brahmas Jack Burchers, "In the finals, we played Breckinridge and they were tough. The rumor was that the fathers of good players in the area would get oil field jobs in Breckenridge so their kids could play for them."

It was believed to be a common practice starting in the 1920s and carrying on through the 1960s that oil field towns in West Texas would get families to move to their respective cities with the promise of a good-paying job in the oil patch if they would bring their talented sons to play football. Allegedly, Breckenridge took it to another level. Certain football boosters in Breckenridge were very vigorous about recruiting players and their families to their dusty little town. Eventually, though, by the early 1960s, the talent pipeline had run dry in Breckenridge. Carrie Lynn Sandefer, wife of one of the most prominent Breckenridge boosters, Jake Sandefer, lamented, "It just hasn't been the same since we had to start playing with our own boys." In 1958, however, the Breckinridge Buckaroos were at the top of their game.

Breckenridge was one of the dominant Texas high school football programs of the 1950s. The Buckaroos' record for the decade was 98–20–4, with state titles in 1951, 1952, 1954, 1958, and 1959. After Joe Kerbel left Breckenridge at the end of the 1954 season to head to the college coaching ranks, the Buckaroos were led for the next five seasons by one of the legends of Texas high school coaching, Emory Bellard. Bellard began his high school coaching career as an assistant at Alice High School (ironically, only thirty miles from Kingsville). He got his first head coaching job in Ingleside, racking up a 32–3 record from 1952 to 1954, with two regional championships. He then led the Buckaroos from 1955 to 1959, compiling a 45–14–3 record, with the 1958 and 1959 state titles. In 1960, Bellard went to Class 4A San Angelo Central High School, racking up a 59–19–2 record, and in his last season there in 1966, the Bobcats won the Class 4A state championship.

From San Angelo, Bellard joined Darrell Royal's staff at the University of Texas, and in 1968, Bellard designed and installed the "wishbone offense," which proceeded to become the dominant offense in high school and college football from the 1970s well into the 1980s. Following head-coaching stints at Texas A&M and Mississippi State, Bellard ended his career in the high school ranks at Spring Westfield High School from 1988 to 1993 and compiled a 41–22–5 mark.

Ten years before Emory Bellard developed the wishbone offense, his 1958 Breckinridge squad ran the "split T offense." Going into the state championship game, Kingsville outweighed Breckenridge by about seven pounds per man in the lines. Breckenridge, however, made up for that disadvantage by being even quicker than the Brahmas. Both teams were 12–1 with Breckenridge, only losing to Class 4A quarterfinalist and traditional state power Abilene High School. The Buckaroos' star player was halfback Joe Ed Pesch, who had run for 1,071 yards on 141 carries during the season.

The championship took place before 8,000 fans, about 1,200 of them Kingsville fans who had journeyed 450 miles to watch their team. The Breckenridge Buckaroos, led by Joe Ed Pesch's 194 yards rushing on just eighteen carries, pounded the Brahmas 42–14. Kingsville sealed their fate when they fumbled the first three times they had the football, and Breckenridge turned all three errors into first-quarter touchdowns. The Brahmas faced a 20–0 deficit but eventually closed the gap to 28–14 via Preacher Pilot's second touchdown on a forty-six-yard pass from Doug Harvey in the third quarter. But Breckinridge immediately struck back with a touchdown of its own to make it 35–14. The Buckaroos added a fourth-quarter score to make the final score 42–14. Besides his 194 yards on the ground, Pesch scored touchdowns on runs of two and twenty yards. Breckenridge also dominated the statistical battle, with a 389–246 advantage in total yards, which included 371 yards rushing. For Kingsville, Preacher Pilot had seventy-five yards in eight carries, while Harvey had sixty-five yards on twelve totes in the losing effort.

Doug Harvey reflected on the loss more than sixty years later: "Against Breckenridge at their place, it was really warm. It was like eighty degrees. It was way colder against Sam Houston in San Antonio, and it was even colder when we played Cleburne in Kingsville. The players on Breckenridge weren't big, but they were fast, quick, and would knock your head off. They had a really good lineman by the name of Charles Huddleston, who went on to play at Texas Tech. Their other big player was their running back Joe Ed Pesch. Man, he was fast. We found out later from our coaches that he had beaten Preacher at the state meet in the hundred-yard dash." (Pesch came in fourth in the 1958 State 3A meet; Pilot came in seventh.)

Like Doug Harvey, many years later Fred Hobrecht recalled the 1958 season and the championship game against Breckenridge: "Our team got the whole student body and town excited. We were all pumped. We were so thrilled to be playing for state. They were some really good times. It's crazy—in the playoffs, it was really cold in South Texas. We had freezing rain for one of our playoff games. When we played Cleburne in Kingsville, it was really cold, too. It never got that cold in South Texas. What's funny is when we went to play Breckenridge in West Texas for the championship, it was eighty degrees. However, because it had already been cold there, the grass on the field was brown because it had died. Being from South Texas, I had never seen that before. Even though we lost, that whole year was a great experience."

After the 1958 dash to the state finals, Kingsville football returned to mediocrity fairly quickly. The three wins in the 1958 postseason were the only playoff wins in school history until 2012. The Brahmas did make the playoffs in 1959, Russ Holland's last year as head football coach, but lost their first-round playoff game to Falfurrias 20–19. Holland's overall record as a head football coach at Brady and Kingsville was 145–62–5. He continued to coach cross-country and track at Kingsville for a few more seasons before retiring in 1974. Holland was named to the Texas High School Coaches Association Hall of Honor in 1970.

More than sixty years later, Doug Harvey looked back on the Kingsville Brahmas' historic run to the 1958 State 3A finals. He quipped, "We had a great time, and I wouldn't have traded that season for anything. We had great coaches, and the whole town got behind us. We had the talent on our team. About ten guys eventually got scholarships. Myself, Preacher, Ronnie Johnson, and Dean Bass went to the University of Houston. The juniors behind us were pretty talented, too. Woody Houston went to New Mexico State. On the team, we were all friends. We ran around together, and we had no animosity toward each other—and that includes our Black players. I wish nowadays both sides, Black and white, could get along with each other better, like the way we did all those years ago."

Archer City

The McMurtry-esque Saga of the 1964 Class A State Champion Wildcats

ARCHER CITY lies nestled in the heart of North Texas, about twenty-five miles southwest of Wichita Falls and just over one hundred miles northwest of Fort Worth. The year was 1964. And the hometown high school football team, the Class A Archer City Wildcats, had a relatively unremarkable reputation. Needless to say, they were not known for their football prowess.

The Wildcats began playing eleven-man football in 1923, and through 1963 (a total of forty-one seasons), the Wildcats' overall record stood at 153–191–22, with no district titles or playoff appearances. Archer City's most famous native son, future Pulitzer- and Oscar-winning novelist Larry McMurtry (of *Lonesome Dove* and *Brokeback Mountain* fame), made light of the Wildcats' football team in his 1966 semiautobiographical novel *The Last Picture Show.* The novel went on to Oscar-winning movie fame in 1971.

The Last Picture Show chronicles a declining North Texas town called Thalia (a fictitious name that McMurtry substituted for Archer City) in the early 1950s. Following protagonist Sonny Crawford's bleak high school football career, the novel makes several references to actual towns that the real Archer City Wildcats regularly played during this period, including Crowell, Chillicothe, and Henrietta. McMurtry pulls no punches regarding "Thalia's" (or Archer City's) poor record on the field, detailing Sonny's grim experience: "Four years of playing for Thalia had inured him to defeat." However, the year after Sonny graduated, Thalia finally experienced success, winning the district title.

Sometimes the truth is stranger than fiction. And McMurtry himself couldn't have written a more unlikely storyline than what happened to the 1964 Archer City Wildcats in real life: a smalltown Texas high school team, never having made the playoffs in its history, wins district and goes to the playoffs for the first time, proceeding to march to the state Class A title.

1964 Class A State Champion Archer City Wildcats. Courtesy of Archer City Independent School District

The road to this unlikely state title for Archer City began when Coach Grady Graves accepted his first-ever head coaching job at Archer City in the spring of 1961. He was thirty-five years old. A native of Italy, Texas, and a 1955 graduate of Texas Tech University, Graves arrived from Olney High School, where he had worked as an assistant coach. He made an immediate impression on his soon-to-be high school players when he met with them in the spring of 1961, at the end of their eighth-grade year.

Ray Bussey, who played end and safety for the Wildcats, recalled the initial meeting. "Coach Graves came when we were eighth graders getting ready to go into high school. He had a meeting with us and said, 'We have a history of being a doormat.' He told us he thought we could change that if we went along with him and bought into what he was doing. I knew I was going to play football no matter who the coach was, so I was all-in regardless."

Mike Stewart, a key player for Archer City at halfback on offense and cornerback on defense, recalled that meeting. He added, "Coach Graves got all of us together at the end of our eighth-grade year. He said, 'Boys, if you do what I ask you to do, you'll win state.'"

Bussey, Stewart, and several other players reminisced on what it was like playing for Coach Graves.

"Coach Graves was very exacting, demanding, and strong," Bussey recalled. "In the preseason, we thought he was trying to kill us. Coach

Graves supposedly went to the football booster club meeting before his first season began and told them, 'Give me your boys for four years.' At practice, he very seldom would holler. He had this way of folding his arms and looking at you. The longer he looked at you, the shorter you got. He would eventually break the silence by saying something like, 'Son, were you ever thinking about what you were doing?'"

"I was born and raised in Archer City," Mike Stewart added. "I even married my high school sweetheart, Judy, who was a cheerleader. Coach Graves came in right when we were getting ready to start high school. I thought he was the meanest rascal I ever knew, but he was a heckuva coach. He was tough but fair. He made men out of us. I tore my knee up at the first practice of my senior year—an injury that eventually kept me out of the army. In fact, a lot of my teammates went into the military, and they said it was a picnic compared to what Coach Graves put us through."

Barney Oliver, who played end on both offense and defense and who went on to play football at Texas Tech, probably knew Graves better than any of the players. He recalled, "I moved from a small school to Archer City in the eighth grade. I had never so much as seen a football before I came to Archer City. We stuck together, though, as a team throughout high school. Coach Graves was a tough coach. He had our respect. He could dish it out to us. And we earned his respect eventually. When he found out we could handle whatever he would throw at us, he learned to respect us. He eventually became my mentor; I wanted to get into coaching after playing at Texas Tech, and Coach Graves hired me on to his staff at Iowa Park when he was the head coach there. He had this way of looking at you. He could holler when he had to. He treated us all the same. We met his demands. I think he was successful because he didn't play favorites."

The players then talked about Graves's coaching philosophy. Graves was mostly a defensive-minded coach. On offense, Graves did what most coaches back during this time did: run the football. Gary Tepfer, Archer City's all-state fullback, said, "Defense was where Coach Graves put his key players. Quarterbacks were not that good back then, so he didn't worry about the pass that much." Ray Bussey also described the Wildcats offense: "We ran a straight T offense. We ran mostly and didn't throw much. That's what most teams did back then. We figured if we gained three and a half yards per play on offense, we would have a first down." Barry Morrison recalled, "Coach Graves believed in the old adage that three things can happen when you pass the ball and two of them are bad. However, everybody we played knew that we could throw when we had to—the threat was always there. We had big touchdown passes in the semifinals against Big Lake and in the finals against Ingleside."

The Wildcats had shown steady improvement in Graves's first three seasons at Archer City. They finished 1–9 in 1961, 3–7 in 1962, and in 1963 they lost to rival Henrietta 16–0 in the last game of the season to finish 7–3, falling just shy of the district title and the first playoff appearance in school history.

After their relative success in 1963, Archer City had some hope going into the 1964 season. The Wildcats were dubbed "the team to watch" in the preseason by the *Abilene Reporter News*. They had ten returning lettermen, including Morrison, Stewart, and Tepfer in the backfield. In the preseason coaches' poll conducted at the coaching school in Fort Worth in August, the Wildcats were also chosen to take the District 11-A title.

Grady Graves primed his players for victory, setting out to make a statement for the 1964 season. Fullback Gary Tepfer described a meeting between Graves and his returning players just before the start of the season. "Coach Graves got all of us upcoming seniors together in the gym. He told us that he and the coaching staff had evaluated the past season, including our team and the teams that we had played. In addition, the coaches had evaluated some other teams around the area and state that they thought could challenge us. Coach Graves assured us, 'I feel we have a shot at it'—meaning the title.'"

The 1964 season started slowly for the Wildcats, who lost two of their first three contests. The Wildcats opened their season on September 4 with a 14–0 road loss to Nocona, a Class 2A school that would go on to a 9–2–1 record for the season. Nocona scored two first-half touchdowns only a few minutes apart and held on for the win. They dominated the statistics as well as the scoreboard, with a 276–137 advantage in total yardage, as well as a 14–6 edge in first downs. Archer City did not help matters any by turning the ball over five times, with two fumbles and three passes intercepted.

Another Class 2A squad, Electra, was the next Archer City opponent for the Wildcats' first home tilt on September 11. Electra, who defeated Archer City 26–0 in the previous year's contest, had dropped their opening game to Haskell 20–6. Archer City got off on the right track against Electra by taking the opening kickoff and proceeding to drive fifty-four yards for a touchdown, with quarterback Billy Holder hitting Gary Tepfer with a five-yard scoring pass. In the second quarter, Mike Stewart, in one of his rare early season appearances, burst up the middle for a sixty-eight-yard touchdown run as Archer City went into halftime with a 13–0 lead. The Wildcats drove ninety-four yards in the third period, with Mike Stewart scoring his second touchdown from one yard out. The Wildcats failed on the two-point conversion and the score remained 19–0, Archer City, which ended up being the final score. The team got their ground attack going in this contest, rolling up 290 yards. The Archer City defense gave up only six first downs in their shutout of the Haskell Tigers.

Next up for the Wildcats was a September 18 home game against a tough Class 2A opponent, the Olney Cubs. Olney was rated, along with their rival Iowa Park, as the favorites in their district race. The Cubs ripped Archer City, 41–0, opening the scoring with a forty-yard punt return for a touchdown in the first quarter, and adding another first-quarter touchdown to go along with two more in the second, hitting halftime with a 27–0 lead. The Cubs added a touchdown each in the third and fourth quarter to make the final score 41–0. Olney held Archer City to what would be their lowest offensive output of the season—116 total yards.

Archer City was now 1–2 to start the season. Ray Bussey explained, "One reason we started slow is that we had some injuries. Mike Stewart had a bad knee. I was out for the first three games because I had part of my hip bone removed and put into my foot to help repair it. We weren't healthy."

Indeed, Stewart ended up missing the majority of the first three games due to his knee injury, and it looked like the Wildcats might be without his services for the 1964 season. Stewart recalled, "As far as my knee, luckily the annual Oil Bowl all-star game was being held in Wichita Falls. Coach Graves took me there, and I met with the trainers, who showed us how to tape my leg so I would be able to play. I had to get my knee drained after every game. I hardly practiced during the week. You know, I had a great bunch of teammates. They could have been resentful—with me not practicing but then getting to play in the games—but they accepted it. We had great chemistry on our team."

Barry Morrison offered another theory regarding the Wildcats' slow start. "The first part of the season didn't go that great," Morrison recalled. "To me, it was because Coach Graves kept moving players around. You play by instinct. Since players were being moved around so much, they were thinking too much instead of just reacting instinctively, because when you know your position and you know what to do without thinking, you're just reacting. I decided to go talk to Coach Graves about it. I got out of study hall one day, and I went to go have a heart-to-heart with him. I was scared to death. I figured I might get kicked off the team. For four years, Coach Graves had hammered it into my head about being a leader. If he had gotten angry with me, that was going to be my comeback: 'Well, you told me to be a leader, so here I am.' Luckily, it never got to that point. I told him what I thought, we got everything squared away, and we didn't lose another game the rest of the season."

After an off week, the Wildcats opened district play in a road contest on October 2 against the Henrietta Bearcats, the team that had beaten them for the district title in 1963. Henrietta entered the game with an uncharacteristic 0–3 record. Like Archer City, they had played three Class 2A squads in nondistrict play—Iowa Park, Bridgeport, and Nocona. With time running out in the fourth quarter, Archer City finally broke a twelve-all deadlock when Barney Oliver rammed his way into the end zone from three yards out, with just 2:32 to play, as the Wildcats came away with a hard-fought 19–12 victory. Archer City struck first just forty-three seconds into the game when on the second play from scrimmage Gary Tepfer went off right tackle for a sixty-eight-yard touchdown. After the Bearcats came right back to tie the score at six, Archer City went up 12–6 in the second quarter when Billy Holder scored from three yards out. Right before halftime, Henrietta scored the tying touchdown. The third and the majority of the fourth quarter were mostly a defensive struggle until Oliver scored the winning points.

In their second district contest, Archer City faced county rival Holliday on October 9 at the Eagles' home field. Holliday came into the contest with a 2–2 record. Although the Eagles broke out to a 6–0 lead, it was all Archer City after that as the Wildcats rolled to a 35–6 victory. After the Holliday score, Archer City tied the game when Mike Stewart scored from five yards out. The Wildcats added two second-quarter touchdowns—one on a Stewart one-yard plunge and the other on a six-yard score by Gary Tepfer—to lead 19–6 at the break. Stewart added two more second-half scores—one on a six-yard run and the other on a seventy-one-yard pass reception from Barry Morrison. Archer City had a 335–176 total yardage advantage and held Holliday to just thirty-eight yards rushing. The win made Archer City 3–2 overall and 2–0 in District 11–A play.

October 16 brought a 250-mile round trip to district foe Paducah. The Dragons had won but one game on the season—a nondistrict victory over Valley View. Paducah was no match for the Wildcats as Archer City scored in every quarter and rolled up 297 rushing yards in a 27–6 victory. Sophomore Billy Holder turned in a big performance as he carried the ball eight times for seventy-nine yards and added a fifty-yard interception return for a touchdown. Mike Stewart had seventy yards on seven carries with a score, and Gary Tepfer had eighty-five yards on eight totes with a score himself.

Next on the schedule was an October 23 home game with Crowell, in a battle of two teams that were undefeated in district play at 3–0. Crowell, like Archer City, had overcome early season injuries and had defeated Turkey 47–0 the previous week. Archer City scored touchdowns in the first, second, and fourth quarters to claim a 21–6 win over Crowell. The Wildcats rolled up 314 yards on the ground. Billy Holder scored from three yards out in the first quarter, and Gary Tepfer scored from one yard out in the second after the Wildcats drove fifty-nine yards in fourteen plays, with Mike Stewart contributing twenty-seven yards rushing on six carries during the drive, and Stewart scored from two yards out in the final stanza. Crowell's only score came on the first play from scrimmage in the third quarter, on a forty-five-yard touchdown run by Lee Looney. Archer City now stood alone atop the 11–A district standings with a 4–0 record.

On October 30, the Wildcats took on the Throckmorton Greyhounds, the three-time defending regional champs in Class B, in a nondistrict contest. The reason for the unusual nondistrict contest during the middle of district play was because Archer City had an early season game with Chillicothe canceled because they couldn't field a team. Throckmorton also had Chillicothe on their schedule, so the two schools arranged to meet in a nondistrict contest.

The Wildcats took down the tough Greyhounds 27–14, with thirteen fourth-quarter points to break a 14–14 deadlock. Barry Morrison scored from fourteen yards out in the final stanza, and Billy Holder went around left end for a thirty-yard score to ice the contest. Archer City dominated the statistical battle, with twenty-five first downs to eleven for Throckmorton. The Wildcats also rolled up 463 yards total offense, including 338 yards rushing, with Gary Tepfer leading the way with twenty-eight rushes for 174 yards and two touchdowns. The Wildcat defense held Throckmorton to just seventy-seven yards rushing on the night.

Now 6–2 for the season, the Wildcats faced two tough district foes to end their regular season. They played a home contest against the 3–1 Knox City Greyhounds on November 6 and came away with a 14–0 victory to move the Wildcats to 5–0 in District 11–A play. Knox City fell to 3–2 in district play and was eliminated from the playoff spot. Although the Wildcats did not dominate the scoreboard, they did dominate the statistics. Archer City held Knox City to just five first downs and 109 yards of total offense. Archer City, on the other hand, had thirteen first downs and rang up 323 yards of total offense, including 283 rushing yards. Gary Tepfer led the way for the Wildcats, with 166 yards on twenty-four carries, and Barry Morrison added 60 yards on the ground. Archer City also picked up forty yards through the air, all of it coming on a Morrison touchdown pass to end Barney Oliver in the fourth quarter.

The Wildcats' win over Knox City set up a winner-take-all showdown for the District 11–A title and accompanying playoff appearance with the Munday Moguls at Archer City's homecoming on November 13. Both teams entered the contest with 7–2 overall records and perfect 5–0 district marks. In district play, the Moguls had given up but fourteen points in five contests, while Archer City had given up thirty. The winner of the contest would take on District 10–A champion Keller the following week.

Gary Tepfer said about the Munday game, "I didn't want to lose to Munday. Going to the playoffs meant a lot to me. Henrietta had beaten us the year before to knock us out of the playoffs. They ran a lot of sweeps to beat us, and Munday was going to try the same thing. Barry Morrison and I were the team leaders and captains. Barry pretty much handled the offense; on defense, I did the talking. I wasn't too verbal, and I led mostly by example. When we got into the defensive huddle at the start of the Munday game, however, I spoke up. I said something like, 'We're going to have to do something to stop their sweeps. Let's get it done!' For the most part, we did."

Archer City came to play, beating Munday 20–7. The Wildcats spotted a Mogul 7–0 first-quarter lead and came roaring back in the second quarter to take a 14–7 lead into halftime, the highlight being a fifty-five-yard Mike Stewart run to set up the go-ahead touchdown. Neither team tallied in the third quarter, and Barry Morrison passed seventeen yards to Ray Bussey with 9:10 left in the contest to account for the final margin. The game was well played, as neither team had a turnover. Although Munday had a 13–11 advantage in first downs, Archer City outpaced the Moguls in rushing yards, 241–167, and in passing yards, 75–42.

Almost lost in the excitement of winning the district title and advancing to the playoffs for the first time in school history was the fact that it was Archer City's homecoming. Judy Crowley was named the Band Sweetheart, and Judy McMurtry (ironically, the younger sister of Larry McMurtry) was named Football Sweetheart.

Judy McMurtry, sister of Pulitzer Prize- and Academy Award-winning author Larry McMurtry, 1964 Archer City Football Queen. Courtesy of Archer City Independent School District

The Wildcats were now in uncharted waters as they prepared for their first playoff game in school history, to be played in Decatur on November 20. Their foe was a playoff regular, the Keller Indians. Keller was in the middle of a streak that saw them win eleven district titles in a thirteen-year period from 1955 to 1967. Going into the bi-district matchup, the two teams had identical 8–2 records. In terms of size, both physically and roster-wise, Keller held the advantage. In fact, Keller had enough players to have only two or three players playing both offense and defense. This was not the case for Archer City; with just twenty-one players on their roster, most of their starters had to play both ways.

The Archer City Wildcats made a fine showing in the first-ever playoff game in school history by downing the seasoned Indians 7–0 on a cold, wet, and rainy night in Decatur. A cold front hit during pregame warm-ups, and players, coaches, and fans ran to find warmer clothes. All except Grady Graves, though. Graves, who had a number of superstitions, always wore short sleeves on the sidelines and shunned wearing a coat, no matter what the weather. The weather got so bad in Decatur, however, that Graves finally relented and put on a coat at halftime.

Ray Bussey confirmed, "Coach Graves was very superstitious. He always wore a short-sleeve shirt on the sidelines; it didn't matter the weather conditions. Well, it was sleeting and so cold in Decatur that he gave in and put a jacket on at halftime."

As far as the game, defense ruled the night, as neither team could garner much offense, especially through the air. Each team only completed one pass on the evening—Archer City for five yards and Keller for nine. Archer City had a slight advantage in first downs, 11–10, but had a larger margin in rushing yardage, 255 to 183. The Wildcats lost four fumbles on the night, and Keller lost three. Archer City finally broke through in the third quarter as the Wildcats marched fifty-four yards and Gary Tepfer started the drive with a forty-yard run to the Keller fourteen, scoring the winning touchdown on a one-yard run, with Barry Morrison kicking the extra point. Tepfer finished the game with thirty-two carries for 157 yards.

Mike Stewart recalled how important the team managers were in helping defeat Keller and win state: "To show you how winning state was a total team effort, our team managers did their part to keep us on the field. It was so cold against Keller that our face masks started shattering. The managers got to where they could replace the face masks very quickly, so we didn't have to stay on the sidelines for very long."

With one playoff win under their belts in their first-ever attempt, the Wildcats turned their attention to the Goldthwaite Eagles in a game that was played in Abilene on November 27. Goldthwaite, the District 9–A champion, had advanced to the second round of the playoffs with an 8–6 bi-district win over District 10–A winner Baird. Goldthwaite started the 1964 season slowly, winning but one of their first five games. When the Eagles hit district play, their defense shut out their last four opponents to take the district title. Once again, Archer City appeared overmatched in the trenches. The Eagles line averaged almost two hundred pounds per player, easily more than the Wildcats.

Archer City capitalized on three second-half Goldthwaite fumbles and held on for a 13–6 win that advanced the Wildcats to the state quarterfinals. After a scoreless first quarter and almost eight minutes of the second, Goldthwaite's Jim Childress scored for the Eagles from four yards out to give Goldthwaite a 6–0 lead. The Eagles' two-point conversion try failed, and they went into halftime with a 6–0 lead. Archer City capitalized on Goldthwaite's second fumble in the third quarter as lineman Jimmy Reeves recovered it and the Wildcats moved forty-one yards in nine plays for the score. Gary Tepfer, who ran twenty-five times for seventy-nine tough yards, scored the Wildcats touchdown from one yard away with 2:41 left in the third quarter. Barry Morrison's extra-point try was good and broke the six-all deadlock. The Wildcats added an insurance touchdown with 5:04 remaining in the contest when sophomore Billy Holder sprinted around left end for a touchdown from fifty-two yards out. Morrison's extra-point attempt was blocked, and Archer City led 13–6. Goldthwaite never seriously threatened the rest of the way, and the Wildcats went on to the quarterfinals. They won the statistical battle with thirteen first downs to eight for Goldthwaite, leading in total yards 258 to 161.

Gary Tepfer recalled the significance of Billy Holder's third-quarter touchdown: "There was one play that made the difference in the Goldthwaite game. Barry Morrison claims he changed the play that Coach Graves sent in, but it wasn't true. We noticed that one of their defensive ends was cracking back to the middle, leaving his side of the field open to a sweep. It was third down and short yardage, and they faked me the ball up the middle. We ran a twenty-six off-tackle play. Barry called the off-tackle play, and he pitched it to Billy Holder, who ran around that unprotected side of the field for a touchdown. Holder was the only one out there. The defensive end for Goldthwaite had cracked back, and everyone else on their team thought I had the ball. There was nobody even close to Billy. I could see him all the way because I was at the bottom of the pile in the middle of the field, and I watched him score."

Archer City's path to the state title didn't get any easier with their quarterfinal matchup against the Clifton Cubs—a 47–0 winner over Honey Grove in their previous game. The two squads faced each other on December 4 in Arlington at Arlington State College. The Wildcats were a decided underdog in this contest. Clifton, like Archer City's first-round opponent, Keller, was in the midst of a strong playoff run where they won nine district titles in ten years from 1962 to 1971. Clifton was unbeaten on the season, 11–0–1, with the only blemish on their record being a 0–0 tie in their first-round playoff game against Midlothian. Clifton advanced by having a 2–0 advantage in penetrations. The Cubs defense limited Midlothian to fifty-eight total yards. The Cubs boasted a strong ground attack, as evidenced by their rolling up close to three hundred yards rushing against Honey Grove in the first half alone. Clifton's defense was no slouch either, giving up just one yard rushing in the same first half against Midlothian. The Cubs had outscored their opponents on the season 428–39.

Besides making it to the state quarterfinals, a first for Archer City, another first occurred when the Wildcats faced off with the Cubs. Archer City was competing against African American players for the first time. Clifton High School integrated for the 1964–65 school year, and it gave the Cubs' football team a shot in the arm talent-wise. Clifton was the only integrated team in their district and one of the first to integrate in Central Texas. The Cubs' leading rusher was James Haywood, one of five African American players who went out for the football team in August 1964. Haywood led Central Texas players during the regular season in scoring, with 172 points on twenty-eight touchdowns and four extra points.

"Clifton had the top-rated offense and defense in the state," Gary Tepfer recalled. "Nobody gave us a chance. Everybody we played underestimated us. They had this halfback, James Haywood, that supposedly only played half of every game. Clifton would usually have such a big lead that by halftime he would put on civilian clothes for the rest of the night."

What Tepfer said about Haywood was true in Clifton's previous game against Honey Grove. Haywood didn't play in the second half after he rang up 189 yards on fourteen carries and four touchdowns by halftime as the Cubs raced to a 33–0 lead.

On an icy, thirty-degree night in Arlington, Archer City baffled the prognosticators again as they grabbed a 12–0 halftime lead and held on for a 26–14 win over the Clifton Cubs. Gary Tepfer and Mike Stewart scored two touchdowns apiece for the Wildcats. Archer City and Stewart opened the scoring with a two-yard touchdown run early in the second quarter. Barry Morrison missed the extra-point try, and it was 6–0 Wildcats. Moments later, Tepfer picked off a Clifton fumble in the air on a pitchout and returned it forty-seven yards for a Wildcats score. The Wildcats try for two points failed, and Archer City went into halftime with a 12–0 advantage.

Barney Oliver recalled Archer City setting the tone early against Clifton and James Haywood. He said, "A big play in the Clifton game was the first play of the game. Clifton had this really good running back, James Haywood. He was one of the better ones around. Well, he came to my side on a sweep on the first play, and I got a really good lick on him. He didn't seem quite as effective after that."

Oliver appeared to be correct in his observation about Haywood. Haywood struggled the whole first half, as he picked up only twelve yards on seven carries.

Gary Tepfer described his second-quarter race to the end zone: "I had another key play against Clifton. They were running a pitchout to their running back. As a defensive end, the quarterback was my responsibility. As he was rolling out to pitch out the ball, our eyes met. He hesitated because I hesitated. When he pitched it out, I timed it perfectly, and I picked off the pitchout and returned it for a touchdown. I remember saying to myself after I picked the ball off, 'I gotta get this done!' What I meant was, I had to outrun the quarterback for the touchdown. I knew he was faster than me. When I looked back, however, the quarterback was standing where he was when he pitched the ball out. He didn't even move. He didn't even try to catch me. That's when I knew we had them."

Early in the third period, Clifton got on the scoreboard when Tommy Traylor went over left tackle for fifty-four yards to narrow the gap to 12–7. The Wildcats countered shortly thereafter when Mike Stewart widened the Archer City lead to 18–7, racing seventy-eight yards late in the third quarter. Archer City again failed on the extra-point try. Clifton narrowed the gap to 18–14 as they scored a touchdown with just a minute left on the clock. After Archer City recovered the onside kick, Tepfer scored his second touchdown of the evening with a forty-five-yard scamper. Mike Stewart caught the two-point conversion pass from Barry Morrison to make the final count 26–14. Archer City rang up 340 yards on the ground but none passing, as Morrison went 0–7 in the air. Clifton had a little more balanced attack, with 153 yards rushing and 116 passing on 8 of 11. Clifton lost two fumbles and had eighty yards in penalties, while Archer City had no turnovers and just ten penalty yards. Stewart led the Wildcats' ground game with 146 yards on sixteen carries, while Tepfer ran for 139 on twenty-two totes.

The Archer City Wildcats now found themselves in totally uncharted territory as they advanced to the state semifinals against the Big Lake Reagan County Owls to be played on December 12 at Snyder High School Stadium. As usual, the Wildcats entered the game as decided underdogs to the Owls and were outweighed once again, both in the line and in the backfield. Big Lake, about seventy miles southwest of San Angelo, entered the contest with a 12–1 record and had outscored their opponents 413–114 on the season. Like Archer City, Big Lake operated out of the wing T offense. Allstate fullback Don Childs led the Owls offense.

Ray Bussey knew that he and his teammates had a big challenge in front of them. He said, "We played Big Lake in the semifinals. We had twenty-one players on varsity. They came out with around sixty-six. One of our guys said when they saw their team, 'Now I know what the boys at the Alamo felt like.' You know what? In the end, we came through."

And came through they did as they hung on for a tense 7–6 semifinal win over the Big Lake Owls. After both Archer City and Big Lake wasted scoring opportunities in the first quarter, Big Lake went seventy-five yards in fourteen plays and took a 6–0 lead with only seventeen seconds left in the first half as Johnny Howard threw a five-yard touchdown pass to Richard McReavy. Then came what turned out to be the key play of the contest and possibly the season. After their touchdown, Big Lake attempted the extra-point kick, but Archer City jumped offsides. Since the ball was now half the distance to the goal and the Owls had their star fullback Don

Childs at their disposal, they decided to go for the two-point conversion instead of kicking the extra point. Childs took the handoff up the middle but ran into Archer City linebacker Robert Tepfer, Gary's younger brother, and was driven back from the goal line.

Several Wildcats recognized the importance of that play—very likely the most crucial one of the season. Barney Oliver recalled, "I had a good game against Big Lake. We all had to do our best; they were good. The defining moment in that game was when Robert Tepfer waylaid the Big Lake fullback on their two-point conversion attempt. They probably would have beat us if Robert hadn't stopped him."

Ray Bussey added, "The big play in the game was when they went for two points after their touchdown. We had jumped offsides on the extra-point try, so Big Lake decided to go for two because the ball was moved closer to the goal line because of the penalty. Well, they tried to run up the middle for the two points and Robert Tepfer stopped them cold."

Gary Tepfer fondly recalled the efforts of his brother and teammate: "The Owls decided to go for two points because they had this big fullback, Don Childs. He got at least five yards every time he carried the ball. Well, my brother Robert was the middle linebacker for us. He was a great athlete. Before the play, Childs goes up to Robert and says, 'I'm gonna carry the ball right over you!' But Robert stopped Childs going right up the middle, and he never even got close to the goal line and the two-point conversion. We ended up winning 7–6."

The key play for Archer City offensively took place early in the third quarter. Archer City quarterback Barry Morrison hit Mike "Swivel Hips" Stewart with a short down-and-out pass close to the left sideline, and Stewart wove through the Owls' defense for a sixty-three-yard touchdown. Morrison kicked the extra point, giving Archer City a 7–6 lead.

Mike Stewart recalled, "I did score that big touchdown against Big Lake. I was lucky. My teammates got me there with their blocking. I was hardly touched, and I made a couple of extra cuts to get me there."

"Mike Stewart finally lived up to his nickname 'Swivel Hips' during the Big Lake game when he scored his touchdown," Gary Tepfer said, chuckling. "He put some kind of move on their cornerback. He faked him out."

Barry Morrison talked about Archer City's attempts to get their smaller, quicker players into the open field: "Big Lake was so dadgum big we had to get outside on them, and that threat of being able to throw helped us against them. They were so much bigger and faster than we were. I'll remember that until the day I die. We were quicker, though, and what also helped us against them—and against everybody we played—was that we were in great condition. Heck, the week before the finals against Ingleside, we were still running wind sprints."

The teams traded interceptions in the fourth quarter, and Big Lake got the ball one more time at their own forty-five-yard line with three minutes to play. With no timeouts, Big Lake drove down the field, and Tommy Love of the Owls slipped out of bounds at the Archer City nine-yard line with one second left on the clock. A pass by Big Lake quarterback Walter Horton was just a little too tall for Johnny Howard, and the Wildcats held on for their ticket to the state finals.

Archer City had emerged victorious, even though they had lost the statistical battle. The Wildcats compiled 150 yards rushing, 100 yards passing, and 15 first downs. Tepfer had eighty-three yards on the ground, and Stewart had twenty-seven. Quarterback Morrison completed four of eight passes. Big Lake ended up with 235 yards rushing, 38 yards passing, and 17 first downs. Fullback Childs had 125 yards, and Tommy Love had 89 yards.

Barry Morrison added one more component to the win: "The four of us—me, Barney, Gary, and Mike—it was like being in a foxhole. I always felt they kind of looked up to me. I had to be the leader. In the Big Lake game, I took the leadership role. Big Lake had this all-state fullback named Don Childs. In the first play of the game, he comes through the guard and center gap. I'm in the middle, waiting for him, as I was unblocked. Well, he just ran over me. I think he accidentally tripped on my chin as he ran over me and fell down. After that, I told one of our other linebackers, Robert Tepfer, to switch sides with me. I figured he could handle Childs better than I could. Robert was hesitant. He asked, 'What will coach say?' I told him we would address it later. Big Lake ran the same play and Robert dropped Childs for a one-yard loss. Robert helped contain Childs for the rest of the evening. Coach Graves never said anything to me about it. I know he saw it. That switch helped us win the game."

The Archer City Wildcats found themselves where no one thought they would ever end up before the season—at the Class A state championship game. The championship game was to be played in Austin at Nelson Stadium on Saturday, December 19. Once again, the Wildcats found themselves as decided underdogs to the District 31–A champion Ingleside Mustangs. Ingleside had defeated four highly rated opponents on their way to the state finals, including the preseason pick to take the state title,

Hull-Daisetta. The Mustangs were led by four players who were sophomores on the 1962 team and made it to the state Class A finals against Rotan before losing 39–6. Out of those four players, halfback Bobby Jones was the star.

The Ingleside coach, Wayne Wilsher, took over the program in 1962, after the Mustangs had posted a 2–7–1 season in 1961. Under Wilsher's tutelage, Ingleside had compiled a 34–5 record in his three seasons leading up to the state championship game. In addition, the Mustangs had outscored opponents 383–74 on the season. By comparison, going into the state title game, Archer City had outscored their opponents by a much smaller margin of 242–132.

On a chilly forty-degree December night in Austin, Archer City scored two touchdowns within six minutes of each other in the second quarter, both capitalizing on Ingleside turnovers, to pull off an improbable 13–6 win over Ingleside. The Wildcats' first score came on the first play of the second quarter when Barry Morrison spotted Barney Oliver in the clear at the Ingleside ten and connected with him for a forty-three-yard touchdown. Moments earlier, Oliver had recovered a Mustangs fumble at the Ingleside forty-five.

About six minutes later, Mike Stewart intercepted an Ingleside pass at the Ingleside thirty-five-yard line. Eight plays later, Gary Tepfer punched the ball in from the two. Morrison missed the extra-point try, and the Wildcats led 13–0. Ingleside took the kickoff and drove to the Archer City nineteen-yard line just before halftime, but defensive end Barney Oliver threw the Mustangs' Bobby Jones for an eleven-yard loss back to the thirty to end the threat.

Ingleside came out strong in the third quarter and drove to the Archer City ten-yard line, but their drive stalled. On the first play from their own ten, Gary Tepfer fumbled and Ingleside took possession at the Archer City eleven. From there, Ingleside fullback John Garcia scored three plays later from the two-yard line. Ingleside went for the two-point conversion but failed, and the score stood at 13–6, Archer City, with 5:40 left to play in the third quarter.

In the fourth quarter, Ingleside had two more chances to score the tying or go-ahead touchdown but were thwarted both times. With five minutes left in the game, an Ingleside drive stalled at the Archer City thirty-three, and a fake punt attempt from there failed. Ingleside got the ball back once more with just a few seconds left in the game, but Mike Stewart ended the threat with his second interception of the night at the Wildcats twenty-six-yard line.

Mike Stewart said about his victory-clinching interception, "I did intercept the pass at the end of the Ingleside game. It stopped their final drive. I just happened to be in the right place at the right time."

The game was mostly dominated by the defenses. Archer City compiled only 153 yards—102 rushing and 51 passing—for the evening, along with nine first downs. The Wildcats had two turnovers on the evening (one fumble and one interception), while Ingleside had four (three interceptions and one fumble). Ingleside had 189 yards on the ground but just two yards passing. Ingleside's Jones had ninety-eight rushing yards on twenty-one trips. Gary Tepfer led the Wildcats in rushing, with seventy-five tough yards on twenty-five carries. Mike Stewart was stifled with only nineteen yards on twelve totes. Robert Tepfer led the way for the Wildcats defense with sixteen tackles from his linebacker spot.

Gary Tepfer was named to the Class A all-state team after the season at fullback after rushing for 1,536 yards on three hundred attempts. He said the following about the state title game: "I really don't remember much about the state championship game. I got knocked in the head early in the game. I don't remember running the ball one time. In the second half, we ran a lot of quarterback sneaks. Three sneaks and a punt. I watched the game later on film. They had to tell me where to line up at the defensive end. Back then, crackback blocks were legal, and that's when they knocked me out. They had this tough kid out at wide receiver, and he hit me hard early in the game."

Mike Stewart and Gary Tepfer then reflected on different aspects of the 1964 season. Mike Stewart said, "I was fortunate to play with a lot of good players. Every week, we lined up and played. We did our best—one game and one week at a time. We had some talent. Of course, Gary and Barney went off to play at Texas Tech, and Billy Pitts played some in college. Our quarterback, Barry Morrison, was a great baseball pitcher and could have played in college, but he went to work after high school."

Stewart added, "Archer City went crazy. Everybody was going to the games. We had one guy in town, Benny King, and he owned a gas station. Well, it was right before Christmas, and he almost went broke because he let a bunch of people charge their gas. A lot of the people couldn't afford Christmas shopping, going to the games, and buying all that gas, so they just charged it. There was also a story going around that a lot of spouses gave their husbands or wives ticket stubs to our state championship game as a gift because they had spent their Christmas money on going to our games."

Gary Tepfer said about the 1964 season and Coach Graves, "We had a little luck, and we worked hard. That year made an impact on me as a person that has stayed with me for my entire life. I was taught and learned about the team concept. It helped me all through life—what it meant to be a part of a team in the workplace, for example. I was a state trooper for years, and it helped me there—being part of that team. Grady Graves changed things. I know he was hard on us. I found out years later how much he cared when I talked to Mrs. Graves. She gave me a lot of insight into Coach. She said when he would get home from practice, he would discuss all of his players at the dinner table—how we were doing, how he could help us, and so on. I was amazed. Mrs. Graves also gave Coach Graves a lot of input on how to deal with us. Coach was really into it, and deep down he really cared about us."

Ray Bussey summed everything up when he said, "It was an amazing run—something to be remembered. We went into every playoff game as an underdog. It was weird; it was like we caught lightning in a bottle. We had good players, though. I don't think it was a fluke. It was our fifteen minutes of fame."

After Archer City took the Class A state crown in 1964, they immediately tumbled back to mediocrity. The 1965 season ended with a 1–7–2 record. One factor, besides the key Archer City players graduating, was Grady Graves leaving Archer City and going to Burleson, a larger school with better pay. He lasted two seasons there, with a 12–8 record. From there, Graves coached at Coleman, Iowa Park, and Wichita Falls Independent School District (ISD). Graves's overall record as a head football coach was 60–55–0 in eleven seasons. Grady Graves passed away in October 2018 at the age of eighty-nine.

Since winning the state Class A title in 1964, the Wildcats have had mixed success on the gridiron. Archer City has won six district titles and made twelve playoff appearances since 1964, making the state quarterfinals in 1994 and 2008. Their overall record through 2023 is 440–515–34 in 101 seasons.

However, as for the story of that one magical 1964 season, even Larry McMurtry could not have written a better tale. Surfacing from the high-endurance training and intense leadership vision of Coach Graves, to the drama unfolding on the field via high-stakes, high-impact, and intense gridiron matchups, the underdogs had emerged victorious and claimed the championship after decades of hardship and defeat. Archer City was now on the map. They had their claim to fame. Coach Graves had won his title and everything that goes along with it. But worth more than the trophy and the accolades, the words of Tepfer resonate and ring forth as a testament to the power of both what Coach Graves did for the Wildcats during that fateful season and what the players found in themselves: "That year made an impact on me as a person that has stayed with me. . . . I was taught and learned about the *team* concept. It helped me all through life."

Del Valle and Kountze

Underdog Versus Underdog in an Unlikely Playoff Showdown, 1967

THERE WERE TWO CLASS 2A SCHOOLS, a little more than two hundred miles apart, that hit their high-water mark in 1967: the Del Valle Cardinals and Kountze Lions. Besides making gridiron history in the same season, the two schools shared several other similarities, including a long history of drought that left them both thirsty for the taste of victory as they squared off in an unprecedented matchup, the likes of which has not been seen since for either team.

Both towns lie off the beaten path just a stone's throw from a major city. Del Valle, about ten miles southeast of Austin, was home to the former Bergstrom Air Force Base until it closed in 1994. The base was converted into what is today Austin-Bergstrom International Airport, and the area around Del Valle has grown considerably since the airport was placed there, with the population currently approaching twenty thousand. Today, Del Valle High School is a Class 6A high school, the largest classification of schools in Texas. But back in 1967, the school boasted just a few hundred people, and the Cardinals were Class 2A, which in 1967 was right in the middle of Texas's five classifications (4A, 3A, 2A, A, and B).

Kountze is located in the Golden Triangle area of Southeast Texas. The major cities that form the Golden Triangle are Beaumont, Port Arthur, and Orange. Unlike Del Valle, Kountze has remained a small community through the years; untouched by mass commerce or development, the quaint and slow-paced Texas small town is something like a dream. Located in the Big Thicket National Forest of East Texas, twenty-five miles north of Beaumont on US Highway 287, Kountze's population has remained close to 2,100 people since the mid-1960s. Through the years, the town's high school classification also hasn't changed; it remains what was in 1967 a Class 2A school (now 3A).

It was the 1967 football season, and both schools had seen little success on the gridiron since their inception. Del Valle didn't start playing eleven-man football until 1956. Their record from 1956 to 1964 was a dismal 21–64–2, without a single winning season to their name.

Although Kountze had been playing football a little longer than Del Valle (since 1952), their record didn't fare any better, at 55–81–1 from 1952 to 1965. The Lions did win one district title in 1960, albeit with a 3–7 overall record, and were quickly ushered out of the playoffs by Liberty, 54–8.

Both schools' respective fortunes began to change when they both secured new head football coaches in the mid-1960s.

In Del Valle, Steve Shaver came to coach the Cardinals in 1965. Shaver graduated from Bellaire High School in the Houston area and eventually played at Sam Houston State University, where he helped lead the Bearkats to the 1961 Lone Star Conference Championship. After graduation, Shaver spent a season in Orange, Texas, as an assistant before he got the Del Valle job at the age of twenty-five in 1965. Shaver experienced success right away at Del Valle, going 8–2 in 1965. The Cardinals just missed the playoffs when they lost their final game of the season to the Taylor Ducks, 25–8. By Shaver's second year, he had Del Valle in the playoffs for the first time in school history. The Cardinals ended up 6–4–1 in 1966. Del Valle finished with a 3–1 record in District 18–2A and won a coin flip for the right to go to the playoffs. Unfortunately, the Cardinals' season ended with a 23–14 bi-district loss to Cameron.

Shaver's wife, one of his assistant coaches, and several of his players spoke of him fondly, reminiscing on old times and that fateful 1967 season.

Shaver met his future wife, Dee Dee, after taking the position at Del Valle. Dee Dee Shaver described meeting her future husband, his personality, and their time at Del Valle: "I was working on the UT [University of Texas] campus at the student health center," Shaver said. "It was a two-person office. The lady I worked with, her husband was the ag[riculture] teacher at Del Valle, and she set Steve and me up on a blind date. Turns out our first date was the first game he coached at Del Valle in 1965. We got married ten weeks later, the Saturday after his last game of the season. We were married for forty-seven years, until his death in 2013. He was an amazing man. He was very laid-back. I loved being with him. He didn't have much of a temper. I loved his personality. Del Valle was wonderful to us. It was a great place to raise kids. They threw us wedding and baby showers. The players and the parents were great."

Dave Smith, one of Shaver's assistants, reminisced, "I played with Steve at Sam Houston State. We were on the conference championship team in 1961. He asked us to be on his staff. Steve could have been a stand-up comedian. He was a great storyteller. He was just a likable guy. A good athlete, too."

Quarterback John Lamb was one of the Del Valle co-captains. He said, "Coach Shaver was a great man. All of the coaches were instrumental in our success. They were ahead of their time. They brought the program up. We were really good because of them. Coach Shaver could be hard-nosed. I would describe him more as pretty rowdy. As long as you did what he said, you had no problems. If you didn't do what he said or didn't execute, you ran laps. Coach Shaver was one of those coaches you wanted to work hard for. We wanted to please him. He would actually teach you without hollering at you."

Wilbur Williams, who played three years of varsity football for Shaver, recalled, "Coach Shaver came my freshman year. I felt that he really understood the game of football. He was more of a defensive-minded coach. He started noticing me as a sophomore. I was the starting cornerback that year. My junior and senior years, I played offense and defense. I had so much respect for Coach Shaver. He was fair, loving, and kind. To show you the kind of person he was, I grew up very poor. Of course, we had no health insurance. Well, during my junior year, I was injured during an away game. When we got back, Coach Shaver took me to the emergency room. My parents never saw the bill. I don't know if he or the school district took care of the bill, but we never saw it."

Meanwhile, a few hundred miles away in Kountze, Ted Tate took the reins of the Lions football program in 1966. A Kountze native, Tate had come from a family of doctors but decided to pursue a career in education instead. Tate spent his early years in Kountze, but he ended up graduating from Stephen F. Austin High School in Austin in 1949. From there, Tate played baseball for the University of Texas.

When Tate came home to Kountze to coach in 1966, he didn't meet with the same success as Steve Shaver first had at Del Valle—not even close. Whereas Shaver's first squad improved their record from 5–5 in 1964 to 8–2 in 1965, Tate's first team at Kountze suffered through a dismal 1–8 season, being outscored 323–34 for the year. This was a far cry from the 1965 Lions (pre-Tate), which finished the regular season 6–4.

Opinions of Tate differed from some of his former players and coaches. Gordon Gilder, who ended up being the catalyst for the 1967 Lions, remarked, "Coach Tate was good. He was tough but fair. He didn't care what color you were as long as you could play."

Bobby Snyder, who played tight end for the Lions, recalled, "Coach Tate and I did not get along. He was very imaginative, and for a Class 2A coach, he was seen as an innovator. He used a double-wide outset sometimes, which was rarely used back in those days. We also ran some plays out of the shotgun formation. I conflicted with him. I respected him, but we just didn't get along. People either liked Coach Tate or they didn't. He could motivate his players, though. One time, we were getting ready to play Kirbyville, who was a big rival. To motivate us, Coach Tate showed us a box of Kotex pads that he claimed had been sent to us by Kirbyville. It got us fired up to play them. It turns out, we learned later, that it was Coach Tate who sent us the box and blamed it on Kirbyville."

"I was a sophomore on the 1967 team," former player Harrison McMillan added. "I was the fullback, and I was also the placekicker. Coach Tate was a wonderful man. Some didn't like him. He coached his way, and you could take him or leave him. He didn't play favorites. If you didn't have it, you didn't play. It was a great bunch of people I played with. Willie Wilson was our defensive coach. I was honored to have played for those coaches. Fred Williams, an assistant coach, would bring me home after practice most evenings. I lived fourteen miles out of town, and the coaches were strict. They kept a close eye on us. They got the best out of us. You wouldn't find two better men than Coach Williams and Coach Wilson. Heck, they were not much older than us."

McMillan spoke of one of the assistant coaches, Fred Williams. Williams came to Kountze from Houston in 1966, integrating Kountze's faculty and coaching staff. He recalled his time working alongside Tate: "I was the JV [junior varsity] coach in 1967. Ted Tate was head coach; he coached the offense. William Wilson coached the defense. Coach Tate was very knowledgeable. He was also very outgoing. He didn't have a prejudiced bone in his body. Sometimes that didn't go over too well with some of the people in Kountze back then. But if you could play, it didn't matter who your parents were. We were very close. He and I used to come up to school on Sundays and work together. He was a great athlete. He

Kountze assistant coach Fred Williams, ca. 1966. Courtesy of Kountze Independent School District

could play all the sports. He played baseball at UT. His daddy, brother, and sister were all doctors, but he wanted to coach. He could coach everything. He took his football, basketball, and baseball teams to state."

Beyond the efforts of Coach Tate and Coach Shaver, another factor that likely contributed to the memorable 1967 seasons for Kountze and Del Valle was the impact of integration. Both schools integrated before other schools in their respective districts and surrounding areas. Del Valle integrated for the 1963–64 school year. On the 1967 team, some key African American players were seniors, including Wilbur Williams, Louis Overton, Louis Arnold, and Charles Anderson. There were also junior Joshua Brown and sophomore Edwin Collins.

Coach Shaver's assistant at Del Valle, Dave Smith, said, "As far as integration, I think it helped that Bergstrom Air Force Base was right across the street from us. The military had already integrated, so Del Valle integrated before other Austin-area schools. That gave us a bit of an advantage for a while."

African American player Wilbur Williams added, "I would say that integration helped Del Valle football, yeah. I had planned on going to Anderson, the Black high school in Austin, like my older sister did. She changed her address, so that's how she went there. Anderson was really good in football. Well, Del Valle integrated in 1963 before my eighth-grade year, so I decided to stay at Del Valle. My white teammates were great. One of our white guys, John Hilgers—our kicker—his family was super. When we were kids, whites and Blacks played Little League out at Bergstrom Air Force Base. I think that helped integration, too; we all knew each other. John's dad was a lawyer, Bill Hilgers. They were great people. They would give us rides home. Otherwise, I would have had to walk. Sometimes Mrs. Hilgers would take us over to their house."

Kountze integrated in 1966, also a year or two before other teams in East Texas integrated, with Gordon Gilder being the only African American on the Lions' twenty-two-man roster. In 1967, lineman James Sims joined Gilder as the other African American player on the Lions' squad.

Kountze star running back Gordon Gilder. Courtesy of Kountze Independent School District

As mentioned previously, in 1966, Fred Williams became Kountze's first Black teacher and coach. "In Kountze, we had Blacks on one side of town and whites on another," he recalled. "When I was hired, I got to teach driver's education. I remember they didn't want me to ride in the car with white girls. I was never alone in a car with a white girl. I tell people that Kountze was like Mississippi back then.

"I was from Lumberton, Mississippi. I came to Houston to live with an uncle, went to Jack Yates High School, and played for Coach Pat Patterson there. Then I went to college at Texas Southern University. Kountze was my first and only job offer out of Texas Southern University. I had never heard of the place. I was the first Black teacher ever hired by Kountze in 1966. They had the Freedom of Choice plan back then. Blacks in 1966 in Kountze had their choice of staying at the Black school or going to the white school. I think eight kids went to the white school the first year. The next year, 1966–67, they closed the Black school.

"Apparently, Kountze had sent letters to the Black universities in the area, saying they wanted to hire a Black teacher and coach. I decided to take the bus to Kountze to check it out. I talked to Ted Tate, and I more or less accepted the job. I told them I would be back in two days. Ted told me later they didn't think I'd come back, and they were shocked when I did. Like I said, Kountze was like Mississippi back then. Kountze was about a third Black when integration came. All in all, though, we had no real problems. Integration went fairly smoothly."

Gordon Gilder, the first player to integrate the Lions, added, "Things went pretty good in Kountze growing up. I decided to go to Kountze High School in 1966 because I wanted to help integrate and I wanted to play sports. I knew everyone growing up in Kountze anyways. We played Little League together; I think that helped. There was no real Black part of town in Kountze. Blacks lived all over. It helped having Coach Williams there at Kountze when we integrated—not that things were that bad to begin with. We never had problems, either in Kountze or on road trips. I never had an incident during the games or afterwards, like going to get something to eat. Eating out was not a problem in Kountze either."

"Integration was not a big deal," Lions player Harrison McMillan recalled. "I had known most of the Black kids growing up anyways. My freshman year was the first year, and I swear at football practice there were fifty Black players out for the team during two-a-days. I think only three or four stuck with it; the rest decided to stay at the Black school. All of my teammates, Black and white, were great people."

One of the biggest differences between the 1967 Del Valle and Kountze squads were their expectations going into the season. As a result of their run to the playoffs in 1966, with most of their key players returning, Del Valle was expected to contend for the district title and the accompanying playoff spot. They were picked by the *Austin American-Statesman*, along with Copperas Cove, to contend for the 18–2A title. The Cardinals returned eight starters on a defense that recorded four shutouts in 1966; plus, they had offensive weapons like Bobby Moreland, Josh Brown, and John Lamb in the fold.

"We had some good athletes," Dave Smith said about Del Valle's 1967 prospects. "Josh Brown, who went on to Southwest Texas and became their all-time leading rusher and was a Vikings draft pick, was really good. I coached for a long time, and there are not many running backs better than Josh Brown. John Lamb, our quarterback, was good, as was Bobby Moreland, our fullback. Edwin Collins, who was just a sophomore, went on to play at Rice. We felt like we could be pretty good in 1967. We had gone to the playoffs the year before."

Kountze, on the other hand, had gone 1–8 in 1966. Going into the 1967 season, the majority of the football pundits placed the Lions fourth in their district, behind Port Acres Austin, East Chambers, and Hardin-Jefferson. Only Hamshire-Fannett was rated lower than Kountze in the preseason polls. One hope for the Lions was that they had every starter returning from 1966, including senior running back Gordon Gilder, who, despite Kountze's poor showing, was still named District 23–2A back of the year in 1966.

"Gordon was a great back," Bobby Snyder recalled. "He was very fast. He wasn't a big guy, but he was solid. He could break tackles when he had to. We ran a lot of sweeps with Gordon, though. He didn't have an abundance of moves, but the one he did have would leave cornerbacks and linebackers in the dust. Gordon would take a pitchout, and he would fake inside and then cut outside. He could do this at full speed and never lose an ounce of momentum."

Fred Williams reminisced about Kountze: "We weren't expected to do much in 1967, as usual. We had won one game the year before. We had low expectations. We had two Black players on our team, Gordon Gilder and James Sims, who were stars, and everyone else. There were some other good players, though."

"We actually did have some good expectations going into the season, thanks to Coach Tate," Bobby Snyder added. "Fred Williams helped with that, too. He was a super coach. The kids loved him. Both of them instilled confidence in us. Now, my expectations were not the state semifinals. As the season went on, the players started saying to themselves, 'Hey, we've got something here.' We were ready to win some games, and when we did, it gave us confidence and we got on a roll."

Kountze head coach Ted Tate leads a Lions practice. Courtesy of Kountze Independent School District

When the 1967 season opened for Del Valle and Kountze, it went according to form for both schools. The Cardinals, as predicted, were fast out of the gate, while the Lions struggled through their first three contests. The Cardinals and Lions looked like two teams going in opposite directions.

The opening game of the 1967 season, a September 8 home contest, was perceived to be a tough task for Del Valle. They were facing the Schulenberg Shorthorns, the third-ranked team in Class A. Schulenberg had a record of 11–3–1 in 1966, reaching the state final but losing to Sonora 40–14 in the championship game. Del Valle made short work of the Shorthorns, 55–0. Halfback Bobby Moreland started the scoring for the Cardinals in the 1967 season by returning a first-quarter punt sixty-five yards for a touchdown. The Cardinals added three more second-quarter touchdowns on drives of fifty-three, seventy-one, and ninety yards. Del Valle's defense held Schulenberg to four first downs and 56 total yards on the night, as opposed to 590 total yards for Del Valle. Moreland ended up with three touchdowns on the night, and halfback Charles Anderson had two.

John Lamb recalled his team's dismantling of the Shorthorns: "We knew we could be pretty good, but we were not really highly regarded coming into the season. Our momentum built throughout the season. It helped tremendously that we killed Schulenberg in our first game, 55–0. They had made it to the state finals the year before. It gave us a big boost. Our confidence built throughout the season as we continued to win."

Dave Smith added, "After our first game, where we tore up Schulenberg, that told us something right there. All of us coaches realized that we could be pretty good."

Del Valle breezed through their next two contests to start the season 3–0. Against Elgin on September 15, the Cardinals defense pitched another shutout as they defeated the Wildcats 33–0. Bobby Moreland scored two more touchdowns for the Cardinals, and their defense was again dominant, limiting Elgin to just four first downs and sixty-nine total yards.

Giddings was the next Del Valle victim on September 22, when the Cardinals blasted the 1–1 Buffaloes 40–12 in their third straight home contest. Del Valle jumped out to a 27–6 halftime lead and coasted from there. Bobby Moreland ran for two one-yard touchdowns in the first half and added a fifty-yard scoring strike to Louis Arnold. Del Valle had eighteen first downs and 321 yards for the evening, including 226 on the ground.

A little more than two hundred miles east of Del Valle, Kountze's 1967 season started with hope as they beat Class A West Hardin 38–12 on September 8. Gordon Gilder ran for 192 yards, scored five touchdowns, caught two passes for 25 yards, and completed a pass for 39 yards in the rout.

In a road contest on September 15, the Lions tied the Kirbyville Wildcats 12–12. The game did show some hope and promise for the Lions, as Kirbyville, who was favored to win District 22–2A, had beaten Kountze 64–0 in 1966.

On September 22, Kountze lost to the Buna Cougars 19–0. The Lions offense never got untracked as Buna picked off five Kountze passes on the evening. Two of the interceptions were on Gordon Gilder halfback passes, and both set up Buna touchdowns. With a record of 1–1–1, as usual, the Lions season appeared to be going nowhere fast.

However, over their next three games, their last before hitting district competition, Kountze started righting the ship. The Lions faced the Newton Eagles on September 29 and dismantled them 66–6. Gordon Gilder got back on track as he rushed for 220 yards and scored on runs of 70 and 40 yards.

On October 6, Kountze defeated Woodville, who was the favorite to capture the 21–2A crown, 41–12. Gilder had three more touchdowns to go with his 208 yards on the ground, and teammate Rickey Winger picked up 157 more.

Kountze avenged a 42–0 shellacking they received from the St. Mary's Hornets in Orange in 1966 by destroying them at home 67–6 on October 13. It was the Gordon Gilder show once again as he scored rushing touchdowns of two, three, and sixty-four yards. Gilder also returned a Hornets punt eighty-one yards for a score. The win over St. Mary's left the Lions with a nondistrict record of 4–1–1.

Meanwhile, Del Valle had but two nondistrict contests remaining after their 3–0 start before district play began on October 13 against Burnet. On

September 29, Del Valle faced their first road test of the season as they squared up against the unbeaten Llano Yellowjackets. Louis Arnold came up big for the Cardinals as he caught two touchdown passes from John Lamb in the second quarter to give Del Valle a 14–7 halftime lead, and the Cardinals held on from there for a 21–7 win. Del Valle intercepted four Llano passes and blocked two punts. The Cardinals were now 4–0 for the first time in school history.

They next traveled to Smithville on October 6 to take on the 2–2 Tigers. Smithville was no match for the Cardinals as Del Valle rolled to a 47–0 victory. Wilbur Williams caught two touchdown passes, and Charles Anderson caught another for the Cardinals. Bobby Moreland chipped in two rushing touchdowns and had a third on a thirty-eight-yard interception return in the third quarter. Del Valle limited Smithville to just 171 total yards and eight first downs. The Cardinals also recovered two Tiger fumbles and picked off a pair of passes. Del Valle's 5–0 start pushed them into the state rankings for the first time in school history, at number ten.

October 13, 1967, marked the opening of District 18–2A play for Del Valle, facing the Burnet Bulldogs in a home contest. The Bulldogs put an early scare into Del Valle as they returned the opening kickoff eighty yards for a touchdown and a 6–0 lead. After that, however, it was all Del Valle, who roared to a 66–6 win. Bobby Moreland scored four touchdowns for Del Valle on runs of seven, eight, and twelve yards, and he returned a third-quarter interception forty yards for a touchdown. Wilbur Williams pitched in with two touchdowns—one on a forty-yard pass from John Lamb and the other on a fifty-five-yard run. The Cardinals' defense dominated again, just as they had all season, giving up just 135 yards and forcing three turnovers.

Wilbur Williams recalled the Burnet game and how he incurred Coach Shaver's wrath on the sideline: "I remember that Burnet game because I learned that Coach Shaver could get on your case when he had to. We knew we were going to wax them, but they returned the opening kickoff for a touchdown. Then they kicked off, and I returned it fifty yards, but I fumbled the ball. Not long after that, I dropped a pass. Coach Shaver got really upset with me. Later, though, I scored two touchdowns and we won 66–6. I got kind of angry at Coach Shaver for getting on my case. I have to admit, it woke me up, though."

Now 6–0 overall and 1–0 in district play, on October 20, Del Valle entertained the Round Rock Dragons, one of the teams that had tied the

Cardinals for the District 18–2A title the previous season. Round Rock entered the game 1–0 in district play, having beaten Georgetown the previous week. A capacity homecoming crowd of 5,500 saw Del Valle pull out a hard-fought 18–6 win. The Cardinals' defense dominated again, only giving up 112 yards of offense and forcing three turnovers. Round Rock's defense held Del Valle to 214 total yards and four turnovers. The eighteen points by Del Valle turned out to be their lowest output of the season. The Cardinals broke a 6–6 halftime deadlock with a touchdown in the third and fourth quarters. The key play was in the third quarter, when Round Rock fumbled at their own four-yard line and Charles Anderson scored for Del Valle on the ensuing play. The win over Round Rock elevated Del Valle to a number-seven ranking in the state 2A poll.

Del Valle now had but two district contests left, against Georgetown and Copperas Cove, with a nondistrict game against Kenedy sandwiched in between the two. On October 27, the Cardinals traveled to Georgetown to take on the 4–3 Eagles and came away with a comeback 22–13 win before six thousand screaming Georgetown fans. After Del Valle led 6–0 after the opening quarter, thanks to a John Lamb ten-yard touchdown run, the Eagles forged ahead 13–6. Right before halftime, Del Valle knotted the score at 13–13 when Lamb uncorked a fifty-yard touchdown pass to halfback Wilbur Williams. John Hilgers booted a twenty-seven-yard field goal in the third quarter to give the Cardinals a 16–13 edge, and Charles Anderson iced the game midway through the fourth quarter with a one-yard touchdown plunge. The Del Valle defense once again took charge on the evening, forcing six turnovers on three interceptions and three fumble recoveries, and limited Georgetown to 170 total yards.

The Cardinals, now 8–0, next had a November 3 nondistrict road contest against the Kenedy Lions. Kenedy was in the midst of a season that would see them go 3–5–1 overall, and they were no match for Del Valle as the Cardinals rolled to a 26–8 win. The Cardinals clinched at least a tie for the district title and secured a trip to the state playoffs thanks to Georgetown defeating Copperas Cove. Del Valle built a 20–0 halftime advantage and coasted from there. Bobby Moreland scored on a sixty-yard run and then threw a sixty-yard halfback pass for another score.

Del Valle looked to cap off their first undefeated regular season in school history when they traveled to Copperas Cove on November 10 to take on the Bulldogs. Copperas Cove, who had been expected to contend for the district title, was suffering through a 1–7 record on the season, as injuries had taken their toll. The game was close at the half 13–6 in Del Valle's favor, but the Cardinals scored twenty unanswered second-half points to roll to a 33–6 win to spoil the Bulldogs' homecoming festivities. The Del Valle defense turned up the heat in the second half, holding Copperas Cove to minus-eleven total yards and forcing three pass interceptions.

African American player Louis Arnold remembered one of the few times the Cardinals had a racial incident when they traveled to Copperas Cove: "What really brought us together as a team was when we went to Copperas Cove. Their players were throwing racial slurs at us, and our white teammates came to our aid. We took it out on them after that. That's when we became a *team*! Our team chemistry was already great, but what happened in Copperas Cove brought us together even more."

The win over Copperas Cove left Del Valle 10–0 overall and 5–0 in District 18–2A. The Cardinals dominated their opposition in the regular season, outscoring them 361–58. Del Valle finished the regular season with a number-five state ranking, which is still the school's high-water mark after sixty-four years of football.

Meanwhile, on October 20, Kountze entered District 23–2A play with a three-game winning streak when they took on the Hardin-Jefferson Rebels. Hardin-Jefferson was the defending district champion, going 10–2–1 in 1966. The Lions came back from a 6–0 halftime deficit on two Rebels field goals to score two touchdowns in the final two minutes to win the 14–6 nail-biter. As usual, Gordon Gilder came up huge for Kountze as he put the Lions up 7–6 with a thirty-four-yard touchdown run with 1:34 left in the contest. On the next series, Gilder intercepted a Hardin-Jefferson pass and returned it forty yards for an insurance touchdown. Besides Gilder, the other star of the night was the Kountze defense. The Lions defense limited Hardin-Jefferson to just seventy-eight yards rushing and eight passing.

Next, on October 27, was a home game against the East Chambers Buccaneers, a team that ended up 2–7 in 1967. East Chambers was no match for the Lions as they rolled 47–6. Kountze's overall record was now 6–1–1, tying their highwater mark for wins in a season. More important, the Lions were 2–0 in District 23–2A play.

On November 3, the Lions played arguably the biggest game in school history when they took on the undefeated Port Acres Austin Eagles in Port Arthur. The Lions stood at 6–1–1 overall, while Austin was 8–0, and both teams had matching 2–0 records in District 23–2A play.

Bobby Snyder knew what the Lions were up against going into the game. He recalled, "Port Acres was always a tough game, especially in Port Arthur. Those guys could hit. They would knock your butt off. It would hurt when they hit you. We had our work cut out for us."

Gordon Gilder added, "That was a big game in Port Arthur against Austin. We had to beat them if we wanted to go to the playoffs. I had a good game. I returned a punt for a touchdown, threw a touchdown pass, and ran for a touchdown. It was exciting because we all knew since we beat Austin, we were going to the playoffs."

Gordon Gilder was correct in his recollection of having a stellar game against Austin. Gilder had 156 yards on twenty-two carries, and did indeed return a punt for a touchdown, ran for another, and passed for one more as the Kountze Lions took down the Austin Eagles 19–6 at Public School Stadium in Port Arthur before eight thousand fans.

After Austin punted after their first possession of the game, Gilder fielded the ball at his own thirty-four and weaved his way through the Eagles defenders for a sixty-six-yard touchdown. The Lions' extra-point try failed, and with 9:02 left in the opening quarter, the Lions led 6–0. Austin took the ensuing kickoff and marched fifty-nine yards for the tying score as the Eagles' Robert Johnson scored from three yards out, with 3:02 left in the first quarter. The first time Kountze had the ball in the second quarter, they marched seventy-three yards in fourteen plays to go ahead 12–6. On a third and nine play from the Austin eighteen, Gordon Gilder took a pitchout to the right side and pulled up and hit end Bobby Snyder with a pass in the end zone.

Bobby Snyder recalled the touchdown pass that Gilder threw to him: "I was a tight end, and I caught a few passes that season. Mostly eight to eleven yards over the middle. I do remember scoring on a halfback option pass. Gordon took a pitchout, and when everybody on the team swarmed toward him, that left me wide open. There was no one within twenty yards of me."

Kountze got on the scoreboard one more time before halftime as Gilder scored from ten yards out after the Lions went seventy-six yards in nine plays. The extra point was finally good, and the Lions led 19–6 at halftime—which is how the game ended because the second half was scoreless. Austin dominated the statistical battle, as they had twenty-one first downs to just eleven for Kountze. The Eagles had a 254–196 rushing advantage as well as a 94–18 passing advantage. What hurt Austin most was drawing eighty yards in penalties to just twenty for Kountze. The Lions also did not turn the ball over during the game, while Austin lost a key fumble in the second quarter when they were driving for the potential game-tying touchdown.

With the win over Austin, Kountze was now 7–1–1 overall and 3–0 in District 18–2A play, and the Lions clinched the district title and playoff berth that went with it.

On November 10, Kountze took on Hamshire-Fannett in Fannett in their final regular-season game. The Lions ended up taking a tough 28–12 win over the Longhorns. Kountze went into the half with a slight 7–6 advantage. With 4:44 left in the third quarter, Gordon Gilder scored from five yards out to help put the Lions up 14–6. The Longhorns narrowed the gap to 14–12 early in the fourth quarter, when they blocked a Kountze punt and recovered it in the Lions' end zone for a touchdown. However, the ensuing two-point conversion attempt that would have tied the game failed. Kountze added two touchdowns late in the contest as Gilder scored from one yard out and Roger Anderson raced in from twelve yards away with 3:43 left to go to make the final margin 28–12. The Lions ended the regular season with an 8–1–1 record and a 4–0 district mark. It was now time for the Lions to prepare for the playoffs.

With a 10–0 regular-season record under their belts, Del Valle now readied themselves for a rematch of the previous year's bi-district matchup with the 5–4 Cameron Yeomen. Cameron had defeated the Cardinals 23–14 in 1966, with a crucial third-quarter blocked punt being the difference. The two squads faced off on November 18 in Belton. The Cardinals pulled out a rugged 14–0 victory over the tough Cameron outfit, scoring two fourth-quarter touchdowns to win the game. Wilbur Williams scored both touchdowns for the Cardinals—the first one on a thirty-four-yard pass from John Lamb with 10:40 left in the contest and the second on a one-yard run halfway through the fourth quarter to cap off a seven-play, twenty-five-yard drive after a Cameron fumble.

Wilbur Williams said the following about his first touchdown: "I remember the thirty-four-yard touchdown against Cameron. John Lamb had tried to hit me with a couple of long passes earlier in the game, but he overthrew me on them. The thirty-four-yarder, though—he laid it in there for me. We finally connected."

The one negative development that hampered the Cardinals was the fact that star fullback Bobby Moreland injured his right knee on his first carry of the evening and was done for the rest of the season. The loss of Moreland hurt because he had picked up 1,550 yards on 202 carries and nineteen touchdowns during the regular season. On defense, Moreland was in on twenty-three tackles a game and had intercepted seven passes.

John Lamb recalled, "We started getting injuries as the year went along. Bobby Moreland tore up his knee; I tore up my shoulder in the last game before the playoffs. I don't know how Coach Shaver did it, but he got Coach Darrell Royal over at UT to send a couple of his student trainers to our playoff games, home and away, to watch over my shoulder."

Kountze now prepared for just the second playoff game in school history, also on November 18. Their bi-district matchup was in Beaumont against the 8–2 Hull-Daisetta Bobcats—a playoff regular. The Bobcats were at the end of a run where they won their district title and went to the playoffs six times in seven years from 1961 to 1967. Hull-Daisetta's playoff experience apparently didn't impress Kountze, as the Lions ripped the Bobcats 33–6. Gordon Gilder kicked off the scoring for Kountze with 3:17 left in the first quarter as his three-yard run capped off a 72-yard drive. Hull-Daisetta came right back with a second-quarter touchdown, but a missed two-point conversion made the score 7–6 Kountze. Gilder struck again for Kountze on their next possession as he raced forty-eight yards for a score to put the Lions up 14–6. The Lions added another touchdown late in the second quarter when a Bobcats fumble gave Kountze the ball at the Hull-Daisetta fifteen. Quarterback Larry Moody took the ball into the end zone a couple of plays later, and the Lions led at halftime 21–6. With 5:43 left in the third quarter, Gordon Gilder struck again for Kountze as he raced forty-six yards for his third touchdown of the evening. With 7:08 left in the contest, Moody scored his second touchdown of the night, and the Lions led 33–6, which was the final tally. The Kountze defense was as impressive as their offense, with Hull-Daisetta managing just 196 total yards.

Del Valle's second-round opponent on November 25 in Brenham were the Tomball Cougars, who, like the Cardinals, were 11–0 on the 1967 season. The Cougars were a 15–6 winner over Columbus in their bi-district contest. The Cardinals used three big plays to help pull out a heart-stopping 14–13 victory over the Tomball Cougars. The first came on the first play of the second quarter when 140-pound halfback Charles Anderson broke off an eighty-yard touchdown run. Anderson ended the evening with 149 yards on eighteen carries. Then, in the fourth quarter with the score knotted at seven, Edwin Collins blocked a Tomball punt and Del Valle took over on the Cougars' fifteen-yard line. Five plays later, Wilbur Williams scored on a one-yard dive, and John Hilgers's extra-point kick made it 14–7. Then

Williams and Collins combined to turn in the play of the night on defense. With Del Valle up 14–7 late in the fourth quarter, Tomball launched a sixty-two-yard drive and scored the potential game-tying touchdown with little time left. Down 14–13 and behind Del Valle in penetrations 3–2, Tomball had to go for a two-point conversion and the win to advance to the next round of the playoffs. Cougars wingback Henry Doaks took a handoff and headed around the left end, where he was met by Williams just short of the goal line. It looked like Doaks could power his way across for the win, but Collins came up to assist Williams as they turned Doaks away.

Wilbur Williams recalled his game-saving tackle against Tomball: "I remember that play against Tomball. I met up with the ball carrier at the one and then Edwin helped me. Even though I was only 140 pounds, in my mind I thought I was 180. I always had to psyche myself up into thinking that. In my mind, nobody was going to run over me. After that play and us getting the win, I thought we were going to go to the championship game and win it all in 1967."

Next for Kountze on their playoff run were the Crockett Bulldogs on November 25 at Sam Houston State University in Huntsville. Crockett had pulled off a surprising 28–6 win over heavily favored Buna, a team that had defeated Kountze 19–0 in week three. Crockett had started their season slowly, going 3–4 in nondistrict play, but caught fire and went 3–0 in District 21–2A play. With the bi-district win over Buna, the Bulldogs had now won six in a row.

What looked on paper to be a close contest was anything but as the Lions rolled over Crockett 54–20. With 3:41 left in the first quarter, Gordon Gilder took a swing pass from quarterback Larry Moody and raced thirty-three yards to the end zone. The extra point made it 7–0. Before his touchdown catch, Gilder had amazingly returned two consecutive punts eighty-plus yards for touchdowns, but both were called back because of penalties.

Harrison McMillan recalled Gilder's punt returns against Crockett, albeit in a slightly hyperbolic form: "Gordon Gilder was the best I've ever seen. He was something else. He was pro material. In our playoff game against Crockett, I swear he had five punt return touchdowns called back because of penalties."

Years later, Gordon Gilder confirmed the true number of punt returns called back: "Actually, when we beat Crockett in the playoffs, I returned two punts in a row for long touchdowns—both of them were called back because of a penalty. It wasn't five, like Harrison said."

On the first play of the second quarter, Gilder struck again, as he caught a halfback pass from Rickey Winger and jaunted forty yards to the Crockett end zone. Gilder then set up the next Lions touchdown with 3:07 left until halftime when he threw a twenty-nine-yard pass to Larry Moody. Harrison McMillan punched the ball in from the two-yard line, and it was 20–0 Kountze. Crockett finally got on the board just six seconds before the half when they returned a punt seventy-five yards for a touchdown. The score was 20–6 at halftime. Kountze struck first in the third quarter when they went fifty-five yards in seven plays on their opening drive. Moody ran twenty-six yards around right end to make it 27–6. After James Sims recovered a Crockett fumble at their own thirty-five, Gilder scored his third touchdown four plays later, which made it 34–6. Crockett promptly fumbled the ball at their own forty-five when they got the ball back, and four plays later, McMillan bulled his way into the end zone from two yards out with eleven seconds left in the third quarter. Crockett scored quickly at the start of the fourth quarter, but Larry Moody came right back with a seventy-three-yard sprint to the end zone to put Kountze up 47–14. The two teams traded touchdowns to finish out the game and to account for the 54–20 final score.

Both Del Valle and Kountze advanced to the Class 2A state quarterfinals, and this was where their seasons and stories finally converged. As if it was fate, one of the Class 2A quarterfinals matchups was to be between 12–0 Del Valle and 10–1–1 Kountze—two historically unlikely contenders. The contest was scheduled for December 2 in Brenham, the site of Del Valle's previous playoff game against Tomball. Both squads possessed high-scoring offenses and stingy defenses. Del Valle had outscored their opponents 389–71 during the season, while Kountze had rung up 479 points to just 123 for their foes.

It was only fitting that these two Cinderella squads would play a classic game. The contest was a back-and-forth affair all the way to the spine-tingling conclusion. Del Valle struck first in the opening quarter when Louis Arnold caught a twenty-five-yard touchdown pass from John Lamb. Kountze and Gordon Gilder struck back with two second-quarter touchdowns of his own, one of them from twenty-one yards out with 4:01 left before halftime. After Del Valle fumbled the ensuing kickoff, Gilder's next touchdown came with just fifty-seven seconds before the half from six yards away. Del Valle struck back just before halftime on a Lamb four-yard touchdown run around the left end. The Cardinals went for two points, and this time Lamb ran around the right end for the conversion to give Del Valle the lead at halftime, 15–14.

Kountze surged back ahead in the third quarter on another Gilder touchdown as he again went in from six yards away. Del Valle countered in the fourth quarter with two touchdowns to put them up 29–21. Josh Brown hit pay dirt from thirty yards away, and Jesse Lopez recovered a blocked Kountze punt in the end zone for the go-ahead score, with just four minutes to play. That set the stage for the final Kountze drive, with hopes to tie the score at twenty-nine. The Lions got the ball on their forty, and Gilder and quarterback Larry Moody took turns rushing the ball down the field until Harrison McMillan scored on a one-yard plunge with fifty-nine seconds left. Down by two points, Kountze went for the two-point conversion to tie up the game.

Whereas the previous week Del Valle won because they stopped Tomball's two-point conversion attempt at the end of the contest to defeat the Cougars, this time the Cardinals were not as lucky. On the two-point try, Gordon Gilder faked a sweep to the right, and when the Del Valle players went to tackle Gilder, he lofted a pass to Rickey Winger in the end zone, who was wide open. Ted Tate said after the game, "It was a made-up play. I thought it might work, so I sent it in from the bench."

Gordon Gilder, who led all rushers of the night with forty carries for 208 yards, recalled, "I remember throwing the two-point conversion pass to Rickey Winger that let us tie Del Valle, and we beat them on first downs. I just rolled out to the right, and when the Del Valle players went after me, I threw Ricky the ball in the end zone. He was wide open."

Years later, Del Valle's Wilbur Williams reminisced on the two-point conversion play: "It was a great game against Kountze in 1967. We did all we could to win. Kountze had to score the two-point conversion at the end to tie us at twenty-nine. We were tied in penetrations, so they beat us by having more first downs. I knew on the two-point attempt they were going to try and pass. Our other cornerback was Edwin Collins, a sophomore. I yelled over to him, 'Watch out for the pass!' He bit on the fake sweep by Gilder, though, and the Kountze guy got behind him."

The last-minute two-point conversion by the Kountze Lions tied the score at 29–29. When the game was over, the two squads were tied in penetrations (how many times a team penetrates their opponent's twenty-yard line)—the first step in declaring who would advance to the next round—at five apiece, and since Kountze had an 18–12 advantage in first downs—the next step in deciding who would stay home and who would go on—the Lions advanced to the state semifinals.

What the cliffhanger with Del Valle also showed was how close the margin can be between victory and defeat. Fullback and placekicker Harrison McMillan recalled a key play he was involved in: "In our 29–29 tie with Del Valle, I remember the last extra point I kicked, I kind of missed it and the ball went really high in the air and came down on the crossbar, but it bounced over the goalpost and was good. What if it fell the other way and was no good? We probably would have lost."

Ted Tate recalled another potential game-changing play. After the game, he said to the *Kountze Times*, "Del Valle had the ball on the Kountze twenty-two in the first period. Charles Anderson, the Cards' fine halfback, hit over right tackle and reached the twenty; he fumbled the ball to the ten and the Lions recovered. Had Anderson held on to the ball, it would have been a penetration. In the end, it would have been the difference in the game, with Del Valle winning 6–5 on penetrations."

Cardinals quarterback John Lamb reminisced about what is still the best season in Del Valle history: "I remember the playoff games the most, especially Tomball and, of course, the tie with Kountze. It was a great place to be and a great time to grow up. Coach Shaver also pulled off—I don't know how he did it—but he got Greyhound buses for us and the fans so we could ride to the playoff games. Other schools were showing up in the old yellow school buses, but we traveled in style."

Assistant coach Dave Smith added, "It was a fun time. It hurt that Bobby Moreland tore up his knee against Cameron. Besides being a good runner, he was a great safety. It hurt us against Kountze. They had Gordon Gilder, who was something else. We couldn't slow him down. Bobby may have made the difference on that two-point conversion."

As for Steve Shaver, he left Del Valle after the 1968 season and briefly went into private business but reemerged in 1971 just a few miles away from Kountze when he became the head coach at Beaumont French High School. In four years at Del Valle, he compiled a 33–8–2 record. Shaver is still the most successful coach in Cardinals history. However, his career was not over by any means.

By the 1970s, the Del Valle football program had fallen back on hard times, from which they have never really recovered. After Steve Shaver left at the end of the 1968 season, Del Valle's record from 1971 to 1976 was a dismal 4–55–1. Winless seasons followed in 1984, 1990, 1993, and 1995. Del Valle did not return to the playoffs until 2002, after a 5–5 finish netted them third place in District 25-4A and a 29–3 bi-district loss to one-time state powerhouse Austin Reagan. To date, the Cardinals have returned to the playoffs five times since 2002 but have no playoff wins to show for their efforts. After sixty-eight seasons, their overall record stands at 219–458–9. The Cardinals' two playoff wins in 1967 remain the only postseason victories in school history.

Although the 1967 season was over for Del Valle, Kountze had survived the classic showdown with the Cardinals and moved on to the state semifinals against the San Antonio Randolph Ro-Hawks on December 9 at Kyle Field in College Station. Randolph, a school that had only been in existence since 1962, was 12–0–1. They had eliminated the previous year's state champion, Sweeny, the prior week in the quarterfinals, 12–7.

Unfortunately for the Kountze Lions, their dream season ended in College Station at the hands of the Ro-Hawks. Down 7–6 in the third quarter, Randolph capitalized on a Gordon Gilder fumble at his own ten-yard line and scored with 3:02 remaining in the quarter; they hung on from there for the 14–7 win. The Lions offense was stymied by the Ro-Hawks defense, gaining a season-low 132 total yards—125 rushing and just 7 passing. Gordon Gilder was held in check, for the most part, with eighty-two yards on nineteen totes for the evening. He did bust loose in the second quarter for a winding forty-nine-yard touchdown run, which gave Kountze its only lead of the night at 7–6. Ball control was the key for Randolph, as they ran seventy-two plays to just thirty-six for Kountze. Unfortunately for Randolph, their state title hopes were dashed the following week in the finals when they lost to state powerhouse Plano, 27–8.

"Randolph was the toughest game I had ever played in," Bobby Snyder recalled. "We had only twenty-four players. They had about forty or forty-five. Gordon didn't have his best game. They had a couple of fast defensive backs who could keep up with him. They would also rotate fresh players into the game, and it wore us out. They were also a lot bigger than we were, like twenty to thirty pounds per man. I weighed in at 180, and they had guys who were 230 to 240. They were quick, too. They just had a very good team. If we played them ten times, they would win eight. They were just better."

However, Snyder added, "Even though we lost, it was a memorable time. The whole town was behind us. We had a huge following. It was disappointing at the end, but having the whole town and school behind us really meant something. They were still behind us even though we lost. I'm proud of my school and my hometown."

"We were very tight, me and my teammates," Gordon Gilder recalled fondly. "It was a great year. Everyone was excited—the school and the city of Kountze. They had never done anything like this before. It helped race relations some in Kountze, but to be honest, it wasn't bad to begin with. It was a fun time."

Fred Williams summed it up when he said, "Every win in 1967 was a big win. Hey, when you only win one game the year before, every win is big. No one saw that season coming. It was a great team effort. The kids were easy to coach. They were all good kids. That team turned around the atmosphere of the town. They did a lot for integration. I never had a problem with any of the kids. I like them, and they know that. It was a fun ride while it lasted."

After their 1967 drive to the Class 2A semifinals, Kountze fell back to a disappointing 4–6 record in 1968. The Lions expected to have James Sims back for his senior season, but that didn't work out and Kountze's record suffered. Sims left after the 1967 season and finished his senior year at Locke High School in Los Angeles before eventually heading off to the University of Southern California (USC). Sims was a first-team Pacific-8 Conference selection for the Trojans in 1972 as a defensive end and in 1973 as a linebacker. He was nicknamed "Psycho" by his USC teammates because of his hitting ability. Sims was a twelfth-round pick of the New York Giants in the 1974 NFL Draft. He played in the World Football League in 1974 and 1975. In 1976, he played for the Tampa Bay Buccaneers in their inaugural NFL season for his old college coach John McKay.

When asked about James Sims, Fred Williams responded, "No one has heard from James in years. He still has relatives in Kountze, but he pretty much vanished."

Gordon Gilder added, "James Sims was a good friend of mine; we were very close. We lived right by each other growing up. He wasn't very big, but he grew a bunch when he came to Kountze in his junior year, and he grew some more when he went out to California. After he went to California, we lost touch with each other over the years."

Sims's ex-wife Pam and his former USC teammates feel confident that he likely passed away, but no death certificate has ever been found for him. Sims is conjectured to have fallen victim to murder years ago in a bar in a knife- or gunfight—possibly over gambling debts.

Fred Williams also spoke on the reason James Sims headed out to California after his junior season. Race relations in Texas still had a long way to go, and "James left Kountze after his junior year to go out to California because his family sent him out there to live with relatives. Turns out, back here in Kountze, he got involved with a white girl. They were afraid he might get killed."

After he had rushed for more than 2,200 yards and scored thirty-eight touchdowns during the 1967 season, Gordon Gilder, on the other hand, was one of the top football recruits in Texas and the United States. Schools like Texas, Michigan State, USC, and UCLA recruited the elusive halfback. Gilder finally decided to attend Southern Methodist University (SMU), because, as Gilder said, "that's where Jerry Levias went." Three years earlier, Levias, from nearby Beaumont Hebert High School, had integrated the now-defunct Southwest Conference when he chose to attend SMU.

Beyond taking the Lions to the 1967 football semifinals, Ted Tate excelled at coaching basketball and baseball to boot. He coached the Kountze baseball team to the 1972 regional title, which was the furthest a Class 2A team could advance in the playoffs. In addition, Tate took Kountze to the state championship game in basketball in 1977, where they lost to Morton, 63–60. It is believed that Tate is the only coach in Texas high school history to take three different sports to the state semifinals or better. Tate amassed an overall 502–258–5 record coaching football, basketball, and baseball. He passed away in Kountze in February 2019, at the age of eighty-six.

As for the Kountze football program, they fell on even harder times than Del Valle after their 1967 playoff run, and their futility has continued to this day. The Lions endured a then–Texas state record of fifty-three straight losses from September 1977 until October 1982. From 1978 until 1981, when the Lions had four straight 0–10 campaigns, Kountze was outscored 1,398–120. Kountze has returned to the playoffs only twice since the losing streak, losing first-round playoff games in 2013 and 2014 after fourth-place finishes in their district both seasons. In seventy-two seasons, Kountze has a 231–467–12 overall record. As with Del Valle, the Lions' two playoff wins in 1967 remain their only ones in school history.

But during that one magical season in 1967, the stories of Del Valle and Kountze converged briefly for three hours in Brenham on a chilly December night in the playoffs. It was underdog versus underdog in a classic Cinderella matchup on the gridiron—a moment that was the first of its kind and destined never to be replicated since. Theirs is the story of two true Texas underdogs and their fleeting glance at victory, there one second and gone with a flash.

Rule

The Triumph and Tragedy of the 13–1 Class B State Runner-Up Bobcats, 1973

AT THE INTERSECTION of US Highway 380 and State Highway 6, about fifty-five miles north of Abilene, is the town of Rule, Texas. In its heyday, around 1960, Rule's population hovered at about 1,350 people. In the early 1960s, the town had five grocery stores, six service stations, two lumberyards, two pharmacies, a furniture store, and three restaurants. There was one movie theater, along with a drive-in theater on the outskirts of town. Unfortunately, like many small towns in Texas (and in the United States, for that matter), Rule has seen a steady decline in the last sixty years in terms of both industry and population. In earlier times, the town's main industries were farming and oil, but both have declined since the 1960s. Oil-service giant Haliburton once had a facility there but has since moved on. By 1984, the town's population had declined so much that the Rule High School Bobcats had to drop down to a six-man football team. As of 2016, the population of Rule was about 625 people—less than half of what it had been a few decades prior. Today, Rule has a bank, an Allsup's convenience store, a Mexican restaurant, and little else.

Dennis Briles grew up in Rule and eventually returned to his hometown in 1970 to coach football at his former high school. He had a tall task ahead of him with the Bobcats. The town's high school football program had been in the doldrums ever since its inception in 1928. Even legendary Coach Gordon Wood, who got his start in Rule in 1940–41, couldn't garner a respectable reputation for the Bobcats. Wood was a head coach for forty-four years in Texas, and when he retired in 1985, he held the state record for the most wins, compiling a 394–93–15 record. He still holds the record for state titles, with a total of nine under his belt. Yet in Wood's two years at Rule, he led them to a 2–8 record in 1940 (his only losing season as a coach) and 4–3–2 in 1941. Other coaches didn't fare any better. From 1928 to 1969, Rule's overall record was 162–175–23, with one district title in 1949. A young Dennis Briles was a member of the victorious 1949 team, as an all-district end, defensive back, and placekicker. That year, the Bobcats went 8–4 and won the only playoff game in school history—ironically, that is, until Briles himself took over as coach.

There was immediate improvement when Briles became the head coach at Rule in 1970. The Bobcats went 8–3–1, won the district title, and lost in the regional final—the furthest a Class B school could advance at that time. Briles was aided by the fact that his inaugural squad included all-state running back Jimmy Lisle—the older brother of 1973 team member Mike Lisle. Jimmy rushed for more than 2,000 yards with the Bobcats as a senior, before going off to play college football at West Texas State (now West Texas A&M).

Briles's Bobcats also included assistant coach Jasper Wilson, who assumed his role at about the same time as Briles. Wilson spoke about his first encounter with the head coach and how that led to his arrival in Rule: "I'm from Abilene. I went to Abilene High in the late 1950s and played for Chuck Moser for a couple of years after Abilene had won those three straight state titles. He was a great coach—outstanding. One of my teammates at Abilene was Dave Parks, who went on to Texas Tech and was the number-one pick in the NFL draft in 1964. I couldn't afford to go to college after high school. My family was dirt poor, so I went and did oil field work. I went off to Vietnam, and when I came back in 1966, I knew I wanted to coach. I went to McMurry College in Abilene and got my teaching degree in agriculture. Then I was sent to Franklin Junior High in Abilene ISD and worked under Dennis Briles. After I finished, I went off to McCaulley, Texas, and I was coaching at the small school there. When Dennis got the job at Rule, I went for an interview. When I walked in, Dennis greeted me with a smile on his face. I knew then that I had the job. We worked well together. Dennis was quieter than I was, and he didn't panic a whole lot. Me, on the other hand, I was a little more outspoken."

Wilson also talked about Briles and his coaching style: "Dennis was always prepared. Whenever we got the ball at the start of the game, Dennis would call a trick play or use a different formation to try and mix things up a bit. He turned the defense over to me. I appreciated his confidence that I could handle it. On offense, we spread the field and ran outside a lot. If we threw the ball, it was to Larry Barbee. He was a state champion high jumper, and Dennis's son Art would just throw the ball up there and let Larry outjump the defender for it."

Art Briles, Dennis Briles's youngest son and eventual all-state quarterback and safety for the Bobcats, described coming to Rule from Abilene

Rule quarterback Art Briles and teammates celebrate quarterfinal win over Prosper. Courtesy of Rule Independent School District

and what life was like on the field for a coach's son: "Moving to Rule was an extremely difficult time for me. It was a little bitty town. It took me at least two years to adjust. Everybody that was there was already established. Playing sports helped; it was very beneficial. It occupied my time. And playing for my dad was great. Anytime you can be around your dad, it's positive. It was always great seeing how important coaching and interacting with kids was to him.

"About the only negative of playing for your dad is that everything is magnified. It's a tough situation. You're under constant scrutiny. You're the coach's son. I learned so much from him. He was a huge influence. And I took a tremendous amount from him that I've used in my own coaching career. He was very analytical—a student of the game. He tried to be creative. Probably the biggest thing I got from him was to truly care and have compassion for the players."

Bobcats tailback and linebacker Mike Lisle concurred: "Art and I were big buddies in high school. When he came as a freshman, there was a bit of an adjustment. It helped that he was a good player and that the team was successful. It also helped that he was good in track. I'm sure coming to Rule from Abilene was a bit of an adjustment."

Several former players under Dennis Briles and Jasper Wilson described their coaches' personalities, along with their coaching styles. Nolan Pittcock was the center and defensive tackle on the 1973 squad. He offered the following comments about his coaches: "I was born and raised in Rule. Coach Briles was level-headed. He could get upset sometimes, but he never really got out of line. Now, Coach Wilson, I should say, was very enthusiastic. He coached the linemen, so I spent a lot of time with him. Coach Briles coached the backs. Coach Wilson liked to get his linemen fired up to play, and he was good at it. In my opinion, Coach Wilson was the backbone of the team. He might grab you and shake you on the sidelines, but he could get the best out of you. He took care of us both on and off the field."

"Coach Briles and Jasper Wilson came at the same time in 1970," recalled Cole Turner, the Bobcats' all-state tackle. "They knew each other. Our four years in the Rule program were the coaches' first four years at Rule. We steadily improved every year. Coach Briles was pretty laid-back, but Coach Wilson was kind of the opposite. We had a bunch of fast guys who could run. Coach Briles liked to spread things out to take advantage of our speed. We threw the ball a little bit. Art could throw it, and Larry Barbee was pretty good at catching it. We ran a lot of sweeps, quick stuff, pitches, and quarterback keepers. We didn't just run up the middle."

Rob Kittley was an all-area running back and linebacker for Rule, who reminisced, "Coach Briles was laid-back and didn't get too emotional. Coach Wilson—now, he was a fireball. He was a little more boisterous. He was a good man and a good coach. He wasn't afraid to chew on you, though. They both came my freshman year in 1970. Coach Briles came from Lincoln Junior High in Abilene, and Coach Wilson was originally from McCaulley—not too far from here. We ran a form of an "I" formation on offense. We ran off tackle a lot to try and get outside. We had quite a bit of speed. I won state in track in the 880-yard run. Art was fast, and so was our fullback, Mike Lisle. Our main receiver, Larry Barbee, also had speed. We ran some end-arounds. We ran the ball a lot more than we threw it."

Mike Lisle recalled, "Our freshman class in 1970 started a great era in Rule. We had a great four years. Our freshman year, we went 8–3–1 and lost in the regional finals. My brother Jimmy was a senior running back, and he had a great year and went on to play at West Texas State. He was eventually drafted by the Falcons. We went 9–1 the next two seasons. Coach Briles and Jasper brought new life into Rule. Jasper Wilson reminded me of Sergeant Carter on the old *Gomer Pyle* TV show—kinda loud. He could get the best out of you, though. He was really good at coaching the linemen."

Larry Barbee, Rule's all-state receiver and state champion in the high jump, said, "Oh yeah, every year we had high expectations. We started winning games once Coach Briles and Coach Wilson came after our

Rule High School principal and head football coach Dennis Briles. Courtesy of Rule Independent School District

eighth-grade year. We had four winning seasons. Coach Briles was a great coach. Coach Wilson was well respected. He meant what he said. He was a great track coach, too. I was a high jumper. We had a lot of team speed, and I could jump pretty high, so Art would throw the ball and I would outjump people for it. Art had a good arm, though."

Rule steadily improved after Briles and Wilson's arrival. After their district title in 1970, the Bobcats went 9–1 in 1971, with their only setback being a 26–20 loss to Newcastle, who ended up winning the regional championship. The year 1971 marked the last season wherein Class B teams could only advance as far as regionals. The first time Class B squads would play for a state title was in 1972.

Rule followed up their solid 1971 season with another 9–1 mark in 1972. Like the previous season, it ended in disappointment. The Bobcats were the preseason favorites to take the state title, and they lived up to their predictions as they rolled to a 9–0 record. Only one game remained, against rival Chillicothe at the Eagles' home field. Rule held on to a 7–0 lead at the half, but Chillicothe scored two second-half touchdowns to prevail 14–7. The Eagles' win brought the district race to a three-way tie between Chillicothe, Rule, and Throckmorton. As was the standard practice back then, a coin flip was used to decide the district champion. Chillicothe, who finished 6–4, won the coin flip and advanced to the playoffs, where they proceeded to lose to Lometa 25–6.

Several of the Bobcats, like Nolan Pittcock, spoke of their disappointment over missing the playoffs: "We felt we got cheated out of it. It should have never came down to a coin flip."

"In 1972, we were number one in the state," Cole Turner added. "We had high expectations for that season. We missed the playoffs by a coin toss. We lost to Chillicothe, a team we should have beaten, the last game of the season."

Art Briles spoke about the disappointment he experienced in Chillicothe on that November night in 1972 and the lessons he learned from it: "It was a cold, chilly night in Chillicothe. I learned a couple of things that evening that have stuck with me through the years. The first thing was never to take an opponent too lightly. My dad warned us before the game to not take Chillicothe for granted. He told us the same thing at halftime. At halftime, though, we said to ourselves, 'Hey, we got this.' We thought there was no way they could beat us, but they did. That game taught me a valuable lesson in my coaching career, and that was to take your opponent seriously, that you can lose to anyone. It was the ignorance of youth. What I also learned from that loss was how you don't realize, when you're young, that you don't get situations or opportunities like that very often and you have to make the most of it. I learned you have to play at 100 percent every snap, every play."

Briles continued, "Only one team made the playoffs back in 1972. We were really good—probably better overall than our 1973 team. That 1972 team was probably the best I've ever played on. It was disappointing to not be able to try and win a state title, but the loss did serve as motivation for my senior year."

The Bobcats did have a lot of motivation going into the 1973 season. They had experience, talent, leadership, and togetherness.

Mike Lisle recalled, "We had great senior leadership: Art, myself, Kittley, Barbee, Turner. We hauled hay and chopped cotton in the summer for our conditioning. In the preseason, we played Class A teams like Aspermont, Knox City, and Munday. Coach Briles tried to step up our scheduling to prepare us for district play. Most of us grew up in Rule, which was a farming community. We were just a bunch of farm boys who grew up there. Our team in 1973 was blessed with talent, speed, depth, and quickness. Winning was in our blood. Before we came along, Rule had some pretty mediocre teams. Coach Briles and Coach Wilson changed all of that."

Rob Kittley commented, "We thought we had a chance to be pretty good in 1973. We lost eight or nine seniors off of the 1972 team, so we had a few holes to fill. We all grew up together. Ninety percent of us started in the first grade together. That helped us later on because we had played so much together that we could depend on each other; we had that trust."

Rule running back Rob Kittley. Courtesy of Rule Independent School District

At the start of the 1973 season, Rule was predicted to battle it out with rival Throckmorton for the District 5–B crown. As far as the state rankings, the Bobcats came in at number five in

Class B. Rule returned fifteen with lettermen and eleven starters. Seven of the lettermen had three years of experience, including Larry Barbee, Cole Turner, and Art Briles. Mike Lisle, whose late-season injury in 1972 may have cost Rule a district title, was back also, along with running back Rob Kittley. One of Coach Briles's main concerns was inexperience in both the offensive and defensive lines.

Despite this setback, Rule also had the advantage of speed. The Bobcats won the state title in track the previous spring. Rob Kittley was the state runner-up in the 880-yard run. Art Briles was a three-time state qualifier in track. He placed second in the 220-yard dash in 1972 and 1973, was second in the 100-yard dash in 1973, and was the anchor on the state champion mile relay team in 1972. Larry Barbee was a state high-jump champion as a sophomore and runner-up as a junior.

"We were a team, and we had the talent spread around," Nolan Pittcock recalled. "And it wasn't just football. We were good in the other sports at Rule, too. We had a bunch of boys and girls who were good athletes. We were taught to win and to achieve. Most everybody prospered after high school and college. When we played football, we were on a continuous high. We never felt like we would be beat. It was a helluva bunch of guys, and we played some fantastic football. We were ready for our senior season. We couldn't wait."

Game one for the 1973 Rule Bobcats was a home contest on September 7 against the Class A Aspermont Hornets—the favorite to win District 8–A. Rule jumped out to an 8–0 lead in the first quarter on an Art Briles one-yard plunge and two-point conversion pass from Briles to Larry Barbee. Rule added a second-quarter score when Rob Kittley scored on a five-yard scamper. The extra point was no good, and the Bobcats led 14–0 at halftime. Aspermont closed the gap to 14–6 in the third quarter as they picked off a Briles pass and returned it seventy yards. That set up a five-yard touchdown by the Hornets. The rest of the game was scoreless as Rule held on for a 14–6 win. The Bobcats defense ruled the night as they limited Aspermont to nine first downs and 175 total yards. However, their offense was sluggish, as they only had eight first downs and 118 yards rushing. In addition, their only pass attempt of the night was picked off by the Hornets.

Next up for the Bobcats was a short seventeen-mile trip up Highway 6 for their first road contest against the Knox City Greyhounds. Rule used six Knox City turnovers, three fumbles, and three interceptions to beat the Greyhounds 29–6. The Bobcats led by only 8–0 at halftime as Mike Lisle scored the first of his two touchdowns in the second quarter on a two-yard run and then added another two yarder in the third quarter, in addition to scoring on the two-point conversion, to give Rule a 16–0 lead. Rule added thirteen fourth-quarter points on an eleven-yard run by Briles, and a fifty-two-yard scamper by Rob Kittley capped off the night for Rule. Knox City added a late touchdown to account for the final score. The Bobcats defense was stellar once again. In addition to the six turnovers, Knox City was only able to gain 206 yards on the evening. Rule's offense made strides from the previous week—this time accounting for 235 rushing and seventy-three passing yards.

September 21 brought a home game against the 1–1 Munday Moguls. It was the Art Briles show on offense as the Bobcats pitched a 29–0 shutout. Briles had a hand in all but one of the points scored for Rule. Briles ran for two scores, passed for two more, and scored two two-point conversions for the Bobcats. Briles's first touchdown pass of thirty-five yards to Larry Barbee came just four minutes into the game. Halfway through the second quarter, Briles hit Barbee again for a thirty-yard score. Sandwiched in between the two passing touchdowns was a five-yard Briles touchdown run. After a scoreless third quarter, Briles capped off the scoring for the night with a fifty-five-yard gallop to pay dirt. The Rule defense, led by Leonard Rhoads, Jimmy Macias, and Bud Hunt, didn't let the Moguls cross midfield in the first half and held them to five first downs and ninety-one total yards on the evening. The Bobcats' passing game showed improvement, with Briles completing six of twelve passes for one hundred yards and two scores. Rule was now 3–0 for the season and had inched up to number two in the state Class B rankings.

A 26–0 home game shutout was next for the Bobcats on September 28, when they played the Jayton Jaybirds out of District 3–B. After a scoreless first period, Rule exploded for thirteen second-quarter points, courtesy of an eighty-five-yard run from Art Briles, and a seventeen-yard pass play to wingback Larry Barbee. In the third quarter, Briles scored his second touchdown of the night on the ground, this time from one yard out, and reserve quarterback Steve Anders hit Barbee with an eleven-yard strike in the fourth quarter. The hosts limited Jayton to a mere 118 yards rushing and twenty-three passing.

With a record of 2–2, Santa Anna out of District 10–A was next for the 4–0 Bobcats. The October 5 away contest against the Mountaineers was no contest, as Rule rolled to a 41–6 win. Art Briles ran for four touchdowns for the winning cause. Mike Lisle scored another, along with Terry Futch. Rule scored all of their points in the first half, and Santa Anna scored a touchdown late in the contest to avoid a shutout. Rule rang up 367 total yards, and the Rule defense shut down their opponent for the fifth straight game. On the season, the Rule defense had given up just twelve points in five contests.

That all changed, however, in Rule's October 12 home matchup with the 2–2 Loraine Bulldogs. Going into the contest, Rule knew there was a difficult task at hand. Art Briles recalled, "For a nondistrict game, this was about as big as it gets. They were also one of the fastest teams we played because they had great athletes. There were just a lot of fast players on the field, especially for Class B. We knew they were going to be tough."

The Bulldogs scorched the Bobcats defense for thirty-four points. Fortunately, the Rule offense was in high gear as the Bobcats rolled up sixty-nine points of their own to crush the District 3–B Bulldogs. Rule scored on their first six possessions of the night and coasted to a 46–18 halftime lead. The Bobcats had to overcome a stellar passing performance by Loraine quarterback Eddie Merket as he threw for 336 yards and four touchdowns. Rule quarterback Briles countered with 208 yards on fifteen carries and two touchdowns, and he passed for two more, along with a pair of two-point conversions. Rob Kittley pitched in 145 yards rushing on fourteen carries, including touchdown runs of sixty-two and thirty-eight yards. Kittley also returned a kickoff ninety yards for a touchdown. Mike Lisle had 150 yards on twenty-one carries and a touchdown. Rule ran for an astounding 545 yards on the ground during the game.

Mike Lisle recalled, "We had some excellent defensive teams. We shut out several opponents. About our only bad game on defense was against Loraine. Michael Jones, their running back, got away from us. Their quarterback threw for a bunch of yards, too. Luckily, our offense was really clicking that night. Rob Kittley had three or four touchdowns."

The Bobcats now headed into District 5–B play with a 6–0 record and number-two state ranking. Going into district play, Rule was the only team in the district with anywhere close to a winning record. Chillicothe, expected to be Rule's biggest challenger for the district crown, stood at 1–5 for the season, as did Newcastle. Faring even worse were Rochester (Rule's opponent for their district opener) and Throckmorton, each at 0–6.

Rochester was the Rule's first district victim. Although it was an October 19 home game for the Steers, they were no match for the Bobcats as they rolled to a 42–0 win. Like the previous week, the Bobcats racked up more than 500 yards of total offense—319 rushing and 196 passing. Art Briles ran for 143 yards in the first half alone. Rule scored twenty-one points in the first quarter and another fourteen in the second. Mike Lisle was the first to hit the scoreboard with a thirteen-yard touchdown run with eight minutes left in the opening quarter. Art Briles then ran for two scores of forty-five and thirty-three yards. Briles added a second-quarter touchdown strike to Steve Anders from nineteen yards away, and he threw for Rule's final touchdown in the fourth quarter when he sent a three-yard toss to Larry Barbee. Rochester only picked up 109 yards rushing and 4 yards passing for the night as the Bobcats defense redeemed itself after the previous week against Loraine.

Now 7–0 overall, 1–0 in District 5-B play, and ranked number two in the state, Rule next had a home contest against the Newcastle Bobcats on October 26. Rule's defense won the day again, scoring their second straight shutout as they rolled to 47–0. Newcastle dropped to 1–7 and 0–2 in district play with the loss. The Rule defense held Newcastle to just five first downs and only ninety-six yards of total offense, forcing four turnovers for the night. Just as impressive was the Rule offense. Briles completed his only pass of the night to open the scoring as he hit Larry Barbee on a forty-five yarder. Rule was unstoppable on the ground, rolling up 415 yards. Other highlights include an eighty-yard touchdown scamper by Rob Kittley in the second quarter, a thirty-five-yard touchdown by Terry Futch a short time later in the second stanza, and a sixty-eight-yard romp to the end zone in the fourth quarter by Mike Lisle.

On November 2, the second-ranked Rule Bobcats scored a 29–0 away win against the Throckmorton Greyhounds. The Bobcats defense was top-notch again, giving up a mere five first downs and 135 yards on the ground and but two through the air. The Rule defense picked off two passes and recovered one fumble. Although not quite as potent as the previous three weeks, the Rule offense was efficient enough to churn out 263 yards on the ground and fifty yards passing. The rushing highlight for Rule occurred in the second quarter when Art Briles scored the game's first touchdown on a ninety-five-yard run. Briles added a ten-yard touchdown run in the third quarter and a twenty-three-yard touchdown in the fourth quarter. Briles capped off the scoring for the night when he completed his only pass of the night—a fifty-yarder to Larry Barbee. Throckmorton fell to 1–7 and 1–1 in district play.

After an off week, Rule was scheduled to play their final regular-season game at home against their nemesis from the previous year, Chillicothe, who was having a bit of a down season, with a record of 3–5–1 going into the contest, but they stood at 2–0 in district play—meaning the winner of the game would be district champion and advance to the playoffs. This time, Rule left no doubt as they rolled to a 64–3 victory. After three shutouts in district play, the Bobcats defense finally gave up points as Chillicothe kicked a field goal in the third quarter while they were down 57–0. Rule rolled up fifty points in the first half as Art Briles and Leonard Rhoads each scored two touchdowns. The Bobcats rushed for 345 yards for the night and added sixty-two in the air as Briles completed three of six passes. Despite giving up a field goal, the Bobcats defense was stellar again, limiting Chillicothe to four first downs and sixty yards of total offense.

Rob Kittley laughed. "We stomped them for a little bit of revenge. Frank Schatte was at Chillicothe, and he had been the coach at Rule before Coach Briles, when we were in junior high. We always talked to him, even after he left Rule. Chillicothe is where he retired."

After the disappointment of staying at home the previous two seasons in spite of 9–1 records both years, the Rule Bobcats now prepared to play their bi-district game against the Rising Star Wildcats on November 23 in Haskell. Rising Star, out of District 6–B with a 9–1 record, had defeated number-three state-ranked Meridian for the district title. The Wildcats had scored 297 points for the year and given up 67. Rule achieved the first undefeated regular season in school history, and they kept their number-two state ranking in Class B. The Bobcats had been dominant during the regular season, scoring 390 points while giving up only fifty-five (thirty-four of those coming in the win over Loraine). Rule's domination continued into the playoffs as they blasted Rising Star 45–6 and Art Briles arguably had his best game as a Bobcat. Briles ran for 135 yards and four touchdowns, completing nine of ten passes for 142 yards. Rule scored seven of the eight times it had the ball in the game. At first, Rising Star kept the game close. But after a scoreless first quarter, Rule struck for three touchdowns, all of them on runs by Briles—one of eighteen yards, another from twenty-eight yards out, and one of three yards, just before halftime. Rule poured on thirteen points in both the third and fourth quarters, adding up to forty-five points total. Rising Star's only points of the evening came with just five minutes left in the contest on a thirty-two-yard run by Alvin Spencer. Rule rolled up 479 yards for the night, including 337 on the ground. Rob

Kittley had ninety-one yards on nine carries, while Mike Lisle contributed seventy-one yards on nineteen attempts. Each scored a touchdown of their own in the rout.

An 11–0 Rule now entered the state Class B quarterfinals against the Prosper Eagles, to be played in Jacksboro on November 30. Prosper entered the matchup with a 10–1 record. The Eagles had outscored their opponents 374–101 during the season. Prosper took down Saint Jo 35–18 in a mild upset in their first playoff contest. The Rule defense came to play as they defeated Prosper 21–0. The Bobcats held Prosper to fifty-two yards rushing and eighty-one yards passing, in addition to recovering three fumbles and picking off four passes. After a scoreless first quarter, the Bobcats put two touchdowns on the board in the second stanza. A key play in the game came 5:16 before halftime, when Briles swept around the right end for an eight-yard touchdown on fourth and goal. Dennis Briles had called a time-out before the play because he noticed that Prosper's defensive ends were cheating and forcing everything back to the middle. Briles ordered a quarterback sweep, and son Art waltzed into the end zone untouched. Then, with just over two minutes left in the first half, Rule drove ninety yards in nine plays to score seven seconds before halftime. Briles hit Larry Barbee with two big pass completions on the drive. With seventeen seconds left in the half, Briles hit Barbee for thirty-three yards and then followed it up with a twenty-six-yard touchdown pass to Barbee. After giving up five first downs in the first quarter, the Rule defense didn't give up another until there were but three minutes left in the game. Briles rushed twenty-three times for 130 yards and completed three of nine passes for 100 yards. Rob Kittley scored the final Rule touchdown from two yards out in the fourth quarter.

Despite the win over Prosper, a few key injuries during the contest strained the Bobcats. Nolan Pittcock recalled, "I blew out a knee against Prosper in the quarterfinals. I was done for the season. It was the only time that I got hurt playing football."

Besides Pittcock, Art Briles broke a couple of ribs against Prosper and was severely limited offensively for the rest of the playoffs.

Now it was on to the semifinals on December 7 in Floydada against the Matador Matadors. Matador was out of District 2–B and was ranked just behind Rule at number three in the state. The game was played in Floydada, 130 miles northwest of Rule, and just 30 miles west of Matador because Rule had lost the coin flip for the homefield advantage. The Matadors came into the semifinal contest with an 11–0–1 record and had outscored their opponents 306–94 for the year. After an undefeated regular season, Matador advanced in the playoffs after a 3–1 advantage in penetrations in a 6–6 tie with Groom and a 22–12 win over Jayton after spotting the Jaybirds a 12–0 lead. Matador was a physically smaller team than Rule, but the Matadors had one large player—6'5", 220-pound Tom Tilson, who played both offensive and defensive left tackle.

Rule jumped out to a 14–0 halftime lead and held on for a 14–12 nail-biter over Matador. Rob Kittley recounted, "The Matador game was tough. We had lost our center, Nolan Pittcock, the week before playing Prosper. He tore his knee up. We couldn't run up the middle at all. Art banged up his ribs against Prosper, too, so he was limited. Matador was stout; they would run right at you. We barely got by them."

The game was mostly a defensive struggle, as Rule was held to only 182 yards on the ground—well below their average of 300-plus yards per game. The Matadors were held to just 175 total yards and only 42 yards in the first half. Despite nursing cracked ribs from the previous week's game with Prosper, Art Briles led the Bobcats in rushing with eighty-five yards on eighteen carries. Mike Lisle got Rule on the scoreboard first with a four-yard run with 7:07 left in the opening quarter. Briles had a big hand in the Bobcats' next eight points, first hitting Larry Barbee with a twenty-five-yard scoring strike to make it 12–0 Rule and then hitting tight end Steve Anders with a two-point conversion pass. Matadors fullback Tray Taylor scored a third-quarter touchdown to make it 14–6. However, the Matadors failed on their two-point conversion attempt. Taylor added his second touchdown with only 2:39 to play to make it 14–12. The Bobcats' 150-pound Jimmy Macias stopped Matador quarterback Steve Stevens short of the goal line on a two-point conversion attempt that would have tied the score at fourteen points with just 2:39 left. Since the Bobcats were behind on penetrations, Matador would have advanced to the state finals if the score had ended in a tie.

"I had broken my ribs against Prosper the week before," Art Briles recalled. "I was pretty limited in terms of what I could do. They got to within 14–12 and went for the two-point to try and tie us. We were behind on penetrations, so they would have advanced if they converted. Jimmy Macias, our defensive end, all 150 pounds of him, was the guy who stopped their quarterback. I think Rob Kittley came in at the end of the play to help out. It was huge. It put us into the state finals."

Then, on Friday, December 14, in Weatherford, came the matchup the whole state had been anticipating: number-one Big Sandy versus number-two Rule. Like Rule, up until the early 1970s, Big Sandy had been unsuccessful in football. The Wildcats started playing football in 1926 and never made the playoffs until 1971. Over the next five seasons, 1971–75, Big Sandy went 63–1–1, with their only loss being a 7–6 matchup in the 1972 quarterfinals—the first year a state champion could be crowned in Class B.

The Wildcats were rated a fourteen-point favorite over the Bobcats. Rule had to face the second most prolific offense in Texas high school football history. They had scored an impressive 470 points and given up only seventy-three in thirteen contests, but Big Sandy had scored an astounding 597 points during the regular season, surpassing Waco High School's record mark of 588 in 1927. In their last four regular-season contests, the Wildcats rang up sixty-eight, eighty-two, sixty-eight, and ninety-four points. In the playoffs, the Wildcats had outscored their three playoff opponents 93–3.

Big Sandy was loaded with talent, even more so than Rule. The Wildcats' big gun was fullback Bobby Mitchell, who was eventually signed by Texas A&M. Going into the state championship game, Mitchell had rushed for 2,247 yards during the regular season on only 140 carries—an average of 16.1 yards per tote. He had tallied thirty-eight touchdowns. In the playoffs, Mitchell had added 640 more rushing yards and three additional touchdowns. He was helped in the backfield by halfback Lawrence Harper, who had rung up 896 yards on the ground. The previous week in their semifinal win over Runge, Mitchell rushed for 189 yards and on defense returned an interception sixty-one yards for a score, while Harper got Big Sandy on the scoreboard with an eighty-one-yard kickoff return for a touchdown after Runge had kicked a field goal with just five minutes left in the first half, to put Big Sandy behind in a game for the first time that season. Mitchell and Harper also doubled as the starting cornerbacks on the Wildcats defense.

Big Sandy also had two sophomores on defense who grew in fame later in their careers. One was defensive tackle David Overstreet, who eventually switched to running back after Mitchell graduated and went to play for Oklahoma. He was a first-round pick of the Miami Dolphins in 1980. The other player was linebacker Lovie Smith, who continued his college career at Tulsa and later became a head coach in the NFL for the Chicago Bears, Tampa Bay Buccaneers, and Houston Texans. When Smith took the Bears to the Super Bowl after the 2006 season, he, along with Indianapolis Colts coach Tony Dungy, became the first Black head coaches to make it to the NFL championship.

The Rule players and coaches knew they had a tall task ahead of them. Jasper Wilson recalled, "Before the Big Sandy game, I was standing with Larry Barbee, who also played safety, and he said, 'Coach, look over there.' Big Sandy had more than twice as many players as we did. We had around twenty-two or twenty-three players. They ran a 5–3–3 defense, and their three linebackers were these big African American players. They were large, fast, and good. Turns out Lovie Smith was one of them. They were a good bunch of kids, though. They were well coached, and there was no trash-talking."

Rob Kittley also assessed the situation before the game: "Big Sandy had about fifty guys to our twenty-three. They had pretty much separate offensive and defensive teams. Most of our guys played both ways. We never came off the field, and they wore us down in the second half. Bobby Mitchell and Lovie Smith—they were good. I knew Smith was good even before he became famous later."

In Weatherford on a chilly Friday night, the Big Sandy Wildcats defense was the star of the show as they held Rule to their lowest offensive output of the season in a 25–0 win. Rule had but seven first downs and gained a mere ninety total yards for the night, with eighty-two rushing and only eight passing. The Bobcats managed to get into Big Sandy territory only twice—both in the first half. They kept the game close for that first half, with Big Sandy in the lead 6–0 at the break. The Wildcats had started out fast, with Bobby Mitchell scoring on their first possession from thirty-five yards out. After that, Mitchell was held in check for the rest of the half, gaining just ten more yards before the break, and the Wildcats were held to just sixty-one total yards at halftime. Mitchell broke loose in the second half, running for three-yard and twelve-yard touchdowns in the third quarter and a two-yard touchdown in the fourth quarter. Mitchell ended up with 183 yards on twenty-three carries, and his four touchdowns gave him forty-five for the season. Rule didn't help their cause by turning over the ball four times, with three fumbles and one interception. Two of their fumbles were inside their own twenty, and both set up scores by Mitchell. Mitchell's big night gave him 3,070 yards rushing in 1973—only the second time in Texas high school history that a running back had gone more than three thousand yards in a season. Mitchell also wrapped up his career at Big Sandy with 7,260 rushing yards total, which at the time was second place in state history only behind the legendary "Sugar Land Express," Kenneth Hall.

Mike Lisle recalled, "Our final game against Big Sandy was one for the books. They had a lot of talent. Bobby Mitchell really stood out. He was a tall, lanky guy. We were talented, too. It was only 6–0 at the half. But Art was playing hurt, with broken ribs, and that really damaged our offense as far as being able to throw."

Art Briles talked about the state championship years later: "In the finals, we played Big Sandy in Weatherford. Man, they were a dynasty. They were clearly the better team. If we would have played them ten times, they would have beat us at least seven of them. Bobby Mitchell was the guy for them. He was by and large the heart and soul of their team. Lovie Smith was on that team, too. He was tough on defense. We're still good friends today. It did hurt some that I was still hurt and we had lost our starting center, Nolan Pittcock, against Prosper with a knee injury. David Overstreet, who was a defensive tackle for them at the time, just ate us up.

"When you play in Class B, you just don't have substitutes to fill things in. We had a small roster. We gave it our best shot, though. I think not making it to the playoffs during the previous two years hurt us. Sometimes we were happy just to make it to the state title game. If we had made it when we were sophomores and juniors, it would have given us that playoff experience and confidence. It was fun, and we had a great group of guys. It was a great time in my life. We felt it was a good season, just making it that far. That hurt us. Happy teams don't win; determined teams do."

Although they had lost in the state championship game, the 1973 season still brings back fond memories from its participants. Nolan Pittcock fondly remembers, "The town got behind us. It was like Odessa in *Friday Night Lights*. There was nobody left in town. When we got to the playoffs, the farmers in Rule made sure we had charter buses to take the players and fans to the games. It was a real happy time. We won all of those ball games. The town treated us like kings. Still do."

Although football season was over, the Bobcats did get a measure of revenge on Big Sandy when the state track meet rolled around in May 1974. Rule won their third state title in Jasper Wilson's four years as head coach. The state title was decided in the last event—the mile relay. The Bobcats won the mile relay by three full seconds over meet favorite Danbury. Because Danbury was nipped for second place in the event, Rule won the title by the slimmest of margins, 54–53. Big Sandy came in fourth, with forty-six points. The mile relay team of Tommy Cornelius, Rob Kittley, Wes Kittley, and Art Briles set a Class B record of 3:22.2. In addition to contributing to Big Sandy's win in the mile relay, Rob Kittley also won the state title in the 880-yard run.

"Besides being a good football coach, Jasper Wilson was also a great track coach," Rob Kittley recalled. "We won state three times in four years: 1971, 1973, and 1974. I was part of the mile relay team that set a state record. In my senior year, I also won the 880-yard run. For a Class B school, we had some pretty good athletes."

Jasper Wilson added, "We had a lot of success in track. We won state in '71, '73, and '74. The 322.2 mark we set in the mile relay was a state record for many years. Our kids were very competitive. When we won the title in 1974, there were thirty-five thousand people in the stands at UT in Austin. It was a thrill."

Dennis Briles coached two more seasons at Rule, going 6–3–2 with another district title in 1974 and 6–4 in 1975. His record in his six years as head coach at Rule was 51–13–3. Because his son Art had accepted a scholarship to play football at the University of Houston, Briles stepped down as head coach at the end of the 1975–76 school year. He wanted to travel to see his son play for the Cougars.

On the morning of October 16, 1976, Dennis and his wife, Wanda Briles, accompanied by Wanda's older sister, Elsie Kittley, left Rule early in the morning so they could watch Art and the Cougars face the SMU Mustangs at the famed Cotton Bowl in Dallas. Art was a redshirt sophomore wide receiver for the eventual Southwest Conference champions. Trips like these were the reason why Briles had stepped down from the coaching ranks after the 1975 season at Rule. He beamed with pride, watching his son play college football. As they headed east toward Dallas on US Highway 380, they came to Newcastle, some seventy miles from Rule. Three miles outside of Newcastle, Briles's Galaxy 500 crested a hill. A commercial truck on the other side of the slope drifted into Briles's lane, and the two vehicles met atop the hill. The impact sheared the roof off the Galaxy 500, and its three occupants passed away instantly.

Later, two hours away, the Cougars beat the Mustangs 29–6 to go to 4–1 in the Southwest Conference standings. Art Briles looked up into the stands, wondering where his relatives were, but he only saw three empty seats in their usual spot. After the game, Cougars head coach Bill Yeoman informed Briles about the accident. Briles left the team for a few weeks to go home for the funeral. For the residents of Rule, the accident was like a punch to the gut.

Rob Kittley lost several relatives in the ensuing wreck: "It tough on everyone—the whole town. Elsie Kittley was my great-aunt. Elsie and Art's mother, Wanda, were sisters. Elsie was older and actually raised Art's mom. I was in Rule farming at the time of the accident. Someone—I don't remember who—called me to tell me the news. We all went over to the Brileses' house. They held the funeral at the school. It was rough on the whole town. Coach Briles was still the principal at the high school, and he was also the mayor. He had graduated from Rule. My dad actually played ball with him."

Art Briles has rarely spoken publicly about the accident. Jasper Wilson assessed, "It really affected Art. He took it really hard, more so than Eddie, his older brother, I think. It's taken Art a long time to try and get over it."

At one point, Art Briles said the following about the tragedy: "I knew I had two paths. You could wallow in despair and doubt, and whine and wonder. Or you could choose to move forward and honor your parents. I decided I would look for a reason to prevail."

Briles chose to go into coaching to help honor his parents' legacy. He eventually became one of the most successful high school coaches in Texas history, winning four state titles at Stephenville High School in the 1990s. After coaching running backs at Texas Tech from 2000 to 2002, Briles accepted a head coaching job at the University of Houston in 2003. By his fourth season, in 2006, thirty years after the tragic accident that changed his young life forever, Briles led the Cougars to the Conference USA Championship and a Liberty Bowl berth. In 2008, Briles went on to coach eight seasons at Baylor, where he coached the 2010 Heisman Trophy winner, Robert Griffin III. He led Baylor to Big 12 conference championships in 2013 and 2014. Briles was named the Associated Press College Football Coach of the Year in 2013.

Jasper Wilson took over the reins of the Bobcats football program in 1976 after Dennis Briles stepped down, and try as he did, the Bobcats never neared the success of the 1973 squad. Wilson stayed through the 1991 season, coaching six-man football at the high school. Rule's last eight years in eleven-man football with Wilson at the helm of the Bobcats were 37–41–1, with no playoff appearances.

Many agree that Wilson's presence at Rule helped the school and town cope in the wake of the tragedy. Rob Kittley remarked, "When Jasper

Wilson stayed on as head coach after coach Briles stepped down, he provided stability to the school and town after the accident. He stayed for more than twenty years and coached Rule in six-man football after we dropped down. We were lucky to have him."

Wilson recalled the good and bad times at Rule. "Dennis was very competitive," he recalled. "When the talent at Rule started fading, he got out of coaching in 1976 but remained the principal. He also wanted to follow Art's career at the University of Houston. I have great memories of Rule. Good kids, good families. The hardest part was the wreck. It happened close to Newcastle. I was supposed to go to Newcastle that evening to scout a football game, but my wife, Ann, wouldn't let me go. 'Too bad of a road,' she said. It was not a good situation. Dennis and Wanda were very close to us. We did a lot with them socially. We had to rebound quickly, though. When there's a tragedy, you have to go on. You have to work and pray your way through it. I took over, and we enjoyed our twenty-two years in Rule. We eventually went to six-man football in the 1980s, and I left in 1992. For the most part, it was a great time in my family's lives."

Through triumph to tragedy, great victory to even greater loss, the legend of that fateful 1973 Bobcats season lives on as a shining moment in the story of the small town of Rule, tucked away in rural Texas—far from the hustle and bustle of urban life, hearkening back to a simpler time. It was a moment that shaped the life of a man who would become a Texas football legend, with the spirit of Dennis Briles living on through his son Art Briles—at their core, just two small-town boys from a place called Rule who were lifelong students of the game they so loved, played, coached, and cultivated.

Fabens

The Pride of El Paso, 1979 2A Quarterfinalist Wildcats

THROUGHOUT THE HISTORY of Texas high school football, the El Paso metropolitan area in far West Texas has always been considered the competitively weakest. One needs to look no further than El Paso–area teams' playoff results over the years. No team in the El Paso area has ever played for a state title or, for that matter, ever made it to the semifinals. Austin High School in 1937 and Ysleta High School in 1941 each won one playoff game against a non–El Paso school to make it to the state quarterfinals. Ever since El Paso High School first laced up their cleats in 1895, El Paso–area teams have compiled a dismal 58–319–4 playoff record against non–El Paso schools.

Fabens, about thirty miles southeast of El Paso on Interstate 10, followed this same dismal pattern for many years. The Wildcats started playing football in 1927 and had won only four district titles in school history: 1958, 1959, 1962, and 1977. Fabens suffered first-round playoff losses each season. From 1927 to 1977, the Wildcats' overall record for fifty-one seasons of football was 175–248–19. But all that was about to change.

Coach Maurice "Moe" Hodges helped Fabens emerge from the football doldrums when he arrived in 1978. A native of the West Texas town of Monahans, Hodges played as a sophomore on the 1948 Class A state championship team that beat New Braunfels 14–0 for the title. After graduating from Monahans in 1951, Hodges went to Tarleton State College as a freshman quarterback in 1952, played football in the army for two years, then ended up at Sul Ross College in Alpine, where he was briefly a teammate of future Detroit Tigers star Norm Cash. Hodges finished out his college football career from 1956 to 1958 at Eastern New Mexico University in Portales, where he was a quarterback, running back, and punter. Hodges then turned to coaching, and his first stop as a coach was in his hometown of Monahans. He started out as an assistant and then became head coach, compiling a 26–7–1 record from 1968 to 1970, including a couple of district

Fabens head coach Maurice Hodges with his son, star running back Randy Hodges. Courtesy of Randy Hodges

titles and two playoff victories. From there, Hodges spent five seasons at Snyder from 1971 to 1975, going 27–22–2, with one district title. He then left coaching to open up a sporting goods store in Monahans.

Fortunately, he didn't stay off the field for long. Hodges decided to return to coaching at Fabens in 1978, bringing his son Randy along with him. Randy was considered to be the top running back prospect in the greater El Paso area, but unfortunately, UIL rules in 1978 stipulated that if a player transferred to a new school, he would not be allowed to play on varsity for a year (unless he was a senior). Because he was only a junior, Randy was disqualified. John "Rocky" Dyer, Fabens's top defensive player, faced the same circumstances when he moved back to Fabens in 1978. Both Randy Hodges and Dyer explained their situation.

Randy recalled, "After my dad left Snyder, he had a sporting goods store in Monahans. He came out of retirement in 1978 and 1979 to coach me. When we moved, I had to play junior varsity in 1978 because of the UIL rules back then. I had a good friend and teammate, John Dyer, who had to do the same thing. His dad had moved to Fabens with the border patrol. John was a center and strongside linebacker. I was the tailback and weakside linebacker."

John Dyer added, "I started out in Fabens, but we moved to Sierra Blanca, about sixty miles away, because my dad was with the border patrol. I actually got to play varsity football in Sierra Blanca during my first two years of high school. They were really small—a Class B school. My freshman year was the first time they had ever played eleven-man football. In fact, they only played eleven-man football for about four of five years before they went back down to six-man football. When I moved back to Fabens, I couldn't play varsity my junior year because of the transfer rules back then. It was a little disappointing. Randy was on the JV team with me, though, so that made it a little easier. We only lost one game, to Fort Hancock's varsity team."

Quarterback David Rueda talked about the addition of Hodges and Dyer. "Randy was an outstanding running back. He was pretty big for back then—about six foot, 195 pounds. Strong, too. He wasn't able to play for us until he was a senior. He helped get us over that hump. Another guy who really helped too was Rocky Dyer. He had to sit out his junior year like Randy did because his family moved back to Fabens. He was a great center on offense and linebacker on defense."

Rueda then spoke about Coach Hodges: "Coach Hodges was solid," he recalled. "He was a good coach. He was big on fundamentals, and he had a good knowledge of the game. He was not laid-back at all. He would grab me by the face mask all the time. He would smoke these skinny little cigarettes, and the smoke from them would get into my eyes a lot of the time."

Wildcats running back Roy Slape added, "Coach Hodges was more of an offensive-minded coach. He was all business on the field. I had great respect for him and admired him. He was pretty level-headed. He wasn't mean, but he wasn't laid-back. Somewhere in between. Day to day, he did his business. I got into a little trouble in school, and he was fair to me. Another interesting thing about Coach Hodges was that he would carry an eyeball in his hand during games and rub it—some kind of superstition. I think it was a deer's eye."

John Dyer concluded, "Coach Hodges was a heckuva man. I loved him to death. He was a big motivator. He could get you to do what you needed to do without yelling and screaming, like some other coaches. He would always ask us, 'Do you want to be champions?' He would tell us things like, 'Run your laps or don't—it's your choice.' Of course, we always did. I even worked for him at his El Paso sporting goods store in the summertime. He treated me like a son. Another thing about Coach Hodges was that he was as color-blind as he could be. He couldn't match his outfits. He might show up with a green jacket and blue pants and mismatched socks. I guess there was no one at home to dress him!"

Fabens had experienced some success before the 1979 season, having won their district in 1977 and in Hodges's first season at Fabens in 1978, but the Wildcats lost to Kermit in the first round of the playoffs both years. In 1979, there was reason for optimism. The Wildcats returned eight offensive and six defensive starters. Besides Hodges and Dyer being eligible, Fabens returned quarterback David Rueda, fullback Ernie Rivera, and halfback Roy Slape in the backfield, along with tackles Jose Rodriguez and Jerry Ortiz and guards Ramon Ortega and Jesus Gallo on the offensive line. Dyer was expected to take over the center spot. On defense, Fabens had a lot of new faces on defense, but Coach Hodges felt the talent was there.

David Rueda said the following about heading into his senior season: "We had high expectations. We were unbeaten in junior high, and we only lost one game as freshmen to a bigger school. As sophomores and juniors, we won district but lost to Kermit both times. We could never quite get over the hump, though. We were confident as seniors—not cocky, though. Our line wasn't big, but they were quick. One of our guards, Jesus Gallo, would play on Friday night but would then get up on Saturday morning and run cross-country. That shows you the type of quickness and type of athletes we had on the line. They were smart. When I got into coaching later, some of the referees commented that they used to like to call our games because our linemen were quick and intelligent. We were pretty much a running team. When we did pass, it was usually a bit of a surprise, so it was gravy when we threw. In district play, I only threw eight passes total, but I completed seven of them for five touchdowns."

"I was only 5'4", 140 pounds," Roy Slape added. "The coaches called me 'Little Man.' I was pretty strong. I could lift the most. I could even beat some of the linemen. Myself, David Rueda, and Joe 'Burger' Rodriguez were the only sophomores to start on varsity back in 1977. We were pretty good in 1977 and 1978—we won district both years—but Kermit beat us both times in the playoffs. Our senior class was a winning class. We knew in junior high that we would be pretty good. My sophomore year, I started out on defense at cornerback. After our second or third game, our fullback got hurt, so I started playing offense, too. I was more of a blocking back as a sophomore and junior. I could open up our holes for our running backs. As a senior, I would carry the ball maybe four or five times a game. I wish I could have carried the ball a little more. I contributed, though. I did my job opening up those holes."

Fabens was scheduled to play seven nondistrict games, including now-rival Kermit in their last game before district play began. Fabens was picked to take the district title over Van Horn, always tough Canutillo, and Alpine, who Fabens tied for the district title in 1978, advancing to the playoffs not on penetrations or first downs but on total yardage, after a 29–29 tie.

Maurice Hodges had the Wildcats play a tough nondistrict schedule to prepare them for a possible playoff run. "We played some bigger schools in nondistrict. We didn't have a choice," Randy Hodges said. "Socorro,

Silver City, Gadsden—they were larger than us. We more than held our own. Playing some tough competition did get us ready for later."

Fabens's first contest of the football season was an away game on September 7 against a private school in El Paso, the Cathedral Irish. Fullback Ernie Rivera led Fabens with 135 yards on twenty-three carries, while Randy Hodges made his debut as the running back for Fabens and delivered ninety-three yards on twenty totes, scoring on touchdowns of one and thirteen yards, leading their team to a 20–7 win. The Wildcats spotted Cathedral an early 7–0 first-quarter lead, but Hodges's first touchdown of the night in the second quarter knotted the score at 7–7 at halftime. Roy Slape added a third-quarter touchdown, and Hodges's second touchdown in the fourth quarter sealed the win. After allowing the initial first-quarter touchdown, Fabens's defense stiffened, and they held the Irish to 140 total yards the rest of the evening.

Week two brought about a September 14 home game against the Gadsden Panthers—a team Fabens had demolished in 1978, with a final score of 37–7. Gadsden was a Class 4A New Mexico high school, much larger than Fabens. The Wildcats blasted the Panthers 59–0 as they rang up 474 total yards, all on the ground. Randy Hodges scored three of the Wildcats' first four touchdowns on runs of twenty-five and forty-five yards in the first quarter and on a second-quarter punt return of seventy-four yards. Four other Fabens backs, Roy Slape, David Balderrama, Harvey Gonzalez, and Genaro Rodriguez, scored second-half touchdowns. As impressive as the Wildcats offense was, the defense may have been even better. Fabens allowed but four first downs, fifty yards rushing, and only ten yards passing, forcing four turnovers, two fumbles, and two interceptions.

Game three was a September 21 home contest against the Class 4A El Paso Socorro Bulldogs, who had struggled through a 0–10 season in their first 4A season in 1978. For the second week in a row, Fabens ran up more than four hundred yards on the ground as the Wildcats pasted Socorro 42–6. Ernie Rivera and Randy Hodges led the rushing attack for Fabens, as Rivera had 147 yards on twenty-two carries and a touchdown, and Hodges ground out 158 yards on seventeen carries, with touchdown runs of eighteen and twenty yards in the first half. The Fabens defense rose to the occasion again, holding Socorro to 165 total yards and recovering five fumbles. The win pushed Fabens to 3–0 for the season.

One setback for Fabens in the Socorro game was an injury to Randy Hodges that hampered him for the next several weeks. Hodges recalled, "I got hurt against Socorro. I hurt my ankle and knee. I had to get a cast from my ankle to my hip. It was my senior year, though. I had to play, and I had to get to college on a football scholarship."

Despite Hodges's injury, the team's confidence was growing. After three wins, no one had come within two touchdowns of the Wildcats. Roy Slape said, "After two to three weeks of the season, we could tell we were going to be good. Everybody, ourselves included, expected us to win district. We were beating some teams so badly that a lot of the time, the starters would only play half the game. We were on a roll."

Next up for Fabens at home on September 28 was another nondistrict contest—this time against the 2–1 Marfa Shorthorns. The Wildcats avenged a 20–7 loss to Marfa in 1978 with a 34–6 win. Randy Hodges's knee injury from the previous week against Socorro proved not to be as serious as originally thought, and he ran for touchdowns of four yards in the first quarter and five yards in the second. David Rueda completed his first passes in three weeks, going 4–9 for 127 yards and two touchdowns. Both touchdown passes were hauled in by receiver Sonny Rodriguez—one of twenty-five yards in the second quarter and another of thirty-nine yards in the fourth quarter. The Shorthorns actually outgained Fabens, 338 yards to 332, but Marfa coughed up five turnovers, three fumbles, and two interceptions.

Week five, October 5, was expected to be challenging for the 4–0 Wildcats, as they faced the second-ranked team in New Mexico Class 3A at an away game in Silver City, New Mexico. The Colts entered the game at 3–1. They had lost to Fabens's week-one opponent, Cathedral, the previous week 6–0, to drop Silver City from their number-one state ranking. The Colts defense had given up but twenty-three points in four games. Silver City's alleged defensive prowess didn't matter to Fabens as they ripped through the Colts' defense for 384 rushing yards on the night and cruised to a 27–6 win. The running tandem of Ernie Rivera and Randy Hodges scored two touchdowns apiece. The highlight of the night was Hodges ripping off a ninety-eight-yard touchdown run in the second quarter. The Wildcats defense stymied the Colts offense, limiting them to 185 total yards.

John Dyer recalled, "Silver City was a big game. It was their homecoming, I think. We beat them handily. A guy named Eddie Brown was their big running back, and I stopped him a few times. Randy had a heckuva run that game—ninety-eight or ninety-nine yards. It was an I-Right 224. Randy went around the right side, and I remember our tackle Jerry Ortiz blocking downfield for him."

Randy Hodges also recalled his record-breaking run: "Sure, I remember that ninety-eight-yard run against Silver City. They were good; they went to state that year in New Mexico. Actually, it was ninety-nine yards. It was special. It's still a school record to this day. The play was a belly fake to Ernie Rivera from David Rueda, and he would pitch me the ball. We ran the play quite a bit, either to the right or left. I took a pitchout five yards deep in the end zone. I was heading for the right sideline when I was met at about the ten by Silver City's all-state defensive lineman, Dan Fast. We collided, and I swear I didn't wake up until about the fifty-yard line. I don't how I stayed on my feet. Instinct, I guess."

Now 5–0, the Wildcats faced rival Clint, a town just eight miles northwest of Fabens, in a home contest on October 12. The Lions, a member of District 6–A, were 4–1 for the season. As David Rueda recalled, "Our big rival was Clint. They were just down the road from us. The farmers from both towns would bet a lot of money on the game. They were the ones with the money."

Clint was no match for the Wildcats as Fabens rolled to a 69–0 victory. The Wildcats dominated from the start as Randy Hodges returned the opening kickoff eighty-five yards for a score. Hodges added another score right before halftime as he returned an interception thirty yards for a touchdown. Roy Slape raced seventy-five yards for a first-quarter touchdown, and Fabens ran out to a 34–0 halftime lead. After Slate added his second touchdown of the night from only three yards out for Fabens's only score of the third quarter, the Wildcats tacked on twenty-eight fourth-quarter points. Harvey Zavala scored three of the four touchdowns on runs of seven, fifty-five, and twenty yards. The Fabens ground attack was once again in high gear as they gained 520 yards for the evening. Not to be dismissed was the Fabens defense, which limited the Lions to four first downs and ninety-five total yards.

John Dyer spoke about how Clint got the Fabens squad fired up to play them, recalling an incident in the days leading up to the game: "We stomped Clint bad. That week before the game, they sent us a little bitty blue coffin. Inside it were some tampons for us linemen and pantyhose for Randy. Well, Randy ran the opening kickoff back for a touchdown, and afterward, he ran by their sideline and showed them the pantyhose. The linemen threw the tampons on the ground by their sideline. I think their prank backfired on them."

Randy Hodges added, "Clint was our homecoming game. They were just five miles down the road from us. Since I was still fairly new to

Fabens, I didn't realize how big of a rivalry this was. During the week, someone from Clint sent our offensive line a box of tampons with each of their numbers on it. They sent me a pair of pantyhose. I showed them their attempt at humor didn't work when I returned the opening kick for a touchdown. I had the pantyhose on me, and I showed them the pantyhose after the touchdown when I ran past their sideline. I also scored on an interception return in that game. That was special, too, because I wanted to score in as many ways as possible that season. I scored running, receiving, and on kickoff and punt returns, and it was my first interception."

At 6–0, Fabens now faced the Kermit Yellow Jackets in their last nondistrict game, an October 19 road contest. The two squads were quickly becoming rivals, as this would be their sixth meeting in the past three seasons. Kermit, 230 miles east of Fabens, had defeated the Wildcats five times over the previous three seasons. Kermit beat Fabens in regular-season games in 1976, 1977, and 1978. In addition, after the 1977 and 1978 seasons, Fabens faced the Yellow Jackets in first-round playoff matchups and lost both times—14–6 in 1977 and 28–0 in 1978.

In a thriller of a game that was possibly the defining moment in the season, the Wildcats used a forty-two-yard field goal, the only one of his high school career, by Joe "Burger" Rodriguez with 1:35 left in the game to spoil the Kermit Yellow Jackets' homecoming 17–16. Randy Hodges scored a touchdown in each of the first two quarters, a fifty-five-yard run in the first quarter and a twenty-three-yard jaunt in the second quarter.

Fabens lineman Joe Rodriguez, whose forty-two-yard field goal in the final two minutes led the Wildcats to a historic 17-16 win over Kermit. Courtesy of Randy Hodges

Hodges described his fifty-five-yard run as follows: "That run against Kermit was as special as the ninety-eight-yarder against Silver City. It was the same play but to the left. Kermit had a guy, David Fulbright, who was a good quarterback, and he also played safety. He went on to play at the University of Texas. I outran him and everyone else. It was pure adrenaline."

Kermit responded with a thirty-five-yard field goal in the first quarter and a one-yard touchdown run by Shannon Cooke in the second.

The key, however, was when the Yellow Jackets missed their two-point conversion attempt. It would come back to haunt them later. After a scoreless third period, Kermit took the lead in the fourth quarter on a four-yard run by Cooke.

Rodriguez's kick was set up by a fake punt from his own thirty-nine-yard line with under five minutes to go. Ernie Rivera picked up another first down on another fourth-down play moments later, with a twenty-four-yard jaunt. After the Kermit defense stiffened at their own twenty-six, Rodriguez atoned for missing a twenty-yarder in the third quarter. He made his forty-two-yard kick with room to spare. However, Kermit was not finished. The last few seconds were wild. After Fabens kicked off, the Yellow Jackets faced a fourth and five at the Fabens thirty-six-yard line. Kermit quarterback David Fulbright threw the ball up for grabs downfield. Two Fabens defenders tipped the pass, but it dropped into the hands of the Yellow Jackets' Malcom Bryant at the Fabens nine-yard line. On first and goal, Fulbright rammed the ball down to the one-yard line. Running back Cooke was stopped on second down, and after Kermit was called for a five-yard motion penalty, Kermit tried for a game-winning twenty-three-yard field goal. The kick was wide right, and the Wildcats had broken the hex.

Years later, several of the Wildcats recalled what was probably the biggest win in school history, along with Burger Rodriguez's unlikely game-winning kick. David Rueda said, "When we were seniors, we beat Kermit during the regular season with a forty-two-yard field goal. That kick was not a fluke. It had been drilled into us by our coaches that if we executed it, things would work out—and they did. Burger was an excellent kicker. It was a big thrill because Kermit had knocked us out of the playoffs the previous two seasons. It was a physical, tough game. We beat them up. They tried an onside kick against us, and Roy Slape hit the kicker so hard it broke his ribs and knocked him out of the game. We also beat up their quarterback/defensive back David Fulbright. We were a physical team. Even back in middle school, we were that way. The other teams sure would remember who they had just played. It was evident early on that Kermit didn't want any part of us."

John Dyer added, "Kermit had always been a powerhouse. Before we came along, our teams had always been beaten pretty badly by them. Burger had a good leg. We felt he had a good shot at making it. Winning that game motivated us. It proved that we could play with the big boys. I don't think anybody thought we could really beat them."

Roy Slape commented, "Our kicker, Burger Rodriguez, had a brother who was an outstanding athlete; he was really good at baseball. His nickname was 'Burger' first, and it was passed down to Joe, his younger brother. We never had any doubt that Burger could make the kick. He had a good leg. That game was a nail-biter. It was like winning the Super Bowl. We knew then that we could beat anybody. When we played them again, we had a lot of confidence, but we weren't overconfident. We played hard. We were going to hurt you but not in a mean way. We played to win."

During our interview, Randy Hodges had a bit of a different take on Rodriguez's kick than his teammates did. "Did I think Burger Rodriguez was going to make that forty-two-yard field goal? Heck no—it was forty-two yards! I was excited, though. It was special watching my teammates drive down the field. David was giving the ball to Ernie Rivera, and he was getting three to four yards a carry. I was watching from the sidelines. I had hurt my ankle in the second half, and I needed to sit out the fourth quarter. I missed the fireworks at the end of the game against Kermit. I just really don't remember it much. I guess I was so excited about Burger's field goal that I forgot about everything else.

"Their school scheduled us for homecoming. I guess they thought Kermit would beat us. They were really good, though. I thought they were better than Childress, who we played in the playoffs. The game was special for me and especially my teammates. My teammates had a clutch seventy-yard drive without me. I think this was absolutely key to our season. My teammates had never beaten Kermit before, and they did it without me. When they did, it solidified the team. I had been averaging about thirteen yards a carry and scored a lot of touchdowns. It showed them that they could do it without me. I was the only white guy on the team. They were a special group of guys."

After an open date on October 26, all that remained in Fabens's regular-season schedule were three District 8–2A games against Van Horn, Alpine, and Canutillo. The 7–0 Wildcats took on the 0–7 Van Horn Eagles at home on November 2. The Wildcats rolled up 770 total yards on the evening, including 483 rushing, and pounded Van Horn 76–0. The big story, however, was the sudden emergence of David Rueda as a passer. Through the first seven games of the season, Rueda had only completed nine passes for 199 yards and two scores. Against the Eagles, he took to the air only four times, but he completed all four passes for 237 yards and four touchdowns. For good measure, Rueda also ran fifty-five yards for a first-quarter score.

It was in the second quarter that Rueda showed off his arm, connecting on fifty- and seventy-two-yard scoring passes to Roy Slape, plus an eighty-five-yarder to tight end Sonny Rodriguez. Rueda's fourth touchdown pass of the quarter was forty yards to end Sergio Martinez. Not to be lost in the showcase of offensive firepower for Fabens was once again their defense, as they shut out Van Horn and allowed only 212 total yards.

Roy Slape recalled his two touchdown receptions from Rueda: "I remember the two touchdown passes I caught against Van Horn. The first one, at midfield, I was in the left slot. There was a receiver out to the left of me. David just stood up and threw left. I caught the ball in stride and ran to the end zone. The second one, the seventy-two-yarder, I ran a post pattern. The ball actually tipped the defender's fingers but fell into my hands, and I used my speed to get to the end zone. I had 4.3 speed in the forty."

Now 8–0 overall and 1–0 in District 8–2A play, all that remained for the Wildcats were two away contests to wrap up their regular season, against the Alpine Bucs on November 9 and the Canutillo Eagles on November 16.

Alpine came into the contest with a 4–4 overall and 0–1 in district, having lost to Canutillo the week before. After scoring a touchdown in both the first and second quarters, Fabens exploded for twenty-one third-quarter points to easily put away the Bucks 35–0. Fabens's first-quarter touchdown was scored by Sergio Ortiz, on the receiving end of a forty-five-yard scoring strike from David Rueda with 1:16 left in the quarter. Ernie Rivera scored from nine yards out in the second quarter, and David Rueda started the third-quarter onslaught with a sixty-three-yard dash to pay dirt. Less than two minutes later, Jesus Gallo recovered an Alpine fumble in the end zone for another score. Randy Hodges capped off the scoring for the night three minutes later with a forty-nine-yard sprint to the end zone. Hodges said, "My forty-nine-yard run against Alpine was satisfying for me. It was a belly option and a pitchout to me going left. Alpine had a quarterback and safety, Kyle Mackey, who went on to play at East Texas State and then for the St. Louis Cardinals. Well, he had been mouthing at me the whole game, and I went around his side for the touchdown. That shut him up."

The Wildcats defense was once again impressive, shutting out the Bucks and limiting them to 176 yards total offense and forcing four turnovers. Fabens's ground attack was once again in high gear, gaining 353 yards for the evening. After a win against Alpine, Fabens climbed to their highest state ranking ever and since, at number seven.

The Wildcats season now boiled down to a winner-take-all showdown with the Canutillo Eagles on November 16 in Canutillo. Fabens stood at 9–0 overall and 2–0 in District 8–2A play, while Canutillo entered the contest at 6–3 overall and 2–0 in district. Canutillo was hoping to avenge a heartbreaking last-minute 19–13 loss the previous season to the Wildcats. Fabens spotted Canutillo an early 7–0 lead when the Eagles punched it in the first time they had the ball, with Fernie Gomez scoring on a twelve-yard first-quarter run. Roy Slape for Fabens countered later in the opening period with a twenty-five-yard touchdown run, and the score was knotted at 7–7 after one period. A key play occurred early in the second quarter when Canutillo's Gomez fumbled the ball after he had moved inside the Fabens twenty-yard line. Shortly afterward, David Rueda completed his only two passes of the evening for forty-nine yards to put the Wildcats close to Canutillo's goal line. Ernie Rivera punched the ball in from three yards out to give the Wildcats a 13–7 lead. Fabens caught a break when Canutillo jumped offsides on the extra-point attempt, moving the ball half the distance to the goal. The Wildcats decided to go for two, and Rivera crossed the goal line to give Fabens a 15–7 lead just before halftime. The second half was scoreless, and the Wildcats brought home their third straight district title, as well as their third straight meeting with Kermit in the playoffs. After Canutillo's initial scoring drive, the Wildcats shut down the Eagles for the rest of the evening, limiting them to just eight first downs and 130 yards. Offensively, Fabens was a little off but still managed to run up 292 rushing yards to go along with Rueda's forty-nine yards through the air. The 10–0 regular-season mark for Fabens brought Coach Moe Hodges's first undefeated regular season in his coaching career.

"I scored two years in a row against Canutillo," said Roy Slape. "My junior year, we beat them to win district and I scored on a sixty-five-yard run. They usually called two running plays for me—a 443 counter in the X formation. I would line up on the left, close to the tight end, and David would get the ball, turn away from me, and then he'd come around to the left and I'd go right to get the ball. The tackle on my side would pull, and he would help block for me. The other times would be when we were in the T formation. I would do a 245 run through the B or C gap. The touchdowns I scored both years against Canutillo were the 443 counter–X formation. The twenty-five-yard touchdown run when we were seniors helped us win district again."

John Dyer said, "Things got a little crazy after the game. The parents from both sides got into a melee on the field. We had to go straight to the bus and get out of there!"

Fabens was now set for its seemingly annual playoff bout with Kermit, to be played on November 23 in Pecos. Kermit, champions of District 7–2A, ended the regular season 7–3, with a perfect district mark of 3–0. On paper, one would likely mark Fabens as a heavy favorite. Fabens had outscored its opponents 394–48 on their run to an undefeated regular season, whereas Kermit had outscored their ten opponents 175–72.

Kermit's chances at victory looked to be even tougher, as injuries were starting to take their toll on the Yellow Jackets. Running back Shannon Cooke, who had given Fabens problems in their regular-season matchup, was out with a broken thumb. Quarterback David Fulbright had been out with a broken collarbone he suffered in a 35–0 win over district foe Ozona. It was a game time decision whether he would play in the playoff contest.

Fabens erupted for twenty-one second-quarter points and then let the defense do the rest as they took their first playoff win in school history—a 21–0 bi-district win over the Kermit Yellow Jackets. The often-overlooked Wildcats defense had another stellar game, limiting the Yellow Jackets to ten first downs, 113 yards rushing, and only twenty-six yards passing. In addition, Fabens recovered two fumbles and intercepted three Kermit passes in the fourth quarter. Kermit quarterback David Fulbright played but was not really a factor in the outcome of the game. Ernie Rivera led Fabens with 116 yards rushing on sixteen totes, including the opening Fabens touchdown on a twelve-yard second-quarter run. Rivera added a four-yard touchdown run late in the second quarter to give Fabens their halftime margin. In addition, Randy Hodges had ninety-seven yards rushing, including a beautiful forty-four-yard second-quarter scamper where he took a pitchout to the left, cut back against the grain, and raced to the end zone. About the only downside for Fabens was that they fumbled five times and lost three of them.

Randy Hodges recalled his second-quarter touchdown run: "The forty-four-yarder against Kermit was another belly option play. I got to run over David Fulbright again. I hit him in the chest with my shoulder. He had to come out of the game. The only negative outcome of the game was that I broke three ribs that night. I broke one on one play and two on another. That hampered me for the rest of the season."

Roy Slape remembered Hodges's run, too: "I made a big contribution to Randy's forty-four-yard touchdown. I was a helluva blocking back. And it was a perfect play. It was an I-left, 428 option. Basically, it was a sweep to the left, which was my side. I remember looking in the defender's eyes, and I could tell he was going to try and tackle Randy, who was coming up behind me. I hit the defender in the waist and dropped him. From my knees, after the block, I looked up and saw Randy hitting the end zone. I almost scored in the second Kermit game, too. I was close to the goal line, and I got the ball and was tripped up with a shoelace tackle. There was nothing but end zone in front of me. I also helped the team by getting their placekicker out of the game. There was a short kickoff by us, and I smacked their player and put him out of the game. It turns out he was their kicker, and that hurt their special teams."

David Rueda brought up another key point: "When we played Kermit again in the playoffs, they didn't want any part of us. The first time we beat Kermit at their place, it was huge. The game was so physical that they didn't want anything to do with us the second time around. Their quarterback Fulbright was good, but he didn't run the ball himself much against us the second time around. They were an option team, but he didn't keep the ball very much because he didn't want to get hit."

After winning their first playoff game in school history, the Fabens Wildcats were now set to face the Stamford Bulldogs on November 30 in Monahans, Moe Hodges's hometown. Stamford was the champion of District 6–2A and was 10–1 for the season, outscoring their eleven opponents 342–158. Stamford beat Slaton 30–22 in their bi-district battle. Stamford, in the Big Country forty miles north of Abilene, was a Texas football power in the 1950s. Stamford's record in the 1950s was 115–10–1, and the Bulldogs captured four state crowns in 1955, 1956, 1958, and 1959 (later forfeited). Stamford was where aforementioned Texas coaching legend Gordon Wood won his first two state titles in 1955 and 1956 before going on to claim seven more at Brownwood. After their breakout 1950s run, Stamford had mixed success, although they would go on to win seven district titles over the next twenty years.

Stamford's football history apparently didn't impress Fabens, as they rolled over the Stamford Bulldogs 48–14. With the win, Fabens became the first team from the El Paso metropolitan area to win two playoff games in the same season against teams that weren't from the same area. The Wildcats pounced on Stamford early and never looked back. Fabens scored two touchdowns in each of the first two quarters to take a 28–14 halftime lead and then added twenty fourth-quarter insurance points to account for the final margin of victory. Fabens jumped out quickly to a 13–0 lead on an Ernie Rivera ten-yard run and a forty-five-yard David Rueda pass to Chito Ortiz. However, a Fabens fumble inside their own fifteen set up an easy Stamford touchdown to make it 13–8 Fabens after a two-point conversion by Stamford. In the second quarter Randy Hodges broke loose for a thirty-five-yard touchdown and followed that score up with a two-point conversion of his own to extend the Fabens lead to 21–8. Before intermission, Rueda found Ortiz through the air again for a score, this time from twenty-three yards out, to make it 28–8. Stamford, however, scored again just before halftime to make it 28–14 at the break. In the fourth quarter, Fabens scored twenty points, the highlight being Rivera scoring his second touchdown of the night with a three-yard run. Rivera had a personal best 188 yards on the ground, and Hodges had 146, as Fabens ran for 471 for the game.

Roy Slape recalled being a little surprised at the outcome: "I really expected more out of Stamford," he said. "I thought they were easier than Kermit. Canutillo was just as good as them. It was a good win, even though we weren't challenged much."

Randy Hodges had an interesting recollection of the Stamford game. He said, "I remember the Stamford safety ended up at Texas A&M. He was very good fundamentally. I never broke one of his tackles. On my touchdown run, I actually jumped over him, so he never got the chance to tackle me. When I later coached, I used his tackling techniques to teach my players. Also, after I scored the two-point conversion after my touchdown, I reinjured my ribs. I started coughing up blood. There was a coach from Texas Tech there to watch me play. My ribs were killing me, but I had to get off the ground. I had to impress him."

The Wildcats' next playoff contest was assured to be more challenging than playing Stamford, since it was against the number-one ranked team in the state, the Childress Bobcats. From District 2–2A, Childress, like Fabens, sported a 12–0 record on the season. After defeating Muleshoe 20–0 the previous week, the Bobcats had outscored their foes on the season 396–68. While making it to the state quarterfinals was rarified air for Fabens, Childress was in familiar territory, at the end of a run in the 1970s where they compiled a 113–17–3 overall record and captured nine district titles in ten years. The Bobcats made the state semifinals or better from 1975 to 1978, including losses in the finals in 1975 and 1976. The Childress head coach was icon Charlie Johnston, who compiled a 315–94–8 record in thirty-five years with the Bobcats from 1967 to 2001.

The showdown between the two squads was on December 7 at Barrett Stadium in Odessa. Childress was led on offense by quarterback Perry Morren, who had thrown for nearly five thousand yards in his high school career, which, at that time, was third all-time in Texas schoolboy history. Morren had tossed a trio of touchdown passes in the previous weeks' win over Muleshoe.

Randy Hodges observed the following about Fabens's mindset and their lack of playoff experience going into the Childress game: "After we beat Stamford, I don't think my teammates understood or fathomed going two or three more rounds in the playoffs. Our intensity level against Childress wasn't the same. It was like getting to the quarterfinals was good enough. I thought we were good enough to win state."

The Wildcats made a good showing in the first half, taking a 7–0 halftime lead on a Randy Hodges sixty-one-yard run just fifty-seven seconds before halftime. Hodges ran one hundred yards on just eight carries, all in the first half. Fabens had gotten the ball at their fifteen after intercepting a Morren pass. Hodges picked up sixteen yards to the Fabens thirty-one, and three plays later, Hodges had a sixty-one-yard sprint to the end zone. Hodges recalled, "My sixty-one-yard touchdown was right up the middle. It's funny because the field in Odessa had those halogen lamps to light the field, and that really cast some shadows. The shadows were everywhere, and I thought they were Childress players trying to catch me. I guess I ran a little faster because of that."

In the second half, however, Fabens was limited to just eleven offensive plays as Childress played keep-away with the ball, scoring on three time-consuming drives of twelve, sixteen, and fifteen plays to claim a hard-fought 19–7 win. Childress pulled within 7–6 with 7:31 to go in the third quarter on a six-yard Clifton Cornish touchdown reception from Perry Morren. Hodges blocked the potential game-tying extra-point attempt after.

Childress got the ball back from Fabens toward the end of the third quarter and proceeded to go sixty-six yards in sixteen plays, with Morren scoring on a quarterback keeper from one yard out with 10:41 to go in the game. The Bobcats' two-point conversion attempt failed, and the score was 12–7 Childress. Fabens came right back and mounted a threat as David Rueda completed his only pass of the evening for forty-eight yards to Sergio Ortiz, taking the Wildcats from their own twenty-four to the Childress twenty-eight. On the next play, however, fullback Ernie Rivera fumbled the ball, and Childress took over on their own twenty-one. The Bobcats proceeded to march down the field for the clinching touchdown, with 2:18 to go in the game. Tailback Donald Sims was responsible for the four-yard score, capping off a night where he rushed for 171 yards.

Another interesting development in the second half was that Hodges, who had picked up one hundred yards rushing on eight carries in the first half, did not touch the ball on offense in the second half. Hodges explained, "I didn't touch the ball the second half on offense. I did touch it twice, though. Childress went for a two-point conversion and I knocked it down, and I also blocked an extra-point attempt. I remember the reporters after the game asked my dad a bunch of questions about why I didn't touch the ball in the second half. A few years later, I was in Childress for the Green Belt All-Star Game they have there every year, and Charlie Johnston, the coach at Childress, came up to me and said, 'What was your dad thinking?' It was just one of those things. He didn't keep me from the ball on purpose. I know my dad felt as bad about it as I did."

Several of the Wildcats discussed the loss that ended their 1979 playoff run prematurely. Roy Slape said, "Against Childress, it just didn't happen for us. We had a chance to win. That game is hard to recall because I've tried to put it out of my head. It still hurts to talk about it. A key play was when we were getting ready to go ahead in the fourth quarter and Ernie Rivera fumbled. He never fumbled. I was on the sidelines getting the next play from Coach Hodges to take into the huddle, and Ernie went off tackle around the left side, my side of the field, and I saw the ball pop into the air. We would have gone ahead. That fumble brought us down a bit. There was also another play earlier in the game when one of our receivers dropped a touchdown pass. We fought a good battle, though."

"Childress was exceptional," David Rueda added. "Their quarterback went to Texas Tech. He was one of the leading passers in Texas history. They could really throw the ball. They were good. They also had a defensive end who was a man-child. It didn't help us that I tore all of the ligaments in my ankle early in the game. I could only play offense after that, and even then, I was limited. We had a costly fumble in the fourth quarter, and we also gave them a cheap touchdown early on in the game. In the end, though, they were better."

John Dyer had a possible theory for the loss to Childress. He said, half-jokingly, "The whole season, we used to listen to Journey's *Infinity* album and *Van Halen II* on the bus going to the games. On the bus ride to play Childress, some of the guys said they were tired of listening to the same songs, and we changed it up. We decided to blame our loss on that."

Moe Hodges left Fabens after the 1979 season. He went to Dumas, forty miles north of Amarillo in the Texas Panhandle and close to five hundred miles from Fabens. Randy Hodges said, "My dad left for Dumas because they contacted him. They had been good in the 1960s, and it was a larger school, Class 4A. My brother was also coming up, and it was a good opportunity for him."

Moe Hodges coached for three seasons in Dumas, 1980–82, compiling an 11–16–3 record. He finished up his coaching career at Matador from 1989 to 1991, going 15–15 overall. His head coaching record was 91–61–6. He passed away in February 2013 at the age of seventy-eight.

Fabens has grown steadily over the years. The Wildcats are now a Class 4A Division I school with about seven hundred students, up from about four hundred in 1979. The town of Fabens, which had about 3,500 residents in 1979, has grown to about 8,500 today. As was the case in 1979, Fabens has remained an economically challenged community, with 49 percent of its citizens living in poverty and only 55 percent holding a high school diploma. Farming, most specifically cotton, alfalfa, pecans, and onions, remains a big industry in Fabens.

Although Fabens has grown, their football fortunes have not. Fabens made the playoffs seventeen times since 1979 but with no playoff wins to show for it. The Wildcats did win a district title in 1982, with a 5–5 record, but have none since then. Since 1979, Fabens's record stands at 381–503–4. The two playoff wins the Wildcats recorded in 1979 remain the only ones in school history.

The town of Fabens will always have the 1979 version of the Wildcats to hang their hat on. David Rueda, who returned to Fabens years later to work for the school district, said the following about the 1979 Wildcats: "The town had followed our evolution on the field since we were in middle school. You could've robbed any store or home in Fabens on Friday nights because everyone was at our games. We were a special group of kids, starting all the way back in the sixth grade. We played well and worked well together. It was a special year. The town still thinks of us and remembers today, over forty years later." The pride of Fabens, a beacon of hope shining bright in the El Paso area, secured a legacy on the field that continues even today.

Beaumont

Steve Shaver Leads the Underdog 1984 French Buffs to the 5A State Co-Championship

ON JANUARY 10, 1901, the United States was forever changed when oil sprang from Texas soil. Up until that date, Russia was the world's leading oil producer, and the vast majority of US oil came from Pennsylvania. There were 37,000 oil wells in the United States, producing about 160,000 barrels of oil per day. Right outside of Beaumont on that fateful January day, an oil well known as Spindletop was struck. Southeast Texas was never the same.

Early on, Spindletop produced more than eighty thousand barrels per day on its own, raising US oil production by more than 50 percent overnight. The United States became the leading oil producer in the world. Spindletop ushered in an age of inexpensive oil, which coincided with the development of the automobile and the internal combustion engine. The landscape of America was drastically changed, and Beaumont kept in step with the times, growing from about four thousand residents before oil was struck to more than forty thousand by 1920. Thanks to the advent of oil refineries and other World War II industries, Beaumont grew to almost one hundred thousand residents by 1950. Interstate 10 eventually went through Beaumont in the 1960s, and the population eventually reached about 120,000, a statistic that has remained for the last fifty years. In fact, the port of Beaumont annually ranks among the top five in the country for total tonnage.

As Beaumont grew, so did its city limits and school system. The city expanded rapidly during and after World War II, and much of that growth occurred north of the city limits, where tiny French ISD is located. The district was started in 1903, and a high school was built in 1913. When the Buffaloes started playing football in 1926, they were a Class B school—the state's smallest classification. While they were part of French ISD (1926–47), French High School was a mediocre 80–87–18 overall. During this time, the highlight of the French football program was that it produced legendary Texas high school, college, and professional coach "Bum" Phillips, a 1941 Buffaloes graduate.

In 1948, French High School consolidated with Beaumont ISD as a Class A school and immediately won four straight district titles from 1949 to 1952. The Buffaloes, or "Buffs" as they are known, won three playoff games in these four years, including their last one in school history up until 1984. However, from 1953 to 1970, they had no playoff appearances and an overall 59–115–5 record.

In 1971, Steve Shaver came to Beaumont to try and resurrect French High School football. He had left his first head coaching position at Del Valle High School in 1968, one year after leading them to what is still their best season ever. Little did he know that when his 1967 Del Valle team was eliminated by Kountze High School, just twenty miles north of French, he would return to the Golden Triangle area to have lightning in a bottle strike again seventeen years later.

Steve's wife, Dee Dee, described how he left Del Valle and ended up at Beaumont French: "In 1969, Steve left Del Valle, but he didn't find a job in time, so he went into construction and home building for a year with a friend of his. He left there because he wanted a job at a larger high school; Del Valle was just 2A. He didn't get hired in time for the 1969 school year, so that's why he went into construction. In 1970, he got back into coaching as an assistant at Corpus Christi King, and then he went to French in 1971. When he got the job offer from French, he asked me, 'What do you think? It's not that much money.' I said, 'If you take the job, at least I can see you come through the door at night happy.'"

It was a slow start for Shaver at French, as he did not experience the immediate success he had at Del Valle. His first thirteen seasons at French resulted in a 54–66–9 record. The Buffs did win district titles in 1974 and 1975, with records of 5–4–1 and 5–2–2, but were quickly ushered out of the playoffs by Port Neches–Groves High School during both seasons.

But despite the rough start, Shaver and the 1984 Buffs would strike oil—just like at Spindletop in 1901. Going into that fateful season, most forecasters picked French to finish either third or fourth in District 22–5A play. Only one pigskin pundit among eight at the *Port Arthur News* picked the Buffs for a playoff spot, given that only the top two teams from each 5A district qualified for the playoffs from 1982 to 1989. West Brook, who had won the Class 5A state title in 1982 (their first year as a high school), was unanimously chosen to win district, with the majority of sportswriters choosing Port Arthur Jefferson as their second pick. However, the Buffs and Steve Shaver were optimistic that they could contend for a playoff spot. French returned twenty lettermen, including four offensive and six defensive starters.

Beaumont French coach Steve Shaver holds the 1984 Class 5A state co-championship trophy after a 21-21 tie with Odessa Permian. Courtesy of Steve Shaver Jr.

The French mainstays on offense and defense also had high hopes going into the season. Mark Guilbeaux was going to lead the offense, and as a quarterback in junior high, he was undefeated and had lost only twice as a junior varsity quarterback. Guilbeaux recalled, "In ninth grade, we had three middle schools that fed into French: SFA [Stephen F. Austin], Lincoln, and Bowie. We had some good players. We went undefeated as freshmen. We knew that if we could stay together, by the time we were seniors we could be pretty good. My sophomore year, the coaches wanted to put Robert Keil and myself on varsity, but my dad kept me back on junior varsity. We had a good JV team that year. My junior year in 1983, I started as a safety on defense. Halfway through the season, I ended up playing as the quarterback because our starter got hurt. It gave me some good experience going into my senior season. I had played a lot of different positions coming up in football on both offense and defense. In fact, my senior year, I wanted to play quarterback and safety. The coaches wouldn't let me do it. About the only guy they let play both ways was Robert Keil."

Robert Keil, who was the only two-way player for French as a linebacker and fullback, recalled, "Going into the season, of course we had high hopes. Almost every team does. The difference with us was our thought process. We vowed to be in better shape than our opponents and to always come to play. We were focused and disciplined. Execution is paramount in football, and we prided ourselves on that. We were well-coached and well-conditioned. I actually thought our 1982 team in my sophomore year was better talent-wise than in 1984. The difference was that they just weren't as dedicated as we were. Guys like Melvin Turner, Mark Guilbeaux, and myself—we had been together since ninth grade. We had a different thought process than that 1982 team. They didn't have the drive or focus we had. We wanted to do something special."

The Buffs opened their 1984 season on September 7 with an away contest against the Dickinson Gators. Dickinson, from District 24–5A, was district champ in 1983, with an 11–2 record. The Gators featured Andre Ware as quarterback, who later would win the Heisman Trophy in 1989 with the University of Houston.

French had a good start to the 1984 season by taking a 12–0 first-half lead over Dickinson. However, they could not sustain their lead, mostly because of six lost fumbles, as the Gators overtook the Buffs to win 22–12. Robert Keil helped score the first points of the game for the Buffs when he launched a twenty-three-yard halfback pass to Keith Wycoff late in the first quarter. Paul Jones added a second-quarter touchdown for French as they went up 12–0 with 9:49 left in the half. Dickinson closed the gap to 12–7 at halftime and took the lead for good with 1:48 left in the third quarter on a seventy-three-yard run. The Gators added a fourth-period score and two-point conversion to account for the 22–12 final tally. Paul Jones paced French with 102 rushing yards on twelve carries. Both offenses had a little trouble getting untracked, as Dickinson gained 214 total yards while the Buffs were held to 202.

The French record for the 1984 season stood at 0–2 after the Buffs lost 26–8 on September 14 to the Port Arthur Lincoln Bumblebees, a squad that would go on to a 10–3 record in 1984, including a 27–25 upset over Bay City, the top-ranked Class 4A team in the state, in the playoffs. The Buffs' offense never got untracked at Port Arthur's Memorial Stadium. French started off the night right with Paul Jones scoring on a ten-yard run in the first quarter. After that, it was all Bumblebees. French only gained eighty-two yards rushing on forty-two carries and had just twenty-eight yards through the air. Mark Guilbeaux had the worst game of his career, going 0–10 passing and rushing ten times for minus-fifty yards. Lincoln also sacked Guilbeaux five times during the matchup.

Guilbeaux talked about how the Buffs didn't take the Bumblebees seriously enough: "We had always beat Lincoln. They always had good athletes, but we always had their number. I think we overlooked them. Well, they whupped our ass. However, since we knew it was a nondistrict game, the loss didn't concern us all that much."

French finally got on the right track with their first home game of 1984, with a 27–14 win against the Forest Brook Jaguars on September

21 at Zaharias Stadium. The Buffs defense held Forest Brook to nine first downs and 136 yards of total offense, forcing four turnovers. After a poor game against Lincoln the week before, where he accounted for minus-fifty yards of total offense, Mark Guilbeaux rebounded with seventy-three yards rushing and 114 passing for French. Guilbeaux got the scoring started for the Buffs on a three-yard run in the first quarter. Forest Brook returned the ensuing kickoff seventy-six yards for a touchdown to tie the score at 7–7. Just forty-five seconds before halftime, Guilbeaux hit Keith Wycoff with a fifty-five-yard scoring pass to put the Buffs up 14–7 at halftime. Robert Keil's nineteen-yard touchdown run early in the fourth quarter extended the lead to 21–7, and French coasted to the win. The Buffs were now 1–2 heading into District 22–5A play.

On September 29, French played the 1–2 Port Neches–Groves Indians in Port Neches and took the District 22–5A opener 20–14 to even out the Buffs' record at 2–2. French relied on the big play for their first two touchdowns, landing on the board first in the second quarter as Mark Guilbeaux hit Keith Wycoff with an eighty-four-yard touchdown pass. Later, in the fourth quarter, Guilbeaux broke a seven-all tie with a sixty-nine-yard sprint to the end zone. The Indians came back to tie the score at fourteen with 5:49 to play, and with just fifty-nine seconds remaining, backup wide receiver Morris Jenkins recovered a Buffs fumble in the Port Neches end zone to give French the improbable 20–14 win. French had recovered a Port Neches–Groves fumble at the Indians' twenty-three with just 1:47 remaining. Two plays later from the Port Neches–Groves' eight, a missed handoff resulted in the ball squirting into the Indians' end zone, where Jenkins recovered the ball for the winning touchdown. French outgained the Indians on the night 310 yards to 206, but six turnovers hindered the Buffs' efforts. Guilbeaux led the French rushers with 107 yards on seventeen carries and was 3–15 passing for 103 yards and three interceptions.

October 5 brought the Buffs' first district home contest against their nemesis, the Port Arthur Jefferson Yellow Jackets. Mark Guilbeaux explained, "Just like we were Port Arthur Lincoln's nemesis, our nemesis was always Port Arthur Jefferson. We had some decent teams in the early 1980s and they were really good. In our senior year, we talked about our previous teams, which had always lost to Jefferson. It would seem like these former Buffs squads had a shot at the playoffs, but then they would lose to Jefferson and their whole season would turn to crap."

The Buffs left no doubt as they pounded the Yellow Jackets 34–8.

Jefferson was down only 6–0 at halftime before the third quarter did them in. French scored twenty-one third-quarter points despite compiling only sixteen total yards of offense. On the second play of the second half, Jefferson coughed up the football at their own eighteen, and two plays later, Mark Guilbeaux hit Melvin Turner with a sixteen-yard scoring strike to put French up 12–0 with 9:18 left in the third quarter.

On the next series, the Yellow Jackets were intercepted at their own twenty, and Paul Jones scored from two yards out five plays later to put French up 18–0 with 6:04 left in the third. Jefferson was forced to punt on their next series, and Vernon Grant blocked the kick, allowing Detrick Hughes to scoop up the ball and return it twenty-three yards for a score. The Buffs now led 25–0 with 4:18 to go in the third. On the Yellow Jackets' next possession, Robert Keil tackled the Jefferson quarterback in his own end zone for a safety to put French up 27–0 at the 3:28 mark of the third quarter. In less than six minutes, the lead went from 6–0 to 27–0. The French defense was also dominant during the contest. With just 1:21 left in the third quarter, Jefferson had but eleven yards of total offense and ended up with minus-two rushing yards on the night. For the second week in a row, the Buffs defense knocked four opposing players out of the game with their relentless hitting.

Guilbeaux recalled, "Once we beat Jefferson, we knew we had a shot at the playoffs. We never wanted to lose to them. We had to get over the hump. It was personal for me. I had revenge on my mind. I was playing JV basketball my junior year, and we went up against Jefferson. One of their basketball players was also a defensive end on their football team. During one of our basketball matchups, I went for a layup and he elbowed me, and my teeth went right through my lip. When we played Jefferson in football, I saw that same player and he asked as he passed me, 'Do you remember me?' I said, 'I ain't ever forgot you.' Later in the game, a play was sent in from the sidelines, but I changed it to where I would run around that defensive end's side of the field. I ran right over him and, trust me, he didn't get up."

Now 3–2 overall and 2–0 in District 22–5A play, the Buffs took on the 1–3–1 Nederland Bulldogs in Nederland on October 12. French took a hard-fought 14–11 win to go to 3–0 in District 22–5A play. Guilbeaux had a thirty-seven-yard touchdown run in the first quarter to open the scoring. The Buffs defense was relentless again, allowing only fifty-five yards rushing and 136 total yards during the game. Three French fumbles enabled the Bulldogs to penetrate the Buffs' twenty-five-yard line five times during their first five possessions, but they were only able to have a field goal with 2:53 left in the third quarter to make it 7–3. Robert Keil scored from two yards out in the fourth to make it 14–3. Nederland added a touchdown and two-point conversion with just 1:46 left in the contest to account for the final score.

The one negative that came from the Nederland win was that Mark Guilbeaux hurt his ankle and missed most of the Buffs' next game against Vidor; he was also limited the following week against Beaumont West Brook. Guilbeaux said about his injury, "I got hurt against Nederland in the second quarter. We ran a fake handoff to the left, and I kept the ball. As I tried to cut back, some Nederland players tackled me and I landed wrong on the ankle. I ended up going back in the game after they taped me up, and my blood was pumping. After the game, though, it really swelled up and was so painful that I had to miss some time."

Minus Mark Guilbeaux, who completed only two plays in the second quarter and was 0–2 passing, French suffered their first district loss 14–0 in the rain on October 19 at the hands of the Vidor Pirates on their homecoming. Vidor was 4–2 overall and 2–1 in District 22–5A play. Guilbeaux was replaced by sophomore Willie Williams, who was called up from the junior varsity to play quarterback even though he was a receiver. Williams, in his first varsity action, had one hundred yards rushing on eighteen carries and threw for sixty-seven more but could never get the Buffs into the end zone. Three times, French had the ball inside the Vidor ten-yard line, but they turned the ball over each time. Paul Jones fumbled at the Pirates' two, and the ball rolled through the end zone for a touchback in the second quarter. Willie Williams also saw two passes intercepted at the Vidor seven. Williams lost a fumble at the French seventeen to set up Vidor's second touchdown of the second quarter. The Buffs outgained Vidor 276–172 but had four turnovers to Vidor's two. After the contest, French and Vidor were tied for the district lead at 3–1, along with West Orange–Stark High School and Beaumont West Brook.

Mark Guilbeaux recalled, "I tried to play against Vidor, but I only went in for a couple of plays. The field was wet, and Vidor tried everything they could to cheat us out of the game. But, hey, that's Vidor."

On October 26, French played the District 22–5A favorite, West Brook Bruins, at Babe Zaharias Stadium. The Bruins came away with a 31–13 win to put West Brook at 7–1 overall and 4–1 in District 22–5A play. French dropped to 4–4 overall and 3–2 in district and were now looking at the real possibility of missing the playoffs. Although still hobbled by his injured ankle, Mark Guilbeaux split time in the game with Willie Williams, but the Buffs were down 24–0 at halftime thanks to three French turnovers in the second quarter. French closed the gap to 24–13 with two second-half touchdown drives, but West Brook added a late touchdown to account for the final score. French totaled only 154 yards for the evening, turned the ball over six times, and had seventy-three yards in penalties. In addition, the Buffs defense gave up the most yards they had all season, with a total of 298. West Brook and West Orange–Stark were now tied at 4–1 in the District 22–5A with two weeks to go. French and Vidor, who lost to Nederland in an upset, were both 3–2.

Mark Guilbeaux discussed a key moment in the West Brook game that affected the team for the rest of the season: "Against West Brook, Coach Shaver was trying to rotate myself and Willie Williams as quarterback. It just wasn't working. We couldn't get into any kind of rhythm. It wasn't doing us any good. I told Coach Shaver that on the sideline and that I wasn't going to split time with a sophomore—he had to make a decision as to who was going to be the quarterback. Some of the assistant coaches, like Coach Norris Bobb, our receiver's coach, agreed with me. Coach Shaver must have listened because I was the quarterback for the rest of the season. It was after that when we started clicking. Once you have the confidence of your coaches, that's big.

Coach Shaver discusses strategy with French quarterback Mark Guilbeaux. Courtesy of Steve Shaver Jr.

"We also started to open things up offensively. We only used to pass when teams knew we had to pass. Now we threw on first and second down, when teams didn't expect it. Moving Willie out to receiver helped. It stimulated and motivated the other receivers. They always had the talent; they just needed a little push. Winning is contagious, and it's all about confidence. Ours eventually went through the roof."

Robert Keil concurred. "Mark sprained an ankle against Nederland,

and it actually helped us because the coaches brought sophomore Willie Williams up to varsity to fill in as quarterback. He was a godsend to our football team. Willie did the best he could at quarterback. He didn't want to let us down. We didn't want to put any pressure on him. The defense was motivated to play better. We knew we had to step up. The key was that when Mark was ready to play again, we kept Willie on varsity and moved him out to wide receiver. He also returned kicks. Mark now had someone to throw the ball to. Once we got Mark back, our offense started rolling."

Moving Willie Williams out to receiver paid immediate dividends for the Buffs in their next game on November 2 against West Orange–Stark, the District 22–5A coleader, in West Orange. Willie Williams touched the ball only three times, but those three plays made the difference in the game and possibly the 1984 season as French rolled to a 27–16 win over the Mustangs. With Mark Guilbeaux now firmly entrenched at the quarterback position, Williams moved to wide receiver, and the payoff was immediate for the game and the rest of the season. After West Orange–Stark took a 10–0 lead in the second quarter, the 120-pound Williams returned the Mustangs kickoff ninety-seven yards for a score to close the gap to 10–7. With just thirty-one seconds left on the clock until halftime, Williams's second touch of the night came on a forty-two-yard reception from Guilbeaux down to the West Orange–Stark ten-yard line. Two plays later, Robert Keil took the ball in from three yards out and the Buffs went into halftime with a 15–10 lead.

With 9:06 left in the third quarter, Paul Jones scooted around the left end for a fifty-six-yard score, and the French lead was 21–10. Shortly thereafter, Williams touched the ball for the third time—this time hauling in a twenty-yard scoring pass from Guilbeaux to make the score 27–10 French. The Mustangs added a late touchdown, but it was not enough. French rolled up 292 total yards, including 218 on the ground, while the Buffs defense limited West Orange–Stark's district-leading offense to only 197 yards. The win lifted the Buffs' district record to 4–2, tied with West Orange–Stark and Vidor. The Mustangs and Pirates met the last week of the regular season. French needed to beat Beaumont Charlton-Pollard and West Orange–Stark had to defeat Vidor in order for the Buffs to advance to the playoffs.

Steve Shaver Jr., who was a sophomore on the French junior varsity team in 1984, had a sideline view of the Buffs' Friday night games. He reiterated what Mark Guilbeaux had said earlier about the decision to move

Willie Williams to a receiver position: "Willie Williams was so good. The turning point of the season was when Dad brought him up from junior varsity. This opened up the offense a little more. If you throw the ball more, you have to have someone who can catch the ball. Willie was that person. We became a different team offensively. We had the talent."

All that remained in the regular season for the French Buffaloes was a must-win matchup against the 2–6–1 Charlton-Pollard Cougars on October 9 at Zaharias Stadium in Beaumont. The Buffs won 20–7 and got their wish as West Orange–Stark beat Vidor 28–7 to allow French to advance to the Class 5A playoffs as the District 22–5A runner-up with a 5–2 record. West Brook was the district champion at 6–1. West Orange–Stark tied French for second but were out of the playoffs because they had lost to the Buffs the previous week. This meant the Buffs were headed to the playoffs for the first time since 1975.

French scored on their first possession against Charlton-Pollard when Mark Guilbeaux hit Willie Williams with a thirty-six-yard scoring pass. The Buffs expanded their lead to 14–0 in the second quarter as Melvin Turner caught a four-yard strike from Guilbeaux. The Cougars closed to within 14–7 early in the fourth quarter, when they recovered a blocked Buffs punt in the end zone for a score. After the Cougars had a potential game-tying touchdown called back because of a penalty with 5:47 remaining, the Buffs extended their lead to 20–7 when Robert Keil ripped off a thirty-yard touchdown run with just 2:39 left in the contest. Charlton-Pollard actually outgained French 202–197 for the evening, but they were stymied by eight penalties for eighty yards and three turnovers.

"We had played a tough schedule, and we were 4–4 and 3–2 in district when Mark came back for the last two regular-season games," recalled Robert Keil. "We had to win them both if we wanted to make the playoffs. This was only the third year that the second-place team in the district could go to the playoffs. We beat a good West Orange–Stark team at their place on homecoming and followed that up with a win over Charlton-Pollard to end up 5–2 in district. We were going to the playoffs and were on a roll!"

With a 6–4 regular-season record and a 5–2 District 22–5A runner-up spot, not much was expected of the Beaumont French Buffaloes as they entered the 1984 Class 5A playoffs. The Buffs were slated to go up against mostly Houston-area teams in Region 3—traditionally one of the toughest in the state. Their first playoff opponent was the Aldine Mustangs, a suburban Houston powerhouse. Aldine, the District 21–5A champion, had carved out an 8–2 record for the season and were led by Coach Bill Smith, who eventually spent twenty-nine seasons at Aldine from 1975 to 2003, compiling a 237–96–6 record, including a 15–0 record and state 5A title in 1990. The game was played on November 17 in the Houston Astrodome, the first time French had played there and also the first time they had ever played on Astroturf. French was a decided underdog to the Mustangs, and none of the eight sportswriters for the *Port Arthur News* picked French to prevail.

Despite their underdog status, the Buffs opened up their passing game offense and, sparked by four touchdown passes, stunned Aldine 48–13. From his flanker position, Willie Williams opened the scoring when he took a reverse handoff and hit tight end Melvin Turner with a forty-nine-yard strike in the first quarter. Mark Guilbeaux hit Turner on touchdown throws of eleven yards in the second quarter to make it 14–0 at the half and eighteen yards in the third quarter. Guilbeaux had another touchdown pass of thirty-five yards to Cedric Jones in the third stanza as the Buffs rolled up thirty-four second-half points. Guilbeaux ended up the afternoon 11–19 for 185 yards as the Buffs rolled up 379 total yards in their shocking blowout of the Mustangs.

Steve Shaver Jr. reminisced about the upset: "After we blew out Aldine, we said to ourselves, 'Hey, we may have something here.'"

Mark Guilbeaux also recalled playing in the Astrodome: "When we made the playoffs, we opened up the offense even more. We had been pigeonholing ourselves by running too much. We would work on our passing game at practice during the regular season, but Coach Shaver would stick to mostly runs during the games. We really opened up the offense when we went into the Astrodome to play our games. In the Dome, we weren't playing in the elements. We were playing on turf for the first time. We now could really take advantage of our speed. We got hot at the right time. I really didn't see us as a Cinderella team."

The French Buffaloes were now heading into uncharted territory, playing a game after the Thanksgiving holiday for the first time. Dee Shaver recalled, "The community was amazing in 1984. I used to look forward to the end of football season because that meant Thanksgiving was coming. In 1984, I said, 'The heck with Thanksgiving!' This was a whole new experience for us, and we were having a great time."

The next game for French was another contest in the Astrodome, this time on November 24 against the LaPorte Bulldogs. LaPorte, the District 24–5A runner-up to Galveston Ball, was 10–1 going into the game with

French. The Bulldogs had trounced Pasadena Dobie 31–8 in their bi-district matchup.

For the second week in a row, the Buffs rolled to forty-eight points as they took a 48–19 win over LaPorte. Mark Guilbeaux continued his passing assault in the playoffs with two touchdown passes to go along with his 103 yards rushing. Robert Keil added three short touchdown runs from his fullback position. Special teams were also a big factor for the Buffs as Derrick Wilson blocked a Bulldogs punt for a touchdown and Willie Williams broke the game wide open when he returned the second-half kickoff for a 104-yard score to put French up 28–12. French had a 353–270 advantage in total yardage and held LaPorte to just eight yards passing.

Robert Keil and Mark Guilbeaux both talked about the start of French's playoff run in the Astrodome. Keil said, "Once we were in the playoffs, we had tunnel vision. We knew we were going to be facing Houston-area teams, and we had heard from everyone about how good they were and that we didn't stand a chance. We were the underdog in every playoff game. The talk was that we would be home after the first round of the playoffs. We had to prove everyone wrong. Well, we went into Houston and the Astrodome, and we showed those Houston teams a thing or two. We wiped out Aldine and LaPorte. We refused to listen to that talk. LaPorte was about twice our size. It was like playing against grown men. I scored three touchdowns against them, though, and I was only about 190 pounds, which was pretty small for a fullback and linebacker."

Guilbeaux added, "LaPorte was big, and they had LaSalle Harper on their team. He played at Arkansas and in the NFL. Nobody gave us a chance. We were getting on a roll, though. We eventually went up against four Houston-area teams. Those schools were bigger and had more talent. We had a big heart, though. I also believe our district was a whole lot harder than the ones they were in. We had teams like Jefferson, West Brook, Port Neches–Groves, and West Orange–Stark. Those Houston districts would have one to two good teams in them, and the rest usually weren't that good. We were battle-tested."

Next for the French Buffaloes was another contest in the Astrodome, this time on December 1 against the 11–1 Houston Sterling Raiders. Sterling had beaten Houston Waltrip 17–0 and Houston Spring Woods 26–21 to advance to regionals against the Buffs. The Raiders averaged twenty-five points per game for the season, just giving up a little more than six points per game.

After the offense had dominated in the first two rounds for the Buffs, it was the defense's time to shine against Houston Sterling. The French defense was sometimes overlooked, but it was the best in District 22–5A, giving up about seventeen points per game. The Buffs held Sterling to 232 total yards, with just sixty-one of those coming on the ground, as they took a hard-fought 22–14 win over the Raiders. French amassed 316 total yards, including 209 on the ground but shot itself in the foot with eleven penalties for ninety-two yards. The Buffs defense held Sterling's Jeffrey Murray, who had rushed for more than 1,500 yards for the season, to just twenty-eight yards on eleven carries.

Murray opened the scoring in the contest with a one-yard run with 1:06 left in the first quarter, and a subsequent two-point conversion put Houston Sterling up 8–0. French came back in the second quarter as Willie Williams made a big play—like he had done many times since being called up to varsity seven games prior. Williams scored from forty-five yards out on an end-around, and the Buffs tied the score with a two-point conversion of their own when Mark Guilbeaux hit Melvin Turner with a pass to make it 8–8 at the half.

Guilbeaux, who was 10–17 for 107 yards, threw two second-half touchdowns, a fifteen-yarder to Turner to give French a 15–7 third-quarter lead, and a nine-yard strike to Robert Keil in the fourth quarter after Sterling had pulled within 15–14. Paul Jones, the Buffs leading rusher, delivered a key play on special teams when he blocked a potential game-tying extra point after a Sterling touchdown had pulled them to within 15–14. Keil caught an insurance touchdown pass with 2:04 left; then, seventeen seconds later, he joined the defense and added a game-clinching interception.

Finis Vanover was the defensive coordinator for the Buffs in 1984 and had played for Shaver at French in 1971, Shaver's first year with the Buffs. He spoke about the French defense: "We opened up the offense for the playoffs. We really started to

French Buffaloes star running back and linebacker Robert Keil breaks off a large gain against Houston Sterling in a 22-14 playoff win in the Astrodome. Courtesy of Steve Shaver Jr.

click. The defense knew if we could hold on until the offense got healthy, we could be good. That's what happened; it all came together. We had the number-one defense in the state in 1984. Teams only averaged 2.8 yards per snap against us. We had twenty-three interceptions and seventeen blocked kicks during the season. We averaged about two scores per game on defense and special teams. Robert Keil was our undisputed leader. His teammates were more afraid to face him than our coaches."

The French defense would face their stiffest challenge of 1984 in the regional final against the 11–2 Galveston Ball Tornadoes. The December 8 game would be the Buffs' fourth consecutive contest in the Astrodome.

Steve Shaver Jr. said about the matchup, "Galveston Ball was huge. Half of their guys had beards. But our guys were fast, quick, and salty. I remember Robert Keil said, 'I ain't worried.' We had watched West Brook play Ball in the second round, and Ball beat them 34–31. We knew we were in for a fight."

The Tors' big gun was fullback Kimble Anders, who would go on to a stellar college career at the University of Houston and then be a Pro Bowl fullback with the Kansas City Chiefs. Anders had rung up 1,828 rushing yards and twenty-five touchdowns for the 1984 season.

Despite the odds, the Beaumont French Buffaloes scored their fourth straight upset as they beat Galveston Ball 24–13 in the Astrodome on December 8. French held Ambers somewhat in check as he rushed for 104 yards on twenty-four carries, about seventy under his usual output. Mark Guilbeaux threw for 148 yards and three scores, two of them going to Willie Williams. Melvin Turner scored the other touchdown on a twelve-yard pass play. Guilbeaux hit Williams with a thirty-two-yard scoring pass with 7:32 left in the opening quarter to give French a 7–0 lead. French then ate up the last six minutes of the first quarter and the first twenty-four seconds of the second with an eighty-one-yard, thirteen-play drive. French coach Steve Shaver decided to roll the dice on a fourth-and-goal play from the Ball twelve, and it was a success, as Guilbeaux hit Turner with a scoring pass to make it 14–0 French.

Ball countered with a drive of their own, sixty-six yards in eight plays, as Anders took the ball the final seven yards for the touchdown. French pushed their lead back to fourteen in the third quarter when the Buffs went fifty-six yards in eight plays. Guilbeaux hit Williams with a thirty-three-yard bomb with 7:20 left in the third to make it 21–7. French extended its lead to 24–7 on a thirty-seven-yard field goal by Paul Jones with 9:19 left in the contest. Ball scored a touchdown with about five minutes left, but the Buffs ran the clock down to fifty-seven seconds on their next possession before Ball could get the ball back.

Robert Keil recalled, "Galveston Ball really impressed me before we played them. They were huge and talented. They had several guys who went on to play in the NFL, Kimble Anders being one of them, along with Eric Hill and Todd Scott. In the end, though, it was all about heart. You gotta have it if you want to go far. One thing we did have was heart. Sometimes heart can beat talent."

The Buffs were slated to play the San Antonio Madison Mavericks at Kyle Field in College Station on December 15 in the 5A semifinals. Steve Shaver Jr. recalled, "Like Galveston Ball, San Antonio Madison was huge and talented." Madison had won the Region 4 title the week before by upsetting defending state champion Converse Judson 19–16. The Mavericks carried a 13–1 record into the contest.

The French passing game that had been so effective in the Astrodome was grounded by Mother Nature as south winds up to thirty-five miles per hour hampered both teams' passing games. Mark Guilbeaux had a rough game passing, going 2–14 for twenty-seven yards. French ended up churning out 217 yards on the ground and used their stifling defense to upset Madison 22–12 and take a spot in the Class 5A state finals. The French defense held Madison, who had been averaging just a shade under 400 yards of offense a game, to just 127 total yards.

The Buffs led 7–6 at halftime, thanks to Robert Keil blocking the extra-point attempt after a Madison second-quarter touchdown. The Mavericks added two field goals with the wind at their backs to make it 12–7 Madison after three quarters. With 6:56 remaining in the game, French got the ball at the Madison forty-seven, and six running plays later, Paul Jones, who led all rushers with eighty-five yards on sixteen carries, scored the go-ahead touchdown from eleven yards out to give the Buffs a 13–12 lead. Mark Guilbeaux converted the two-point conversion with a two-yard run, and the French lead was 15–12. Madison got the ball back with 4:19 left and faced the daunting task of having to go eighty yards against the wind. On their first play from the scrimmage, Madison coughed up a fumble, and six plays later Jones scored his third touchdown of the day to wrap up the game.

Mark Guilbeaux remarked, "We played Madison at Kyle Field in College Station. It was our first game outdoors after four games in the Dome. There was about a thirty- to forty-miles-per-hour wind blowing, and it really threw our game plan off. It hampered our offense because we had a tough time throwing the ball. Luckily, we had a tough running game that day and our defense really stepped up. It was a nail-biter. We overcame the weather, but it took us a while to get acclimated. They were good and big. They played a little bit dirty, too."

Robert Keil added, "One of my favorite plays of the season was against Madison. They had scored right at the end of the first half to pull within 7–6. I blocked the extra point to recover the ball, and I started running the other way. I remembered that back then, you couldn't advance the ball for a two-point conversion. After running for a little bit, I realized that I couldn't score, so I stopped and handed the ball to the referee. I did it to save my energy for the second half. That was a tough game at Kyle Field. The wind was blowing thirty-five miles per hour, and it really hindered our passing game. It was a great game."

The French Buffaloes now faced their most daunting task yet, as their opponent in the state championship on December 22 at Texas Stadium was none other than the Odessa Permian Panthers, who in 1984 were in the middle of a thirty-year dynasty in Texas high school football. The Panthers, whose 1988 season would be immortalized in the book *Friday Night Lights*, had forty-one all-time postseason wins in school history—which, at that time, was the most in Texas schoolboy history. Permian won state titles in 1965, 1972, and 1980 and was the runner-up in 1968, 1970, and 1975. The Panthers were the first large school to reach the finals seven times. Permian had been ranked number one in the state for most of the season and were the odds-on favorite to take the state title. They had scored 166 points in five playoff contests, the most in Class 5A history. Permian had allowed only forty-two points in five playoff games—another record. Also, if Permian were to score ten points or more in the final against French, the Panthers would be the highest-scoring team in 5A history. Another advantage for Permian was the sheer size of their school. They had about 2,500 students, one of the largest enrollments in Texas, while French was one of the smallest 5A schools at just over 1,300 students.

As with their other playoff games, almost no one gave French a chance against the Permian Panthers. In addition, Finis Vanover recalled, "I felt that Permian had total disrespect for us."

But the French players, most specifically Robert Keil, did not fear the Panthers. Steve Shaver Jr. recalled an event that happened a few days before the game. "We used to watch game films during our Monday or

Tuesday practices. Before we played Permian, Coach Vanover was showing us their films, and they did look impressive. Coach turned the lights on and he said something along the lines of, 'They're going to be a tough challenge coming up.' Well, Robert Keil spoke up and said, 'There's only one problem coach.' Coach Vanover asked, 'What's that, Robert?' Robert replied, 'They ain't never had a hat put on 'em like we're fixin' to put on 'em!' Everybody charged out of that film session fired up, and it carried over to the game."

Robert Keil remarked about the Panthers, "I always thought that Permian didn't play the same caliber of teams that we did in our part of the state. Other teams were intimidated by them. Not us, though. We weren't starstruck. Our mindset changed everything. We felt we were equally matched. We were big underdogs. They were supposed to be one of the greatest teams in state history."

"We really didn't know that much about Permian going into the championship game," Mark Guilbeaux added. "When you get that far, you get ready for the game and prepare for it, just like we had been doing all season. To be honest, they weren't one of the better teams we had faced talent-wise. They were great at fundamentals like tackling, and they stuck to their game plan. They also didn't quit."

For the first time since 1945, in the large school division when Highland Park tied Waco High 7–7, there was a Class 5A cochampion. Beaumont French and Odessa Permian played to a 21–21 tie to share the Class 5A state title. Under UIL rules, state championships that ended in a tie were not decided by penetrations, first downs, or total yardage, but the two schools were instead deemed cochampions. The game was the last tie for a state championship in Texas high school football history. There were no ties for a state title between 1985 and 1995, and Texas high school football went to overtime to settle ties starting in 1996.

The game didn't start well for the Buffs as Greg Anderson of Permian returned a punt eighty-three yards for a score just two minutes into the game. However, the Buffs struck back for twenty-one unanswered points. Robert Keil remarked, "Permian scored first on that eighty-three-yard punt return. Well, me or my teammates didn't get caught up in it. We could've just rolled over and quit. We moved past it, though, and got the job done. We even jumped out to a 21–7 lead. You have to give Permian credit, too—they didn't give up either."

The Buffs' first score, which came from their possession right after

Permian's touchdown, was set by a fifty-six-yard pass from Mark Guilbeaux to Willie Williams down to the Panthers' eleven. From there, Paul Jones took the ball into the end zone, and the extra point tied the score at seven. French took the lead when Guilbeaux hit Williams with a thirty-six-yard scoring strike in the second quarter, and Guilbeaux followed that up with a nine-yard scoring toss to Keith Wycoff.

Permian closed to within 21–14 at the half when they marched eighty yards in seven plays and scored with thirty-three seconds left in the half. On their first possession of the third quarter from their own forty, Permian drove sixty yards and tied the score with 4:28 to go in the third.

But the Panthers hurt themselves with five turnovers. Permian also had two touchdowns called back because of penalties. Two plays after Permian scored the tying touchdown in the third quarter, Permian returned a Mark Guilbeaux interception thirty-eight yards for a score, but the play was called back for an illegal block. In the fourth quarter, the Panthers apparently scored on a ten-yard run, but it was called back for illegal procedure. On the next play, Robert Keil intercepted the ball for the Buffs. Permian saw one more opportunity late in the game from the French thirty-seven, but Charles Goodman intercepted a Panthers pass at his own thirty with thirty-one seconds remaining to preserve the 21–21 tie.

Robert Keil once again gave the Panthers credit: "Permian didn't quit. They got down to us, and they didn't give up. Usually, when we got ahead, the other teams that we played would roll over and quit. Not these guys. They earned my respect. It was a historic game. There will never be another tie for a state title in Texas. They had been averaging about thirty-five points and well over four hundred yards per game. We held them well under both."

One interesting note to consider about the fateful matchup was that Mark Guilbeaux was six of twelve passing in the first half for 156 yards and two scores, but he had no completions in eight attempts in the second half. He explained, "We changed in the second half. We played not to lose. We got really conservative, and we lost our aggressiveness on first and second down. In the first half, we had a lot of third and short-yardage plays because we were aggressive on first and second down. Then, on third down, Permian didn't know if we were going to run or pass. When we went conservative, we were faced with a lot of third and long, and they pretty much knew we had to pass and came up with a defense to stop us on third down. It became a momentum thing in the second half. Luckily, our defense stepped up again. Robert had a big interception, and Charles Goodman had one at the end to preserve the tie. One thing Permian also did in the second half, which a lot of people didn't notice, was put their best athletes on the field for both offense and defense. That helped slow us down. They had a lot of their really good offensive players play both ways."

Robert Keil added, "It's hard to say what happened in the second half. Maybe we were feeling the pressure a bit. I was proud because we battled and didn't fold. We got some big turnovers in the second half. The defensive guys stepped up. For me, those memories remain fresh to this day. I vividly remember a hit I got on Dal Watson, their star running back. He had to crawl off the field. You know what, though? He eventually came back into the game. Like I said, they didn't quit.

"In the end, we got it done. This was for my school, the coaches, my teammates, the parents, the fans, for the French teams that had played before we did, and for the city of Beaumont. It was a pride thing. We made our mark on Texas high school football history. It was a great experience. It seemed like we played football for the whole school year. We started back in August with two-a-days, and we didn't finish playing until just before Christmas."

Finis Vanover gave much of the credit for the Buffs' title to Coach Steve Shaver: "In the end, Steve's personality was the straw that stirred the drink. He always knew which buttons to push, whether it be with the players or the coaching staff. He could adapt to just about anything. He was a master play-caller, too. He could somehow get in those kids' minds and get them to perform. They loved and respected him. He didn't treat everyone the same, though. Every kid is different, and he knew what made them tick. It was a privilege to play and coach with him. He was a close personal friend.

"Steve was instrumental in a lot of people's lives. He expected the most out of his players. He used to say, 'The good ones will,' meaning you could push your better players and that would make the rest of the players better. The good players will do what you ask them to do. The good players aren't going to quit if you push them. Coach Shaver used to challenge them to be better. He knew they wouldn't quit. A lot of coaches are afraid to be tough on their talented players because they think they might quit. Coach Shaver never worried about that."

Dee Shaver shared something her husband said to her on the way back to Beaumont after the state title game: "I remember coming back from Dallas after the Odessa Permian game. Steve kept things in perspective.

I said to him, 'Did we really just play and tie for the state title?' He said, 'It's a short distance from the penthouse to the outhouse.'"

Little did Steve Shaver know that what he said coming back from Dallas in December 1984 would be a self-fulfilling prophecy just three years later. Shaver remained the coach at French for the 1985 season, compiling a 6–4 record. For the 1986–87 school year, the Beaumont ISD school board decided to consolidate their four high schools—French, Charlton-Pollard, West Brook, and South Park—into two high schools. South Park was absorbed by West Brook, and Beaumont Central High School was created by combining French and Charlton-Pollard.

There were four head coaches at the Beaumont high schools, and now there would be only two. Jerry Hentschel, the head coach at South Park, was chosen to be the new head coach at West Brook, taking over for Leo Nolan, who had been the head coach at West Brook. In a somewhat controversial move, Steve Shaver was chosen as the head coach of the Beaumont Central Jaguars over Mike Mitchell, who had been the head coach at Charlton-Pollard for the previous three seasons. Since a large percentage of the Beaumont Central student body and football team was composed of African Americans, many in the community, including some school board members, thought an African American coach would be the obvious choice to lead the Jaguars.

Coach Shaver lasted two seasons as the Beaumont Central head coach, going 8–2 in 1986 and 5–4–1 in 1987. In early 1988, weary of fighting the community and school board, he decided to step down as head coach, and an African American coach, Marvin Sedberry, stepped in as his replacement for the Jaguars.

Steve Shaver Jr. spoke about the situation: "Dad had the résumé to get the head coach's job at Central. He had won a state title at French just a couple of years before. But he decided to step down because

Steve Shaver Jr. and Sr., ca. 1985. Courtesy of Steve Shaver Jr.

of the pressure from the community, and he was also burned out on coaching. He was relieved to get out after so many years. He ended up teaching driver's ed. The district did do right by letting him do that. He taught it for a couple of years at Central and then he went over to West Brook. He had a trailer there on campus where he taught until he retired around 2000. There were some hurt feelings. He won state and then, all of a sudden, he couldn't coach. It eats at your heart. You pour everything into the community, like he did at French for years, and then you get pressured to get out."

Steve Shaver passed away in 2013 at the age of seventy-two. His record in twenty-one years as a head coach at Del Valle, French, and Central was 117–88–14. After his state co-championship at French in 1984, he was named Class 5A Coach of the Year in Texas, and in 1999, he was selected for induction into the Sam Houston State Athletic Hall of Fame.

Steve Shaver left a coaching legacy in Texas high schools, first at Del Valle, where he led the Cardinals to their greatest season in school history in 1967, and then at Beaumont French, where he did the same in 1984.

Steve Shaver Jr. fondly recalled his father's impact as both a coach and community leader: "Dad was like a second father to a lot of these kids, both at Del Valle and at French. French was in the North Beaumont area, which was a rough part of town. The kids there were hard workers, though. He got the most out of the kids, both in school and as individuals. Dad wanted to make sure they became productive citizens."

From Del Valle to Beaumont, the legacy of Coach Shaver and the final draw for the Class 5A state title in Texas history lives on.

Ladonia

The Friday Night Lights of the 1988 Class A Semifinalist Fannindel Falcons

IN 1990, H. G. "BUZZ" BISSINGER wrote his definitive book on the sports and social dynamics of a West Texas town addicted to high school football, the iconic *Friday Night Lights.* The classic nonfiction piece documents the 1988 football season of the Odessa Permian Panthers and has gone on to inspire American sports culture, spawning a movie and television show by the same name.

And while the 1988 Panthers immortalized in Bissinger's book advanced to the Class 5A semifinals only to suffer a tragic loss to Dallas Carter, 430 miles northeast of Odessa, a small Class A school experienced the same triumph and defeat, basking in the glow of those same Friday night lights, if not just for a moment. Ladonia, home of Fannindel High School, is about thirty-five miles south of the Texas-Oklahoma border in northeast Texas, about halfway between the towns of Greenville and Paris and seventy miles northeast of Dallas.

Like Odessa, Ladonia suffered through economic hardship in the late 1980s. The town's population was down to a little more than six hundred residents, a far cry from its heyday when it was home to nearly two thousand folks in the 1920s. Back then, the Gulf, Colorado, and Santa Fe Railroad passed through Ladonia, making it a hub for corn, cotton, and grain crops. At the time, the town boasted around a hundred businesses. But during and after the Great Depression, Ladonia fell into a downward spiral that continues to this day. By 1988, the town's commerce was nearly nonexistent, down to about ten businesses. The downtown area was rife with shuttered buildings and weed-ridden lots. Only one restaurant served the entire population. Something had to give. And then, like a beacon in the darkness, the Fannindel High School stadium lights switched on to brighten the night sky with a dazzling albeit fleeting glimmer of hope.

As documented in Bissinger's classic book, Ladonia's neighbor Odessa, while a much larger city of about ninety thousand residents, was still reeling economically just a few short years after the oil bust of 1986. Discarded oil field equipment lay dormant on Highway 80 leading into the town, unemployment numbers soared, and commerce came to a halt, with streets plagued by abandoned buildings and dilapidated movie theaters.

Similar as their stories may be, Odessa's Permian High School and Ladonia's Fannindel High were two very different places in 1988. Probably the most glaring difference between the two schools was their sheer size. Permian was one of the larger Class 5A schools in Texas, with about 2,400 students, while Fannindel was a small Class A school with only approximately seventy students. On the gridiron, Permian's program (formed in 1959) had a reputation throughout Texas high school football for its successful run, having won state titles in 1965, 1972, 1980, and 1984, in addition to being the state runner-up in 1968, 1970, 1975, and 1985. Conversely, Fannindel's success on the field was very limited.

Fannindel High School was formed in 1960 when several other Fannin County schools consolidated to form Ladonia ISD. The Falcons were practically the polar opposite of Odessa's Permian on the gridiron until that fateful season in 1988, having compiled a grim 91–172–4 record from 1960 to 1987, with no district titles or playoff appearances.

About the only newsworthy item to come out of Ladonia was in 1985 when the Texas Legislature launched the No Pass No Play policy for extracurricular activities. Students involved in after-school activities were now required to pass all of their coursework or risk being ineligible to participate. In 1985, media from around the country converged on Ladonia in the dawn of No Pass No Play, as the Falcons football team was reduced to eleven players because of failing grades, with the team still managing to compile a 5–5 record.

Larry Braley, who was the principal and head football coach at Fannindel at the time, said, "In the early days of No Pass No Play, around 1984–85, we had a lot of athletes and cheerleaders who weren't eligible to play. It got so bad that the national news came out and did a story on us. Our school got the nickname 'Flunkindel.'"

By the time the 1988 school year came about, it seemed like things might be different on the gridiron for Fannindel. The Falcons were predicted to be one of the top teams in the state. *Texas Football* magazine picked Fannindel as the number-ten team in the state in Class A. This was a rare but welcome nod of encouragement for the underdog outfit.

Permian, true to form, received their usual lofty preseason accolades.

They had finished just outside of the top ten in Class 5A according to the *Texas Football* prognosticators, but the Panthers were picked as a prohibitive favorite to win their district. And in their preseason poll, the Associated Press picked Permian to win it all.

Both the Falcons and the Panthers had star players in 1988, each sought out by every major college in the country. And while the saga of Permian running back James "Boobie" Miles is well documented in *Friday Night Lights*, Fannindel had its own star ball carrier and linebacker—Fred Woods. In fact, *Texas Football* magazine actually listed Woods as a higher-rated recruit than the acclaimed Miles. Woods was touted as the seventh-best running back prospect in Texas, while Miles was rated tenth. Both Fannindel and Permian ran the I offense to showcase the talent of their respective stars.

Vic McCain, who started the season as the Falcons' top receiver, recalled the following about his star teammate: "Fred Woods could've been the next Lawrence Taylor. He was a great defensive end and linebacker, in addition to being a great running back. He ran a 10.6 hundred, a 4.5 forty, and was 6'3" and 225 pounds. Oklahoma wanted him so bad that Barry Switzer drove down to Ladonia in a snowstorm to pick Fred up and take him back to Norman for his recruiting visit. Even after he got hurt, they honored his scholarship. I grew up on the same street as Fred in Ladonia, and I had to try and tackle him in our sandlot games. That was no fun, let me tell you."

Falcons lineman Philip Burnett added, "As a senior, Fred was 6'3" and 220 pounds. As a junior, he won the state title in the two hundred meter. He was also the anchor on the mile relay team. I was the third leg, so it was basically my job to make sure Fred got the baton. In all my years of playing and then coaching, he is one of the best athletes I've ever seen."

Fannindel running back Fred Woods. Courtesy of Fannindel Independent School District

Optimism for the 1988 Falcons surged as the team finished with a 7–3 record in 1987, their second straight winning season under veteran coach Larry Braley. However, for the 1988 season, Braley stepped aside from his duties as head coach, staying on as an assistant coach and principal of Fannindel High School. The new head coach was then twenty-three-year-old Doug Williams.

Williams discussed how he ended up at Fannindel:

"In 1987, I was new to the school business. I was from Wolfe City, which is just down the road from Ladonia. In fact, my brother was playing on Wolfe City's team in 1988. I needed to stay in the area, and Larry Braley, who was the head coach and principal at Ladonia, hired me to coach there. Coach Braley had also grown up in the area and was and is just a tremendous man. He called me in before the 1988 season and told me he was going to give me the head coaching job. I think I was ready from an X's and O's standpoint. It was all the other stuff I needed help with. Coach Braley would say, 'Jump' and the kids would say, 'How high?' We ended up being co-coaches. To me, he was the guiding force, though. I was just twenty-three years old. We worked together really well. To this day, we still talk."

Larry Braley added, "I wanted to just be principal of the high school and not coach football anymore, but Doug talked me into staying on as an assistant. Doug pretty much did everything. He ramrodded the whole thing. I was on the sidelines during the games, and I made it out to practice when I could. Doug was really good with X's and O's, and I gave him advice here and there since I had been around it for so long. It was all Doug's doing, though. He's an outstanding coach."

Vic McCain remarked, "Coach Williams and his assistant Steve Guffey came to Fannindel together when we were juniors. It actually was a good thing. My older brothers had played for Coach Braley, and it had gotten to the point on offense where we had become so predictable that the other teams knew what plays we were going to run. Coach Williams changed all of that. He changed our offense and switched some of our personnel around. I was one of them. I played guard as a sophomore, and Coach Williams needed a receiver. He took me and some other guys out and had us run some routes to see who would be his receiver. I grew up on the sandlots playing receiver and running routes, so this was right up my alley. Coach Williams chose me, so it was a big move for me. I got to touch the ball more, and I eventually played in college as a receiver.

"Coach Williams and Coach Guffey were like father figures to me. I didn't have a father growing up; I was raised by my grandmother. If I ever needed anything or needed advice on any kind of manly stuff, I would go to Coach Williams. He would even take me over to Greenville to get my hair cut. There were no Black barbershops in Ladonia, so he would take me to Greenville. He would get some funny looks, being the only white guy in the barbershop. He was like family. We would go over to his house to watch movies, and his wife would bake cookies for us. We would meet up with him at the field house on Sundays, too."

"I think we knew 1988 could be special," Philip Burnett recalled. "There were sixteen of us in our senior class, and we were close-knit. All of us but one had gone to school together since kindergarten. The one who didn't came in first grade. We had been playing sports together for years, like little league and basketball. Coach Fields became our basketball coach when we were in fifth grade, and that's when we started playing together. We were playing a junior high schedule in sixth grade—something like twenty games. I think that's why Coach Braley pretty much turned over the team to Coach Williams. Coach Braley knew that we needed someone like Coach Williams to get us over the hump—someone who could really motivate us and get us there. It was Coach Williams's second year; I remember his first year, he had us so fired up to go to our first track meet that nobody could stop us. We went to win. That was his mentality. He used to say, 'Expect to win.' We didn't know any different. He put that attitude and confidence in us."

Larry Braley commented, "I thought we had the chance to have a good season. We had gone 7–3 in 1987, and we had a great group of seniors coming back. We had decent size and a lot of speed. The kids were also good leaders. Before the season, though, it looked like we were the toughest Class A district in the state."

Braley may well have been correct in his assessment of District 19–A. Two playoff teams from 1987 were realigned into Fannindel's district in 1988: Union Hill and Maud. Maud, which was close to Texarkana and two and a half hours away from Ladonia, had made the playoffs in 1987 and was ranked number six in the state by *Texas Football*, while Union Hill was a three-and-a-half-hour trip south of Ladonia and was a perennial powerhouse in the 1970s and 1980s, winning state Class A titles in 1978 and 1982 and losing in the finals in 1984.

Vic McCain reminisced, "They changed our district up for our senior season. We had missed the playoffs the previous couple of years, and now our district could be even tougher. Maud and Union Hill were added to our district. We were ranked number ten in the state in the preseason, while Union Hill was number five and I think Maud may have been number one."

The Falcons were confident heading into the regular season after their August scrimmages. Doug Williams recounted, "We were pretty good in 1987. We lost two close games to district rivals Celeste and Gunter. One thing we were lacking to compete with those schools was a good offensive line. We had speed and skill position players. We started an offseason program, and those linemen really made some big gains from 1987 to 1988. We knew we were going to be good. We also went to a lot of football clinics in the offseason. You could tell it paid off when we had our scrimmages before the regular season started. During our first scrimmage in August, we scored seven touchdowns in just twenty plays. I could tell we were going to be something on offense, and our defense was going to be pretty good, too. We couldn't wait for the season to get going."

Fannindel's inaugural game of the 1988 season was against their Fannin County rival the Honey Grove Warriors on the road September 2. After a slow start, the Falcons scored on three long second-half drives to earn a hard-fought 28–14 win. Quarterback Bruce Jones led the way for the Falcon offense as he ran for 103 yards on eighteen carries and completed seven of thirteen passes for 112 yards and two scores. The win over Honey Grove vaulted the Falcons into the state rankings for the first time in school history, at number ten in the Class A poll.

A home game against the Chisum Mustangs was next up for the Falcons on Thursday, September 8. Chisum was in their first season of varsity football and had lost to Fruitvale in their opener. Fannindel rolled to an easy 60–12 win as the Falcons led 26–0 after one quarter and only played their starters in the first and third quarter. Fred Woods scored three rushing touchdowns, and Steve Wilburn scored on punt returns of forty-five and seventy-one yards. The Falcons now stood at 2–0 for the 1988 season.

Fannindel's next contest was an away game on September 16 against the Prairieland Patriots, a team that would go 6–4 in 1988. The Patriots pulled off a huge upset by taking down the Falcons by a score of 18–6. In addition to losing the game, the Falcons lost their star player when Fred Woods injured his left knee on the Falcons' third possession of the game. He had gone around the end on a right sweep, but after he was tackled, he did not get up and didn't play for the rest of the game or even the season, for that matter. After Woods left the game, Fannindel's offensive attack was almost nonexistent, as the Falcons were held to only 225 yards for the game and did not score until the final ten seconds.

Fannindel was now faced with completing the rest of the season without one of the most highly sought-after players in the state. This was similar to what happened to Odessa Permian in *Friday Night Lights*. The Panthers' star running back, Boobie Miles, was also injured in an early contest and was essentially out for the entire 1988 season. This is where the stories of the star runners from each school start to diverge.

With Permian being a large Class 5A school and usually having seventy or so players on its varsity roster, the Panthers just plugged in Boobie Miles's backup into the starting role. Junior Chris Comer filled in more than capably for Miles as he starred throughout the rest of the season and then led Permian to a state title in 1989. At that point, Miles was treated as if he were expendable. In a heart-wrenching and disturbing scene in *Friday Night Lights,* Panthers coaching staff casually describe him as just another "dumb nigger" without a football under his arm. According to the book's account, some racist white fans in town suggested that Miles should meet the same fate as a lame horse, put out of his misery since his life no longer had any value. Miles eventually quit the squad, expressing his frustration: "I see what it's all about. . . . I'm a guinea pig." Once injured, he was replaced and discarded in a situation only fueled by racial bias.

However, Fannindel took a very different approach in the wake of Fred Woods's injury. Filling the void would prove most difficult, as the Falcons carried only about twenty players on varsity and there was obviously no one at the talent level of Woods to take his spot. Most small schools that lost a player the caliber of Woods would see their season slide into the abyss. But the injured Woods, along with Doug Williams, seized the moment, regrouped, and in the end, still inspired his teammates.

Fannindel head coach Doug Williams. Courtesy of Fannindel Independent School District

In an unusual move to try and salvage the team, Doug Williams decided to change his offensive attack part of the way into the season, a move that was mostly unheard of at the time. Williams recalled, "Fred tore up his knee against Prairieland. I took Fred to the orthopedic surgeon, and he said it was a torn ACL. I was beside myself. Fred said to me, though, 'Coach, it's not what is; it's what's now.' That became our team slogan. We had to scramble after that. What we decided to do was scrap the I offense and go to the Veer offense. We put Vic McCain at right halfback and Eddie Akins at left halfback. Aside from Fred's injury, we stayed healthy for the rest of the season. That was good because ten of our eleven starters played both ways. Fred was great about the whole situation. He could have sulked about what happened, but he became the heart and soul of our team. Even after his injury, people looked up to him. Eventually, Fred became more or less an extra coach on the sidelines. It even got to where he called the defensive signals. Our team could have gone either way after Fred got hurt, but we rallied and made the most of it. We had a great mix of kids."

Philip Burnett added, "Fred Woods was like a coach on crutches on the sidelines. Coach Williams had instilled that confidence in us—that's why when Fred got hurt, we didn't roll over like a lot of teams would have. We just kept going."

"Obviously, losing Fred hurt," Vic McCain agreed. "Coach Williams shook things up and switched from the I offense to the Veer. He needed another running back to run the Veer, though. I was a receiver, and Coach Williams took Steve Wilburn and me out on the practice field and ran some plays to see which one of us would be a better fit for running back. In the end, I was selected, which was fine by me because that meant I got to touch the ball more than I would as a receiver. Obviously, you never want to see anyone get hurt, but Fred getting hurt did open some doors for some other players to get looked at by college scouts. We had a lot of talent on our team."

After the Falcons regrouped, they played two more nondistrict contests to adjust to their new offense and prepare for district play. Even though they didn't exactly dominate the matchup, they still won a home game 32–0 on September 23 against the young and inexperienced Blue Ridge Tigers. The Falcons followed that win up with another at home on September 30 over the rival Wolfe City Wolves 20–9. Defensive tackle Brian Braley led the way defensively for Fannindel, with four quarterback sacks.

The Falcons' District 19–A opener was an away game on October 7 against the Detroit Eagles, who were in the midst of a miserable 1988 season where they would finish 0–9. Detroit jumped out to a 6–0 lead, and that held up until the final six minutes of the first half. In those six minutes, Fannindel scored three touchdowns to roll to a 20–6 lead. Bruce Jones led the comeback as he threw a forty-five-yard touchdown pass to Vic McCain and then another three minutes later to running back Eddie Akins. Jones capped off the first-half scoring with a forty-one-yard run with 1:13 left in the first half. Akins scored on a seven-yard run in the third quarter, and the Falcons added three fourth-quarter scores to account for the 46–6 final score. Jones hit Steve Wilburn with a forty-eight-yard scoring strike, and running back Marcus Phillips scored twice in the final two minutes of the contest from two and twenty-two yards out. Fannindel was now 5–1 overall and 1–0 in District 19–A play.

The Maud Cardinals awaited the Falcons in a home contest on October 14. Union Hill had defeated Maud 54–26 in their district opener. Maud had started the season 4–0 and state ranked but was now 4–2. Fannindel's recently installed Veer offense started hitting on all cylinders as the Falcons rolled to a 44–8 victory over the Cardinals. Vic McCain was again the big gun for the Falcons as he scored on touchdown receptions of six and nine yards and scored on runs of twenty-eight and sixty-four yards. McCain finished with 134 yards rushing on only ten carries. Quarterback Bruce Jones threw for three scores in the rout. In addition, Eddie Akins ran for ninety-two yards on nineteen carries and had one- and six-yard touchdown runs. Steve Wilburn had an eighty-four-yard punt return for a touchdown in the second quarter. The Fannindel defense held the Cardinals to just 153 yards of total offense and held star running back Joey Missildine to just eighty-four yards on twenty-six carries.

Doug Williams recalled the epic game: "We had never played Maud before. They traditionally had a good program. They were in far East Texas, close to Texarkana. Luckily, they came to our place. We put it on 'em pretty good. As we left the field, we were saying to ourselves, 'This is coming together!'"

After an easy 47–21 away win on October 21 over the Lone Oak Buffaloes, the Falcons followed that victory up with a home game against the Celeste Blue Devils on October 28. Celeste was 1–6–1 for the season overall and 0–2–1 in District 19–A play. Celeste had lost the previous week to Maud 38–0, a team Fannindel had handled 44–8 in the second week of the district slate. The Falcons routed the Blue Devils 45–14, as they moved to 8–1 overall for the season and 4–0 in District 19–A play.

During the last week of the regular season, the Falcons played the biggest game in school history—a home game on November 4 against the eighth-ranked Union Hill Bulldogs. Union Hill entered the contest with a perfect 9–0 mark for the season and, like Fannindel, was 4–0 in District 19–A play. The Bulldogs were led by one of the top running backs in East Texas, Larry Boyd, who had a record-setting night the week before with more than 450 yards on the ground against Lone Oak.

Luckily, Fannindel jumped out to a 21–0 lead as Eddie Akins scored on runs of nine and twenty-five yards, while Vic McCain ran nine yards for another score. The Bulldogs scored before the half to make it 21–8, and

Union Hill closed the gap to 28–23 after three quarters. Fannindel tacked on a fourth-quarter score to take a 35–23 win and take home the district title. Bruce Jones ran for ninety-one yards on eighteen carries and tacked on 158 passing yards and a scoring pass. Larry Boyd was not much of a factor in the contest, as he was held to ninety-eight yards on twenty-seven carries by the Falcons defense. Union Hill was held to 228 total yards on the night, their lowest output of the season, while Fannindel rolled up 365 yards for the win. With the Falcons being District 19–A champions and their regular season complete, Fannindel would now face the District 20–A runner-up, the Mount Enterprise Wildcats, in the first round of the playoffs.

Doug Williams talked about how they helped limit Larry Boyd to under one hundred yards rushing in the Falcons win: "This was the first time we played Union Hill. They were close to three hundred miles south of us, not too far from Brenham. They had to come to our place, too. They had a great running back, Larry Boyd, who ended up at Arizona State. He had been racking up big numbers. We were playing for the number-one and number-two seed. Well, Steve Guffey, who was great at studying films, noticed that Boyd's stance was a little bit different when he was going to get the ball on a pitchout. We knew where he was going most of the time, and we were able to hold him under one hundred yards. This win put us on a roll for the playoffs."

The Fannindel Falcons now prepared for their first-ever playoff game, against the 8–1 Mount Enterprise Wildcats, a game scheduled to be played on November 11 at Canton High School Stadium. The 8–1 Wildcats were knocked from the unbeaten ranks by District 18–A foe Oakwood in their last game, 38–6. Oakwood would go on to lose to District 19–A runner-up Union Hill, 22–7, in their first-round playoff contest.

Philip Burnett recalled an event leading up to the Mount Enterprise game: "To show you Coach Williams's intensity, on the Tuesday before the Mount Enterprise game, we were supposed to be running sprints. We were feeling good about ourselves because we had won a few games and had made the playoffs. We were kind of half-assing around, and Coach Williams got so mad he stormed off the practice field, marched straight past the field house where his car was parked. He stomped all the way home, which was four or five blocks away. He was pissed. We got the message. We did our sprints on our own plus some extra ones. We ended up playing well that Friday night."

And play well they did. Fannindel flattened the Wildcats, 49–18. The Falcons recovered a fumble on the Wildcats' opening kickoff at their twenty-four-yard line and scored five plays later on a pass from Bruce Jones to Eddie Akins. The rout was on. Jones found Steve Wilburn with a fifty-seven-yard scoring strike later in the quarter to put the Falcons up 14–0. After a fake punt failed for Mount Enterprise, Fannindel scored another touchdown with just five seconds left in the opening quarter on a Jones eleven-yard run to put them up 21–0. The Wildcats caught Eddie Akins in the end zone in the second quarter to make the score 21–2, but right before the half, Jones intercepted a Mount Enterprise pass from his defensive back position and returned it eighty-six yards for a score. Fannindel led at the half, 28–2. In the third quarter, Vic McCain scored two touchdowns from one and eighteen yards, and Akins scampered sixty-eight yards for another score to put Fannindel up 49–2 after three periods. Mount Enterprise added two more scores in the fourth quarter, but it was nowhere near enough.

After winning their first playoff game in school history, the Falcons took on a familiar opponent, the Gunter Tigers, who had been in Fannindel's district the previous two seasons. The Tigers had gone 10–0 in both of those seasons and beat Fannindel 27–6 in 1986 and 38–21 in 1987. Gunter was champion of District 17–A and had received a first-round bye in the playoffs. The two teams squared off in Bonham on November 18.

For the second game in a row, the Falcons recovered a fumble on their opponent's twenty-four-yard line to start the game and turned it into a score. The Falcons took a 6–0 lead on an Eddie Akins two-yard run. From there, Fannindel coasted to their second easy win in a row, 39–7 over Gunter. After Gunter struck back and took their only lead of the night, the Falcons scored again on a three-yard run by Eddie Akins but missed the two-point conversion attempt to lead 12–7. That was the halftime tally, as there was no scoring in the second quarter. The Falcons blew the game open on the first play from scrimmage in the second half as Akins ran sixty-four yards for a score. With 4:30 left in the quarter, Jones hit Vic McCain with a six-yard scoring pass to make it 26–7 after three quarters. The Falcons added two fourth-quarter tallies, both on one-yard runs by Jones and Steve Wilborn, respectively. Fannindel had ten fumbles on the night but rolled up 455 yards of total offense, compared to just 191 for Gunter.

Philip Burnett recalled, "I remember that night in Bonham when we played Gunter—it was really foggy. We couldn't even see the sidelines from the field. What I remember more, though, is a sign I saw in the Bonham locker room before the game. It said, '11 Brothers Are Hard to Beat.' That sign kind of fit us. We had been going to school together all those years and had been playing together, too. We knew each other and what we were going to do. We trusted each other. We knew we were going to step up and play together."

Now 11–1 for the season, the Falcons' next playoff contest was scheduled for November 24, Thanksgiving night, at Homer B. Johnson Stadium in Garland. Their foe would be the Wortham Bulldogs. This was the first time Fannindel had played in a regional semifinal, on artificial turf, and on Thanksgiving. Wortham was 9–2–1 and no stranger to the playoffs. The Bulldogs were 11–3 in 1987, losing in the regional final to Class A powerhouse Bremond. Wortham beat Normangee in their playoff opener 27–6 and followed that up with a 14–7 win over Apple Springs.

Despite fumbling ten times for the second consecutive game, the Fannindel Falcons held off the Wortham Bulldogs 21–16. Fumble number ten almost brought a horrendous ending to a hard-fought game. After Fannindel recovered an onside kick by Wortham, quarterback Bruce Jones coughed up the ball on his own forty-seven-yard line with thirty-eight seconds left in the contest. Luckily, on first down, the Falcons' Cody Derrick sacked Wortham quarterback Jerrod Lemmons back on his own forty-six. However, after the play, Fannindel was flagged for an unsportsmanlike conduct penalty, good for fifteen yards. With the ball now at the Fannindel thirty-eight, Wortham gained seven yards on a quarterback keeper. After a Wortham timeout, Lemmons for the Bulldogs dropped back to pass but was brought down by Fannindel's Gary Nichols behind the line of scrimmage. With Wortham out of timeouts, the clock went down to zero before they could get off another play.

Before the fireworks at the end of the game, Wortham had jumped to a 10–0 lead in the first quarter, thanks to a pair of Falcons fumbles before Fannindel finally got on track. The Falcons started their comeback in the second quarter as they held on to the ball long enough for Jones to score on a fifteen-yard quarterback keeper to make the score 10–7. Fannindel took the lead with fifty-one seconds left before Jones hit Vic McCain with a twenty-eight-yard touchdown pass on a fourth-and-goal play. On the second play of the third quarter, Jones struck again as he raced fifty yards to pay dirt down the left sideline. The extra-point kick made it 21–10 Fannindel. The two teams traded possessions and field position for the rest of the half until the final thirty-nine seconds. On a fourth and seventeen play from the Fannindel twenty-seven, Wortham quarterback Lemmons found receiver Lamonte Chambers in the end zone to make it 21–16. The Bulldogs' two-point conversion try failed and that set up the dramatic finish in the final thirty-nine seconds.

Looking back on the game, Doug Williams humbly admitted to an error he made that could have possibly led to a Falcons defeat: "We played Wortham in Garland on Thanksgiving night. They were good. They scored late to make it a one-score game. They tried an onside kick, but we recovered it. Then I made a mistake. I thought they had three timeouts left and that we would need a first down to run out the clock. It turns out they only had two. All we had to do was fall on the ball. Well, we handed it off, thinking we had to get a first down, and we fumbled. Wortham recovered. Luckily, our defense bailed me out."

Now advancing to the regional finals for the first time, Fannindel took on a playoff powerhouse in the 1980s, the Bremond Tigers, with the game set to be played on Saturday, December 3, in Greenville. Bremond won the state Class A title in 1981 and lost in the finals in 1983 and 1987. The Tigers had won twenty playoff games over the past seven seasons, while Fannindel had just wrapped up winning their first three playoff games ever. After winning their first-round game against Frost, 10–1–1 Bremond squeaked by Burkeville on penetrations after a 0–0 tie. The week before they played the Falcons, the third-ranked Tigers beat Fannindel's District 19–A rival Union Hill, 28–12.

Bremond's big gun was quarterback and linebacker Bo Robinson, who was 6'5" and 240 pounds. Robinson had accounted for more than 3,500 yards of total offense over the past two seasons. He was the son of Bremond coach Wendell Robinson, who spent thirty-two years as a head coach in the Texas high school ranks, compiling a 197–126–7 record.

In a scene reminiscent of *Friday Night Lights*, controversy arose regarding the decision of when and where the Bremond contest would take place. In *Friday Night Lights*, Buzz Bissinger described how Odessa Permian and Dallas Carter chose the playoff site for their Class 5A semifinal game. Instead of negotiating over the phone, the meeting occurred at the Midland airport the Sunday before the game. Representatives for both schools went into a back room of the coffee shop they met at to negotiate issues like the site for the game, the money involved, where the fans should sit to minimize the outbreak of possible violence at the game, which team would wear their home jerseys, and how many Blacks and whites should be on the officiating crew. Carter officials changed the location of their "home" site from Texas Stadium to the Cotton Bowl in Dallas. The Cotton Bowl was on the east side of Dallas, close to the heart of the Black community. Permian chose Ratliff Stadium in Odessa as their "home" site. After tense negotiations, the two sides chose Memorial Stadium in Austin as the site for the game.

Like the wrangling that took place between Odessa Permian and Dallas Carter, Doug Williams described how the Falcons negotiated with Bremond and how they got to play close to Greenville: "Getting everything sorted out for the Bremond game was something. We had played on Thanksgiving; they played two days later on Saturday. Well, Bremond was set on playing on Saturday so they could have a full week to prepare. Their superintendent was adamant about it. We wanted to play on Friday. We agreed that we would play on Saturday if they agreed to play in Greenville. It was less than thirty miles for us, but it was 150–200 miles for Bremond. We knew that in Greenville, we would get a lot of coverage and a good crowd. It would be like a home game for us. Our kids would be comfortable, and it would be a three- or four-hour drive for Bremond."

As they prepared to face Bremond, the Falcons were met with considerable disrespect. Both Doug Williams and Philip Burnett each had a story to tell about the incidents leading up to the game. Williams recalled, "The Friday night before our quarterfinal game with Bremond, we went to go watch Bartlett play Flatonia in Austin. If we beat Bremond, we would meet the winner of that game in the semifinals. Flatonia won, and after the game, the PA announcer said, 'Next week, Flatonia will play Bremond in the semifinals.' We hadn't even played Bremond yet, but nobody thought we were going to beat them. In our locker room before the game against Bremond, I told them that story and then said to our team, 'Guys, nobody respects us!' Our guys came out of that locker room fired up."

Philip Burnett added, "We got to go see Bremond play Union Hill the Saturday before since we had played Wortham on a Friday night. I went with Coach Williams, Coach Guffey, and a couple of other players. We sat in the press box on the Bremond side. At halftime, the players went down to the concession stand and their fans saw our Fannindel letter jackets. The Bremond fans started giving us a hard time, telling us we 'ain't shit,' stuff like that. When we got back up to the press box, we told Coach Williams what had happened. He was wanting to go into the stands and fight their fans! On game night, we went out and warmed up before the game, and when we went back into the field house, he gathered us together for his pregame speech. He basically told us that Bremond thought we were a bunch of ghetto kids and white trash and that we didn't belong on the same field as them. He was a motivator, though. He told us we could beat them, and he convinced us that we could. We would not have won that game without him. Then, to top it off, he had us run through the Bremond victory line on our way out of the field house. We were ready to play!"

Fannindel's Bruce Jones partially blocked a twenty-six-yard field goal attempt by Bremond's Darrol Scott with just twelve seconds remaining in the contest as the Fannindel Falcons punched their ticket to the Class A state semifinals with a heart-stopping 37–36 victory over the Bremond Tigers.

The teams were knotted at halftime at 21–21. Bremond took a 28–21 lead with 10:53 left in the game when Bo Robinson scored on a one-yard plunge. After the ensuing kickoff, Jones guided the Falcons back down the field. After a fourteen-yard sack that put the Falcons back at their own five-yard line, Jones scrambled for twenty yards, hit Steve Wilburn for twelve yards, and then launched a sixty-three-yard scoring pass to tight end Rodney Cuba. Fannindel decided to go for two, and Jones found Eddie Akins alone in the corner of the end zone to put the Falcons up 29–28. Akins then intercepted a Robinson pass on Bremond's next possession at the Fannindel forty-yard line, and two plays later, Vic McCain turned the corner on the right side and dashed fifty-three yards for the touchdown with 5:12 remaining. The extra-point kick made the score 37–28 Fannindel.

Bremond wasted little time striking back as Robinson, from his own twenty, hit receiver Nicky Hayward on a seventy-eight-yard pass that went all the way down to the Fannindel two-yard line. Charles Bailey ran for a two-yard touchdown, and Robinson passed for the two-point conversion to make it 37–36 Fannindel with 4:53 to play. Bremond eventually took over on their own twenty-one-yard line, with 1:17 remaining, and advanced the ball to the Falcons' nine-yard line. After an incomplete pass on first down, Bremond was forced to try for the potential game-winning field goal on second down because they were out of timeouts. A high snap forced Bremond kicker Scott to hesitate, and that's when Fannindel's Jones got a piece of the ball.

Doug Williams recalled, "It was a back-and-forth game all night. Basically, they were big; we were fast. We were going to lose on penetrations, but we got two scores in a row to put us nine points ahead. We couldn't get one last first down to put the game away, so they got the ball one last time, went down the field, ran the clock down, and tried the game-winning field goal. I never saw the kick. If they would have made it, there would have been time for a kickoff. I was talking to Steve Guffey about what we would do. We decided on a trick play. We were going to throw the ball across the field and try to have a wall set up to run the kick back. We never saw Bruce Jones block the kick."

Doug Williams didn't see the game-winning block by Bruce Jones, and there was also no film of the play, as Philip Burnett explained: "Coach Williams was the reason we beat Bremond. He had instilled that confidence in us. We had no doubt at the end of the game that their kicker wasn't going to make that field goal. Sure enough, Bruce Jones got a piece of the ball. What's crazy is, there's no videotape of Bruce's block. Coach Fields, our basketball coach, was filming the game, and he got so excited at the end of the game that he accidentally hit the Stop button instead of record."

So, in one more parallel between the 1988 seasons of the Odessa Permian Panthers and the Fannindel Falcons, both squads advanced to the state semifinals—Permian in Class 5A and Fannindel in Class A. And both teams' seasons ended during their December 10 semifinal matchups, with Permian losing to Dallas Carter at Texas Stadium, 14–9, and Fannindel falling to top-ranked Flatonia at Tyson Field in Waco, 28–0.

Fannindel lost on a chilly, rain-soaked night in Waco. Flatonia's Wesley Scott rammed his way for 142 yards on thirty-four carries and scored touchdowns of three and five yards, and the Bulldogs defense held Fannindel to its lowest output for the season, just two yards rushing on twenty-three carries and only sixty-three yards passing. Despite their lack of offensive firepower, the score at halftime was 7–0 Flatonia. However, the Bulldogs added two touchdowns in the third quarter and one in the fourth to account for the 28–0 final margin of victory.

Doug Williams recalled how he sensed potential trouble in the week leading up to the game: "After we beat Bremond, it was hard to get refocused. We started getting a lot of media coverage. Channel 8 in Dallas came out and did a story. I think we were a little distracted that week before we played Flatonia. We played them on a Saturday night in Waco. It was thirty-six degrees and freezing rain. Flatonia was good, though, don't get me wrong. We were never really in the game."

Phillip Burnett added, "When we played Flatonia in Waco, man, it was cold. That's still the coldest I've ever been in my life. Remember, this was back when there was no Under Armour gear you could wear to keep you warm. We wore sweatshirts underneath our pads and wore cotton gloves. We also had mesh jerseys back then that weren't very warm either. The rain froze on our face masks. By halftime, we were all soaking wet. The weather was not conducive to running the Veer offense either. Bruce Jones got hurt in the first half. He dislocated his shoulder, and we had to pop it back in place so he could play.

"The Flatonia game was the only one we ever chartered a bus to. Our booster club paid for it. Before that, we'd always just ridden the old yellow school bus. Well, after the game, after everyone else had gotten on the bus, Steve Wilburn, who has since passed away, got on and said, 'We're never getting a charter bus again. We beat all of these other teams where they rode the charter bus and we rode the yellow bus. We ride the charter bus one time and we lose!' Sure enough, when we later went to Austin for the state basketball tournament, we didn't take a charter bus; we rode the old yellow school bus."

Although their football season came to a close on that cold and rainy night in Waco on December 10, basketball season brought renewed hope for the Falcons. Several of the Fannindel's key football players, Bruce Jones, Vic McCain, Steve Wilburn, Steve Gaffney, and (when he was healthy and up to the task) Fred Woods, had helped the school reach the state finals in basketball the previous season, where they lost in double overtime in the state championship game 72–71, to Dallardsville Big Sandy. Although the Falcons had to cancel some of their early-season nondistrict games because they did not have enough players, with most of them still playing football, they were still favored by many to take the state title in March. By February 14, Fannindel was 17–1 and ranked number one in the state in Class A. Philip Burnett, who was a reserve on the team, said, "We lost to Flatonia on a Friday night, had our first official basketball practice the following Monday, and then played Honey Grove on Tuesday. We beat them by twenty. We had played together for so long we hadn't missed a beat."

The Falcons basketball team was led by Ladonia native Glenn Fields, who was in his sixth year at Fannindel. The Falcons, under the tutelage of Fields, had steadily improved from their freshman year. As freshmen, Fannindel went 25–6 and won their first district title in twenty-three years.

As sophomores, they went 33–2 and lost in the regional finals. Every starter was a senior and had gone to school together since kindergarten.

Frustrated, isolated, and hurt, Odessa Permian's Boobie Miles of *Friday Night Lights* fame was essentially done with football and athletics after an injury took him off the field, and team politics and social dynamics seemingly barred his reentry to the game. However, after making a full recovery, Fred Woods of Fannindel seized the opportunity to return and help his team to a state title in basketball and then went on to the University of Oklahoma. Almost miraculously, Woods had recovered enough from his knee surgery and returned to the Falcons lineup for the playoffs, scoring twenty-six points in the regional final defeat of New Summerfield. At the state tournament in Austin, the 23–2 Falcons beat Clyde-Eula on March 9 in the semifinals 82–72, as Woods scored thirty points, pulled down eighteen boards, and blocked three shots. Eddie Akins scored eleven points off the bench. Fannindel then beat Moulton 75–58 in the finals on March 11, with a twenty-nine-point second quarter being the key to the Falcons running up a 45–29 halftime advantage and coasting home from there. The five Falcons seniors' scoring totals were Jones with nineteen points, Woods with sixteen points, Wilburn with twelve, Gaffney with eleven, and McCain with seven. They finished their championship season with a 25–2 mark.

Vic McCain said, "We loved basketball, and we had gone to state the year before. We were 121–12 in four years. We expected to win state. We lost the year before in the finals, where we missed twenty-one free throws. I was more of a defensive player. They would put me on the other school's best scorer. In the semifinals against Eula, I held their star player Byron Barnes to about fifteen points under his average. We loved basketball. We were always outside playing it. Back then, there were no computer games or things like that. We couldn't have afforded them anyway."

As for football, after the graduation of the 1989 senior class that made the state semifinals and captured the state basketball crown, Fannindel sports returned quickly to mediocrity. The four playoff games the Falcons won on their drive to the 1988 Class A semifinals were the only ones in school history. Odessa Permian, on the other hand, won the state Class 5A title in 1989, again in 1991, and remained a football power in Texas until the late-1990s.

The Falcons went 6–3–1 in 1989 under Doug Williams but missed the playoffs. Williams then left Fannindel and went on to coach at Leonard and Winnsboro, compiling a 66–49–2 record in his three coaching stops. He then went into school administration and has been the superintendent of Sunnyvale ISD, in a suburb of Dallas, since 2007.

Since Doug Williams's departure after the 1989 season, from 1990 to 2003 Fannindel had only one more winning season before dropping down to six-man football in 2004. From 1990 to 2003, Fannindel's record stood at a paltry 37–101–2, with no playoff appearances. Although the team could not sustain their football success of 1988, for one brief moment in the history of high school football in Texas, the 1988 Fannindel Falcons had their own version of *Friday Night Lights.* Their light shone hope and new life into their small Texas town for but a brief moment, in a way that was perhaps not as bright or as flashy or even memorable as their Odessa counterparts. Theirs was a quiet light, indeed, but soothing, radiant, and stunning, all the same.

Groesbeck

The 1991 Goats Grasp the 3A State Championship

GROESBECK, TEXAS, about forty miles east of Waco at the intersection of Texas Highways 14 and 164, is the county seat of Limestone County and has a present-day population of a little more than four thousand. The town, incorporated in 1871, was an early trade center for farms and ranches and was named for Abram Groesbeck, director for the Houston and Texas Central Railway.

Whereas traditional state football powers Bremond, Mart, Cameron, and Chilton are within a few miles of Groesbeck and have a combined eighteen state titles, the Goats historically haven't fared as well on the gridiron as their close-by counterparts. In seventy-eight years of football before Groesbeck's 1989 season, the Goats' overall record was 284–351–27, with just five playoff appearances and a mere two playoff wins, both coming in 1986.

But in 1989, Groesbeck's football fortunes changed. That was the year Jerry Bomar took the reins as the team's head coach. A 1971 graduate of Sherman High School, Bomar played safety and quarterback at Texas Tech. After college, Bomar went into coaching and got his first head coaching job at Atlanta High School in 1982. He completed four years in Atlanta and three more at Addison Trinity, a private school in the Dallas area, and then took over at Groesbeck.

Bomar recalled his first days with the Goats: "There weren't really any high expectations when I got to Groesbeck. We had no history of success in football. I remember Frances Whitehurst, who has an elementary school named after her here in Groesbeck, told me when I took the job, 'If you just go 5–5 every three years, we'll be happy.' I told her, 'I didn't come here to go 5–5.' There were 150 applicants for the job, one of the reasons being that Groesbeck had great athletic facilities. We had the only artificial turf field in Class 3A. The turf was a huge advantage for us. We only lost one game on it in the three years I was there, and that was a last-second loss to

Mexia. Our complex got into people's minds. They would arrive to play us, and we would watch the teams look around in awe.

"We had to change some things once we got to Groesbeck. All the kids wanted to do was play basketball. We had to convince them they could play both basketball and football. Our basketball coach, Richard Reagan, had a great program and also ran a great offseason program. We had to assure everyone that they could do both sports. We started turning things around. We went 3–7 in 1988, the year before we got there. In 1989, we went 7–3. We lost two heartbreakers in district play in back-to-back weeks to Mexia and Palestine Westwood.

"We flirted with the playoffs again in 1990. We were 5–0 in nondistrict, and we had an open date before we started district play. It was the end of the six weeks, and one of our English teachers had failed our starting quarterback and two of our other starters. I had been told that they were going to be OK, that they were going to pass. It was a mess. The local TV stations came out, and the town was going nuts. It was a huge deal because we were getting ready to start district play. I stayed out of it. Without those players, we went 2–3 in district. We took some lumps."

Bomar concluded, "One positive thing did come out of it, though. Brandon Bennett was our starting quarterback for the rest of the season and he got some valuable experience. Truth be told, he should have been starting all along. Our other quarterback was a good player, but he was only about 5'10", whereas Brandon was 6'5" and a great athlete. The problem with Brandon was that he was more into basketball than football. He just wouldn't commit to working hard for us—that's why he wasn't the starter. He finally did, though, and he became a great quarterback."

Brandon Bennett agreed with Bomar. "Obviously, you would never wish bad on a teammate, but when we lost our starting quarterback halfway through my junior season, it made me the starting quarterback. It forced me to grow up. I got some valuable experience, and it upped my leadership skills. It gave me confidence going into my senior year."

Bennett also discussed how the Goats football program changed when Jerry Bomar arrived on the scene: "The football program was losing in a major way. After our freshman football season, we were all going to quit to focus on basketball. We loved basketball. It was not a good situation. Coach Bomar came in at the end of our freshman year, and he changed our minds. We needed someone to come in and lead us, and he did. He had a vision. He ran an up-tempo offense that featured a lot of throwing and catching. It was fun to play in. Coach Bomar came in on day one and led us. He taught us little things, like being on time, responding properly during roll call, and learning to go full speed all the time at practice. No one was comfortable around Coach Bomar. You would walk on eggshells. He had this way of pushing the right buttons with his players. He could get into your head. He demanded your best in offseason, practices, and games. There was no half speed. Great coaches take you out of your comfort zone to make you and the team better, and Coach Bomar was good at it. He expected a lot.

"We were also always well prepared, and he was extremely creative on offense. Most teams in 1991 were still running the ball most of the time. The Wishbone was still a popular offense. Coach Bomar's offense was very balanced between the run and the pass. I threw for something like 2,800 yards as a senior, which was quite a bit for those days. We utilized the tight end a lot, and we used swing passes to our backs coming out of the backfield.

"One more thing Coach Bomar believed in was having a separate offensive and defensive unit. We really only had one player, Lenoy Jones, who played offense and defense. It showed our depth as the year went along, and we wore teams down in the second half, especially in the playoffs. Another thing Coach Bomar did was make us study film, and he would also grade us. We got to where we didn't want low grades on our game films. It motivated us."

All-state defensive back Lenoy Jones also spoke about Bomar's coaching technique: "Coach Bomar brought his system with him to Groesbeck. He liked mixing it up and throwing the ball. He had a lot of weapons here. Back then, teams were still running mostly, and what we found was we would get teams down in a game because of our offense, and then they would

Lenoy Jones celebrates on the Astrodome field after the Goats' 7-0 Class 3A state championship win over Burnet. Courtesy of Jerry Bomar

have to try and throw the ball to catch up—which most of the time they weren't very good at. Teams weren't used to throwing the ball to try and come back.

"Coach Bomar was a confident coach. It would rub off on you. He would also talk to me as a team leader. He would bounce ideas off of me. It made me feel important, like I mattered."

What Bomar also brought to Groesbeck that Brandon Bennett alluded to earlier was Bomar's philosophy on rarely letting his players play both ways, instead having them play either offense or defense. While this was common at Class 5A schools, it was a rarity at a Class 3A school like Groesbeck. Bomar said, "I've believed in two-platoon football ever since I started coaching. You can take an average kid at, say, the defensive end, and you can teach him better technique with specialized coaching. He also practices at the defensive end for the whole practice. Also, if you run multiple schemes, it's very hard to master if you're playing both offense and defense. In addition, in the fourth quarter, the player is fresh and not worn out from playing both ways." This philosophy would pay off later in the season.

While Groesbeck was expected to field a good team in 1991, they were in possibly the toughest Class 3A district in the state. Groesbeck was picked no better than fourth in the District 18–3A race. Other top teams in the Goats district were Mexia, who won the state 3A title in 1989; Crockett, who lost in the 3A finals in 1990; and Fairfield, which returned six offensive and ten defensive starters from a 9–2 playoff team.

The Goats had twenty-one returning lettermen, including four offensive and defensive starters returning. Lenoy Jones, who played free safety as a junior, was also slated to take snaps at receiver, thus becoming the Goats' only two-way player. Jones eventually went on to play at Texas Christian University (TCU) and then played seven seasons in the NFL with the Oilers, Titans, and Browns.

Brandon Bennett talked about the anticipation of his upcoming senior season. "We had never as a school made a deep run in the playoffs," said Bennett. "When we were sophomores, Coach Bomar's first year, we had a really good senior class that just missed the playoffs. We came close our junior year, too. We felt like we had a very talented senior class in 1991. Coach Bomar was an established coach, which helped, and during the summer we worked really hard. Coach Bomar wanted me to be a leader, so I would pick up the guys that lived on my side of town since I had a car to take them to summer workouts. My cousin who lived on the other side of town would pick up players and bring them to workout. We threw the ball a lot and practiced running our routes and timing, and eventually we developed a great rhythm."

Groesbeck quarterback Brandon Bennett. Courtesy of Jerry Bomar

The Goats met their nondistrict rival the Mart Panthers on the road to open the 1991 season on September 6. This would be the sixty-seventh meeting between the schools, one of the oldest matchups in Texas state history, with Mart holding a 38–24–4 lead. Mart used three first-half Groesbeck turnovers to take an 18–0 lead and then held on for an 18–14 win on a rain-soaked field. A fifty-six-yard interception of a Brandon Bennett pass on Groesbeck's opening possession of the season set up the first Panthers touchdown. Mart stretched their lead to 12–0 at 6:13 of the second quarter on a twenty-one-yard touchdown pass and extended their lead to 18–0 on an eighteen-yard touchdown pass that was set up by a Groesbeck fumble. The Goats made it a game in the fourth quarter as they scored their first touchdown of the 1991 season with 10:08 to play as Bennett hit receiver Tyrone Brown on a thirty-three-yard touchdown pass to make it 18–7. Groesbeck closed the gap to 18–14 with just over a minute to play as Dwrain Cooper scored from one yard out, but Mart ran out the clock for the victory.

Brandon Bennett said about the Mart game: "At Groesbeck, we have two big rivalry games every year: Mart and Mexia. We were at war every time we played either one of them. Well, we went to Mart our first game of the season, and we go and lose to them. They were a pretty good team, but we thought we would handle them pretty easily. Losing to them shook us up. I also didn't play very well. I turned the ball over a few times in the rain. The loss made us look in the mirror. If there's ever such a thing as a good loss, this was it. It woke us up. My experience at the end of my junior year helped me get over this loss quickly. I had been taught by the coaching staff to always focus on the next play; don't dwell on your previous mistakes or bad plays. We moved forward with the help of Coach Bomar. He got us back on track. We got right back to work and put the game behind us."

Lenoy Jones also recalled how Coach Bomar made a change after the Mart game: "I didn't play any offense against Mart. Coach Bomar believed in players playing either offense or defense. After Mart, they put me on offense, too. I played some receiver but a lot of tight end. It changed the dynamics of our offense. It gave us another weapon. Our offense started clicking after that."

The Groesbeck offense did indeed click against the St. Pius Panthers at home on September 13 as the Goats evened their record at 1–1 with a 62–0 win. Groesbeck rolled up forty-three first-half points and coasted home from there. Defensively, the Goats held St. Pius to 110 total yards and minus-one-yard rushing.

September 20 brought a home contest versus the Waco Robinson Rockets. Robinson entered the game with a 2–0 record. With eleven seconds to play, Elgrick Tatum nailed a twenty-three-yard field goal to lead the Goats to a heart-stopping 33–30 comeback win over Waco Robinson. The Goats dug themselves a 17–0 first-quarter hole as turnovers led to ten Robinson points. Groesbeck climbed back into the game as they scored fourteen points of their own in the second quarter, but Robinson extended their lead to 24–14 at halftime. The Rockets extended their lead to 30–17 in the third period, but Groesbeck struck back with their own touchdown when Derrick Morgan crashed over the goal line from the two to close within 30–23. In the fourth quarter, the Goats tied the game at 30–30 when Brandon Bennett found Tyrone Brown on a twenty-five-yard scoring pass down the right sideline. With three minutes to go, Groesbeck got the ball back for their final sixty-two-yard drive. The big play in the drive was a pass from Bennett to Tyrone Brown down to the Rockets' thirty-one. Three plays later, Tatum hit his game-winning field goal.

Brandon Bennett recalled, "The Robinson game was huge. The game went back and forth. We had to fight back from being way down in the first half. It was a great feeling when Elgrick Tatum hit that field goal at the end. Once we slipped past Robinson, we got on a roll as a team."

And roll the Goats did as they beat their last two nondistrict opponents: Franklin in an away game on September 27, 47–12, as Brandon Bennett rang up 264 yards of total offense, and Hillsboro in another away game on October 4, 46–0, the highlight being a seventy-yard bomb from Bennett to Lenoy Jones in the third quarter. The two wins gave the Goats a 4–1 record and some much-needed momentum heading into District 18–3A play.

Groesbeck's first district contest at home on October 11 was with their most fierce rival, the Mexia Black Cats. The annual game was nicknamed the "Battle of Limestone County." The two teams first met in 1901, and the Goats had not beaten the Black Cats at home since 1963. Mexia had a 33–13–3 lead in the series and had won the previous five games in the series, including a 35–16 win over the Goats in 1990. In 1991, though the Goats left no doubt as they rode five Mexia turnovers to a 38–0 win over the Black Cats. Besides the five forced turnovers, the Goats held Mexia to 167 total yards and only 113 rushing yards on 43 attempts.

Week seven brought an October 18 road game against the Palestine Westwood Panthers. Westwood was 4–2 on the season but lost their first district contest to fourth-ranked Crockett 34–12. The Panthers put up a fight but in the end lost to the Goats 34–15. The Groesbeck defense was once again extremely opportunistic, forcing three turnovers, and scored two fourth-quarter touchdowns—one on a forty-seven-yard interception return by Rock Smith and the other on a twenty-eight-yard fumble return by Marty LeNoir. The win lifted the Goats to 6–1 on the season and 2–0 in District 18–3A play, while Westwood dropped to 4–3, 0–2 in district.

October 25 brought a District 18–3A showdown at home with the Crockett Bulldogs, who were state 3A finalists in 1990. Crockett had continued their winning ways in 1991, as they were off to a 7–0 start and a number-three state ranking. The Goats, however, pulled off probably their biggest upset in school history by shocking the Bulldogs 31–25. Groesbeck jumped out to a 24–7 first-half lead and held on from there. The Goats defense once again made a difference as Rock Smith for the second consecutive week returned an interception for a touchdown, which gave the Goats a 24–7 second-quarter lead. After Crockett closed the gap to 24–13 at halftime, Groesbeck got the ball to start the second half and proceeded to drive the ball ninety-eight yards down the field for a score to give the Goats a 31–13 lead. Crockett scored a couple of touchdowns late in the contest, but it was not enough to overcome the Goats. The loss for Crockett broke a string of thirty-four consecutive regular-season victories. Groesbeck was now alone in first place in District 18–3A with a 3–0 mark.

Jerry Bomar said, "Even though it was a great win, after we beat Crockett we didn't look ahead. We were just trying to focus on our next game. Once again, the thought of going to state never entered our minds. We just wanted to get to the playoffs, and beating Crockett was just one hurdle to get there."

Brandon Bennett added, "Even though we were 6–1, we weren't ranked. People didn't give us much respect. Crockett was a huge game. They had made the finals the year before, and they'd been ranked all season. Getting past them was important because back then, only two teams made the playoffs, and it looked like it was going to be a three-team race between us, Crockett, and Fairfield, which was our last game of the season."

Groesbeck's homecoming game came on November 1 against the Teague Lions. The Goats made their homecoming a happy one as they rolled to a 55–13 win. Rock Smith returned an interception for a touchdown for the third week in a row, this time from forty-one yards out. Lenoy Jones also snatched a Teague fumble out of midair and ran twenty-seven yards to pay dirt for a second defensive touchdown. On offense, the Goats racked up 401 yards of total offense, including 268 on the ground. The Goats led 55–0 early in the fourth quarter before Teague finally got on the scoreboard with two late touchdowns against the Goats' second-team defense.

With the win, the Goats were now 8–1 overall and 4–0 in district, clinching at least a tie for the District 18–3A title with one game to go. However, the last game of the regular season was a November 8 road contest against the Fairfield Eagles, who, like Crockett, had only one district loss, and because only two teams advanced to the playoffs in Class 3A back in 1991, one of the three teams was staying at home.

Fairfield, led by all-state nose guard and future UT star Tony Brackens, came into the contest with a 7–2 overall record and were ranked tenth in the state in Class 3A. Fairfield was 3–1 in district play, having lost to Crockett 20–13, who Groesbeck had defeated earlier. If Fairfield were to defeat the Goats, then there would be a three-way tie for the district crown. The two representatives from 18–3A would be decided by the highest net point average in head-to-head competition.

Although Groesbeck fell to Fairfield 26–7 in a lackluster performance, the Goats qualified for the postseason as the second-place team in District 18–3A. Crockett, Fairfield, and Groesbeck, all finished with 4–1 district marks, but Crockett stayed at home despite a 9–1 record. The Goats had their worst offensive showing of the season as they gained only 188 yards on the evening, with just fifty-five rushing yards. Brandon Bennett had a poor night for the Goats, as he was only seven for twenty-four on the night and suffered three interceptions. The Eagles' powerful Wishbone running attack rang up 333 yards on fifty-two carries.

Jerry Bomar recalled, "We had the big heads for the Fairfield game and it showed. We did qualify for the playoffs, though. If there was a three-way tie for the district title, it was determined beforehand that point differential between the three schools would decide who would go to the playoffs. Remember, back then, only two schools went, so one of us was going to be left out. What it came down to was the last five minutes of the Fairfield game. We were down 19–7, and Fairfield had the ball. My defensive coordinator came up to me and said, 'You know, if the score stays the same, we're out of the playoffs. If we lose by twelve or less, we're done. Do you want me to let them score?' I said, 'Not right now.' I thought about it for a minute. Letting the other team score on purpose went against all of my beliefs as a coach. Luckily for me, the problem was solved because before I could say anything or make the decision, the Fairfield fullback burst up the middle against our defense for about a thirty-yard touchdown. Our problem was solved! Crockett, who had a great team, was out of the playoffs. To this day, there are some people in Crockett who accuse me of throwing the Fairfield game just to keep them out of the playoffs."

"Fairfield was something we needed," added Lenoy Jones. "We were kind of full of ourselves, and we weren't ready or prepared. After we lost, a lot of us thought we were out of the playoffs. Some of the guys, especially the seniors, were crying and everything. We thought we had played our last game. Coach Bomar then explained to us that we did qualify for the playoffs because of the point differential with Fairfield and Crockett. We were relieved. It was like we got a second chance."

Brandon Bennett added, "Fairfield at the end of the season was another bump in the road. They had a good team. Tony Brackens, who went on to play at UT, was one of their linemen. It was a cold night, and they kicked our butts. It was close at the half, and I thought we had a chance to come back and win. I didn't play very well, like in our first game of the year against Mart. Luckily, we qualified for the playoffs by a point differential or something like that. Crockett had to stay home while us and Fairfield went. This was another one of those 'good losses.' Coach Bomar got us back on track and focused for the playoffs. We ramped up our intensity level. Once we hit the playoffs, we were off and running."

After surviving the tough District 18–3A gauntlet, the Goats' opening playoff game was on Friday, November 15, at Bryan's Viking Stadium. The contest was a rematch with the Waco Robinson Rockets, who the Goats nipped 33–30 in week three. Robinson won District 17–3A with an 8–1–1 overall record, their only loss being the nondistrict defeat to Groesbeck.

Jerry Bomar wanted to be sure his team wasn't overlooking Robinson. He said, "After we lost to Fairfield, we had to get our focus back. We were playing Robinson in the playoffs, and we barely got by them 33–30 on a last-second field goal early in the season. We were playing them in Bryan at the high school stadium. We took the players to Bryan a day early and made them work out there. We took the players back to our August workouts, and we hit a lot. We got our point across. We got our edge back. We got back to being physical."

Bomar's return to the intensity of early season practices must have worked on his players' psyches because the second matchup of Groesbeck and Robinson had nowhere near the drama of the first contest as the Goats rolled to a 34–0 win. Groesbeck got off to a much better start in this affair, not falling behind 17–0 like in the first contest. This time, it was Groesbeck who jumped out to an early first-quarter lead, as they rang up two touchdowns to lead after one quarter 13–0, with Charles Gibson running for two scores. The Goats extended their lead to 20–0 at halftime when Gibson scored again, this time from one-yard out, to cap off a sixty-one-yard, ten-play drive. The Goats then all but put the game away on the first play of the second half as Brandon Bennett hit Lenoy Jones on a sixty-three-yard bomb. Gibson added one more touchdown in the fourth quarter, his fourth touchdown of the night, this time from two yards out, with 8:54 left in the contest. Besides Gibson, the Goats' defense took center stage, limiting Robinson to just 102 yards and seven first downs on the evening.

Brandon Bennett added, "We played a rematch with Robinson, this time in Bryan on a wet field. Once again, our intensity level was ramped up. This was our first time in the playoffs, and we were going to make the most of it. Probably the biggest difference between the first time we played them and the second was that our defense was starting to play lights-out. They really got the ball rolling. What I really remember about that game was the first play of the second half, where I hit Lenoy with a long bomb. It was a play-action pass, where I faked it to the tailback before throwing it. I could get sloppy with my play fakes, but the coaches made me really work at it in practice, and on that play, I executed a really good fake to our tailback, and Lenoy was wide open down the left sideline. Robinson bit on the fake, and there was no one around him."

Next up for the Groesbeck Goats in the 1991 Class 3A playoffs were the Bellville Brahmas. Bellville, out of District 20–3A, beat Elgin 17–7 in their bi-district matchup. The matchup took place at Conroe's Buddy Morehead Stadium on November 22. Groesbeck ended up taking a 22–13 decision over Bellville. The Goats took the opening kickoff and drove sixty-three yards to jump to an early 6–0 lead as Brandon Bennett hit Tyrone Brown with a seven-yard scoring pass. The next time Groesbeck had the ball,

Bennett and Brown again hooked up on a touchdown pass, this time from twenty-seven yards out. The Brahmas, however, struck back on their next possession for a score to narrow the Groesbeck lead to 12–7. Groesbeck got a field goal right before the half to make it 15–7. Bellville made a game of it in the third quarter when, after they picked off a Brandon Bennett pass, they scored four plays later to make it 15–13. Bellville went for the two-point conversion to tie the score, but they were stopped short of the goal by the Goats' senior linebacker Keith Sherrod. Groesbeck took the ensuing kick-off and drove sixty-three yards in eleven plays for an insurance touchdown with Dwrain Cooper, taking the ball in from four yards out. In the winning effort, the Goats' Lenoy Jones picked off three Bellville passes.

Brandon Bennett recalled, "I had a pretty good game against Bellville, but it was our defense that came up big again. We moved the ball well all night, but we just couldn't get it in the end zone. We learned that we could win in all different ways. That night, the defense had our back. Lenoy came up big with three picks."

Jones said about his defensive effort, "I picked off three passes against Bellville, but it should have been four. I missed one I should have had. Coach Bomar also got on my case about one of my interceptions. It was a fourth-down play, and instead of batting the pass down, I went ahead and picked it off. If I just would have knocked it down, we would have gotten the ball in a much better field position. But, hey, I was seventeen years old, what did you think I was going to do? I wanted that interception!"

Next up for the Goats were the Hamshire-Fannett Longhorns on November 30 at Sam Houston State's Bowers Stadium in Huntsville. The Longhorns entered the game with a 10–2 record, the same as Groesbeck, and had defeated Liberty and Navasota in the first two rounds of the play-offs. The Longhorns were led by senior tailback Spence George, who had run for more than 1,700 yards on the season.

It was the Groesbeck defense that rose to the occasion again as Groesbeck pulled off a hard-fought 10–0 victory that propelled the Goats to the regional finals. Groesbeck held Hamshire-Fannett to nine first downs and 186 yards on the night and limited Spencer George to sixty-nine yards rushing on seventeen carries. Groesbeck took a 3–0 lead after they recovered a Hamshire-Fannett fumble on the Longhorns thirty-five-yard line and Elgrick Tatum hit a twenty-five-yard field goal with 7:14 to go in the opening quarter. In the third quarter, the Goats put together an eleven play, fifty-two-yard drive that was capped off with a Brandon Bennett eleven-yard touchdown pass to Tyrone Brown. Hamshire-Fannett threatened to score in the final minutes, but the Goats broke up a fourth-down Longhorns pass in the end zone.

"Hamshire-Fannett was really good," Brandon Bennett recalled. "They were highly ranked and had a really good option quarterback and a really good running back. Their defense was tough, too. It was just one of those games where you just grind it out. Our defense was locked in again. We were only up 3–0 when I hit Tyrone Brown in the third quarter with a fade route in the end zone. Tyrone was an NFL-caliber-type wide receiver. I would compare him to Steve Smith of the Carolina Panthers. Tyrone was fast, had great hands, and was quick out of his routes. Something else Coach Bomar was good at was that he would come up with schemes to get the ball in Tyrone's hands. That's what you do in high school—get the ball into the hands of your best players."

The opponent for the Goats in the Region 3 final was another familiar foe, District 18–3A rival Fairfield, the team that had beaten Groesbeck soundly 26–7 on the last night of the regular season. The rematch was scheduled for December 7 at Waco's Midway Stadium. Fairfield had beaten Waco LaVega, Columbus, and Anahuac to reach the regional final.

Jerry Bomar recalled, "The first time we played Fairfield, it was twenty-eight degrees, we had won eight in a row, and our players were getting a little full of themselves. We just didn't show up to play that first time. Fairfield changed their defensive scheme for the first time we played them, and it was effective. They kept it the same for the rematch. You know, I lost every coin flip in the playoffs that year. We wanted to play Fairfield the second time at Baylor, who had artificial turf, just like we had. We ended up playing at Midway Stadium in Waco, which is a high school stadium with a grass field."

Lenoy Jones talked about an incident in the days leading up to the Fairfield game that got the team fired up for the rematch: "I was watching the sports on one of the Waco TV stations during the week before the game. They had a piece on our upcoming game with Fairfield. Well, Fairfield's running back, Lee Cyrus, said about us when they interviewed him, 'When you come out for revenge, you don't play your best game.' We took that personally. Also, there were rumors going around—I don't know if they were true or not—that Fairfield was saying they weren't too worried about us. It may have just been my teammates telling me that to get me fired up. Trust me, I didn't need any help there. I had a laser-like focus. We were ready for the rematch."

In the rematch with Fairfield, the Groesbeck Goats left no doubt as they routed the Eagles 31–0. Fairfield gained just thirteen total yards in the first half and ended up with four first downs and 102 total yards for the game. Unlike the first game against Fairfield, where the Goats offense never could really get on track, the Groesbeck offense clicked, for the most part, the second time around. The Goats had eighteen first downs and 337 total yards. Brandon Bennett was twelve for twenty-one for 191 yards and three touchdowns. Lenoy Jones hauled in five passes for 124 yards and a score, while Tyrone Brown had four catches for sixty yards and two touchdowns. Charles Gibson chipped in ninety-three yards on fifteen carries.

"Like I said, that first Fairfield loss was a good loss," Brandon Bennett said. "It got our attention. We played them at Waco's Midway Stadium, and that place was packed; it was standing-room only. It was a game between a couple of heavyweights. To be honest, nobody gave us much of a chance. Coach Bomar got us ready. He took us over to Midway's stadium to have us practice there to get used to the conditions, and he also put in a few new wrinkles on offense and defense. He put in a few trap plays to run against Tony Brackens. We were totally prepared. We were the better team that night. We took the ball right down the field on our first possession to go up 7–0, just like that. After that, we didn't take our foot off the gas. They couldn't move the ball against our defense, and offensively we put the heat on them."

The Goats now faced a daunting task in the state semifinals. Awaiting the Goats were the undefeated and top-ranked Edna Cowboys on December 13 at Austin's Berger Center Stadium. Quarterback Adrian Robinson was the big gun for 14–0 Edna in their "I" offense, as he had rushed for 1,250 yards and passed for 867 more, and accounted for twenty-seven touchdowns. The Cowboys' stingy defense had five shutouts and had given up but seventy-five points in fourteen games. Edna beat Hallettsville, Devine, Lyford, and Sinton on their road to the semifinals.

Edna coach Buzzy Whitely insisted on a coin toss to determine the site for the game. Goats coach Bomar wanted Kyle Field in College Station with their artificial turf, as the Goats were the only Class 3A school in the state with an artificial turf field, which enabled them to take advantage of their speed. Whitely wanted a grass field since that was all the Cowboys had played on during the season and opted for the Berger Center, an Austin ISD stadium, over UT's Memorial Stadium.

Lenoy Jones recalled, "You know, in a way, I thought it hurt Edna playing in the mud and not on artificial turf. They had some really athletic players, like Adrian Robinson, their quarterback. They had as many or more weapons as we had. It actually benefited us playing in the mud. And, besides that, it was fun! We didn't get a chance to do that back in Groesbeck, since our field was artificial turf."

"We wanted to play at the biggest venue possible for our players," added Jerry Bomar. "Since Edna chose Austin as the city to play in, we wanted to play at UT's Memorial Stadium. We ended up playing at Berger Center, a high school field in Austin. We were playing on a Friday night, so our superintendent let us go to Austin early so we could work out at Berger before the game. We took a Trailways bus, and the players got to eat some nice meals. Well, it was raining in Austin and it kind of ruined our plans. We used to like to walk the field with our players a few hours before the game, but we couldn't do that either because of the weather. It was still wet at game time."

Sparked by 246 passing yards by Brandon Bennett, the Groesbeck Goats punched their ticket to the Class 3A state finals with a 21–13 win over the Edna Cowboys. Two of Bennett's eleven completions went for touchdowns, a 75-yard scoring pass to Lenoy Jones that put the Goats up 14–7 with 2:49 left in the first quarter, and a fifty-yard bomb to Tyrone Brown in the third quarter. A nine-yard run by Edna's Adrian Robinson closed the gap to 14–13 in the second quarter, but Groesbeck blocked the extra-point try and the Goats led by one at halftime. After Bennett hit Tyrone Brown with a fifty-yard touchdown bomb on the Goats' first possession of the third quarter to put Groesbeck up 21–13, Edna was unable to move the ball against the Groesbeck defense until late in the game.

Jones said about his seventy-five-yard touchdown play, "I was lined up at tight end on the left. I just ran a streak route, which is basically straight up the field. Brandon hit me in stride. It was hard to get my traction at first because of the mud. I kind of had to tiptoe and move gingerly to the sideline until I could get my balance. Once I had gotten to the sideline, I was able to go full speed to go in for the touchdown. It all happened right in front of our fans."

Jerry Bomar talked about what he thought was a key to the win over Edna: "Us playing two-platoon football showed up in the semifinals against Edna. Our guys were fresh, but they had several of their players that played both ways and by late in the game they were tired. Adrian Robinson, their quarterback and safety, was exhausted by the fourth quarter."

Brandon Bennett said about the win, "They had a really good quarterback and some athletic receivers. We weren't afraid of them, even though they were number one in the state. We honestly didn't know that much

Coach Jerry Bomar congratulates running back Dwrain Cooper after Groesbeck's 21-13 semifinal win over Edna. Courtesy of Jerry Bomar

about them. Once again, our coaches prepared us to play. Our depth did wear out Edna. Their quarterback was worn out by the fourth quarter. We kept the pressure up on them. It was a wet and rainy night. We went at each other early. We could've scored again late in the game, but I threw a ball up for grabs that they picked off. I should have taken the sack."

Jerry Bomar gave his thoughts about advancing to the Class 3A finals: "After the Edna game, as I was leaving the locker room, I sat down on the curb by the buses and I said to myself, 'Wow, we're going to the state finals.' It was hard to believe.

"After I regrouped, we decided to go to Texas Stadium in Arlington that Saturday night since we had already played on Friday to watch the other semifinal game, Southlake Carroll against Burnet. I really didn't want to play Southlake Carroll. They ran a multiple offense that was really hard to handle. Burnet, on the other hand, ran the Wishbone, and we had seen that several times that year, especially in the two games against Fairfield. It gave us a fighting chance. Well, we got our wish. Southlake Carroll was up 7–0 late in the fourth quarter, and Burnet tied the score on a trick play. They advanced on penetrations. That was their third tie in a row."

Lenoy Jones remarked, "I know the coaches may have felt a little different, but a lot of us wanted to play Southlake Carroll. Even back then, they were really good and they already had that reputation of being one of the best programs around. We wanted to play them because they were the team to beat. You want that challenge. You know, we still didn't get much respect from anyone. Our district had a team playing for a state title for the third year in a row, and most people were saying that Burnet was going to walk over us."

After Burnet had rolled through their first two playoff opponents, Comanche and Big Lake, Burnet pulled off a rarity that had never been done in the Texas high school playoffs. The Bulldogs tied three consecutive playoff games against Vernon 20–20, Marble Falls 14–14 in the quarterfinals, and Southlake Carroll 7–7 in the semifinals, but since the penetration rule was still in effect in 1991, Burnet advanced each time because of an advantage in penetrations. Many felt that Burnet's tying three consecutive playoff games led to the rule change in 1996, where teams would now play overtime in both regular-season and playoff contests.

Jerry Bomar recalled, "We got to play the title game in the Astrodome. Everyone was thrilled. Back in 1991, the Dome was still a great place to play. We got to play there because our superintendent got a call from a booking agent wanting to know if we wanted to play at noon on Saturday. They said they would pay our expenses. We didn't really like playing at noon. It got us out of our routine. That's how we got to play there. We went in and practiced on that Friday, and I noticed that the NFL goalposts for the Oilers were still up. They were narrower than the high school ones that should have been put up. When we came back the next day, the NFL goalposts were still there and I couldn't believe it. What if the game had been decided because of that?"

"I remember we were very disappointed that we couldn't play Edna at UT when we played them in Austin," said Brandon Bennett. "Teams in the playoffs wanted to keep us off of Astroturf because that's what our field at Groesbeck was and turf helped our passing game. We could've played at Kyle Field instead of in Bryan, at Baylor instead of Midway Stadium in Waco, and UT instead of Berger Center. We wanted the experience of playing on college fields. Luckily, after we beat Edna, the final game against Burnet was set to be played in the Astrodome. It was unbelievable to play there. When we found out we were playing there, we were excited. When we went to Houston, we got to work out there, and we all just looked at the roof in awe."

Bennett added, "We were so excited about playing for a state title in the Astrodome that we were locked in. We had great senior leadership, and we wanted to win the whole thing. We were hungry. We had the whole community behind us, and we knew deep down we were going to win. We had great practices all week."

Lenoy Jones agreed, "We were excited about playing in the Dome. Back then, it was like playing in the Cowboys stadium nowadays. I remember being interviewed about going there to play and I said, 'It's great to going to Houston to play in the Astrodome, but we're not going there to sightsee.'"

On December 20 in the Astrodome against the Burnet Bulldogs, the Groesbeck Goats captured the Class 3A state title with a tense 7–0 win over the Burnet Bulldogs. The game ended up being a defensive struggle, with Burnet finishing with 161 total yards and Groesbeck with 160. The biggest play of the game occurred in the second quarter, and it set up the only touchdown of the game. From the Burnet thirty-eight in the second quarter, Mitchell Maxwell, the 5'10" Burnet safety, went up against 6'4" Lenoy Jones for a jump ball on a Brandon Bennett pass. Jones came down with the ball for a thirty-two-yard gain down to the Bulldogs six-yard line. On the next play, Dwrain Cooper took it in from the six for the game's only touchdown, with 1:58 remaining until halftime. Groesbeck held Burnet to just three first downs and sixty-four yards total offense in the first half. The Goats' defense made sure that Burnet would not be able to beat them on penetrations in case of a tie like the previous three weeks. The closest the Bulldogs got to the Groesbeck twenty-yard line was the Goats' twenty-seven in the third quarter.

Brandon Bennett recalled, "It was a tough battle against Burnet. We were a little surprised to be playing them. We thought Southlake Carroll would beat them in the semifinals, but they didn't. It was another grind-it-out game. We scored after Lenoy caught that jump ball down on their six. Lenoy was 6'4" and went and got the ball. We got that seven points, and our defense carried us the rest of the way."

Jones talked about his big catch: "Brandon threw it up for grabs, and I outjumped the defensive back. I lost my balance, and I saw the pylon for the end zone. I thought it may have been the pylon in the back of the end zone, and I thought if I dove, I might score. It turns out it was the front pylon, and I ended up about five yards short."

Bennett then recalled how he felt after the game was over: "When that last second ticked off the clock, we cried tears of joy. I couldn't believe it! Our senior class had won a state title! I thought back to when we were in seventh and eighth grade, and we didn't win a football game. We had come a long way thanks to Coach Bomar and the other coaches. It was something no one could take away from us. Even today, when I go back to visit, people still want to talk about it. We hung out together; we loved each other. When we got back to Groesbeck on the charter buses, our fans were waiting for us and they were all yelling and screaming. It took a lot of hard work and sacrifice. For a lot of people in Groesbeck, it gave them hope. It brought the community together. We learned that if you want something worth having, you have to sacrifice and work hard for it."

Jerry Bomar added, "We were never ranked. We were picked no better than fourth in our district. I never really could have predicted what happened. We had no expectation of winning state. It never entered my mind."

Lenoy Jones remarked, "I have fond memories of winning state in the Dome. I went back there twice when I was playing at TCU when we played the University of Houston, and then when I was with the Oilers in 1996, I played there eight times. I would walk into that building and the memories would come flooding back. What I really remember the most, though, was how bad we were a few years before and how far we came. When we were in seventh and eighth grade, we were horrible. We were probably the worst team ever to go through Groesbeck Junior High. When I think about where we were compared to where we ended up, it was very satisfying."

After football was over, many of the Goats football players promptly went to basketball season. Like the Fannindel Falcons in 1988, Groesbeck was expected to compete for a state title. In 1991, the Goats finished 27–7, losing in the regional final to eventual state champion Hardin-Jefferson 58–53. If the Goats were successful, they would be only the second school in UIL history to win a state football and basketball title in the same school year, Dumas being the first thirty years earlier in 1961–62.

Groesbeck had to cancel all of their nondistrict basketball games due to not having enough players, since most of the basketball players were playing football. When District 18–3A play started, the Goats tore through their competition and reached the state tournament in Austin with a perfect 16–0 record.

Richard Reagan coached defensive ends on the football team and was also the head basketball coach. He recalled, "I had no idea we'd be that good in football in 1991. I knew we were going to be good in basketball. They were good kids, they were very coachable, and we had been there before. We had some good athletes playing both football and basketball. Lenoy Jones, Brandon Bennett, and Tyrone Brown were all good basketball players. We had one guy, Chuck Phillips, who was 6'7", and he didn't play football.

"Because of our success in football, we had to delay the start of basketball season. We played no nondistrict games. I don't know if Coach Bomar knows this or not, but while we were in the football playoffs, the kids were slipping off and playing basketball on the weekends. If Jerry would have found out back then, he would have had a heart attack. We ended up going to the state tournament undefeated at 16–0. We beat Hardin-Jefferson, who had won state the year before, in the regional finals, 121–93. It was the best basketball game I've ever been involved in."

"I loved playing basketball," Lenoy Jones remarked. "It's what we grew up with. There was no peewee football in Groesbeck, but we had Little Dribblers from about the time we were ten or so. It was all we knew, and we would play it all the time. That's why after football season was over, it was no problem transitioning to basketball. We also had great chemistry from playing together all of those years."

"I liked playing football, but I loved playing basketball," Brandon Bennett added. "So did most of my friends. We actually won a national championship in Little Dribblers when we were around ten years old. Basketball season was on hold until football was over. We would practice on our own during football season. We would get into the gym at the elementary school, mostly on Sundays. Coach Bomar didn't like us messing with basketball during football season, so we kept it quiet. As kids, it never crossed our minds that one of us could have gotten hurt.

"We knew we had a good chance to win state. I got hot at the regional tournament. We beat Hardin-Jefferson in the regional final 121–93. We ran them out of the gym. We felt like no one could beat us. We won our first game at the state tournament and then played Stafford in the 3A final. They beat us 73–72. We played awful. Later, when I was going to Sam Houston State, one of the Stafford players, Marty Schott, and I would cross paths every now and then, and he would remind me about them beating us."

After Groesbeck won the state title, Bomar left the Goats for a head coaching job at Killeen High School, just ninety-five miles southwest of Groesbeck. The Kangaroos had won the Class 5A Division I state title in 1991, and their coach, Bobby Etheredge, had left to join the college coaching ranks.

Bomar explained why he left Groesbeck: "After we won state, I had stars in my eyes. We had just won, and I wanted to coach at the highest level in the state, which at the time was Class 5A. When I did that, though, it didn't fulfill me. I look back, and it's overrated sometimes. It was a hard decision to leave Groesbeck. There were some hurt feelings."

In four years at Killeen, Bomar had a 30–14–1 record and reached the playoffs in three of his four seasons. After that, he spent eight years at Class 5A Grand Prairie, seven years at Callisburg, and five years at Orange Grove; then Beeville High School came next, where he had a 21–12 record in three seasons from 2016 to 2018. After the 2018 season,

Bomar's record stood at 229–143–3 in thirty-four seasons as a public school head coach.

After Bomar left Groesbeck, the football program returned to mediocrity. The Goats made the playoffs in 1992 but promptly lost in the first round. Groesbeck did win two other playoff games in 1994, before losing to eventual state champion Sealy in the third round. Since then, the Goats have qualified for the playoffs eight more times but have lost in the first round each time. The six playoff wins the Goats secured on their way to the state title in 1991 is more than all the other seasons of Groesbeck football combined. Since 1991, the Goats' overall record stands at 129–178–1.

However, after his 2018 season in Beeville, Bomar made a surprise move by returning to Groesbeck to coach the Goats for the 2019 season. Bomar explained how he ended up back in town: "I was at Beeville. It was a good job at first. There were no expectations, and we had a blast. We were 9–3 my first year, and we won district. The next year, we went 6–4. We had a young team. I was happy there, but I started to have problems with the administration and it took the fun out of everything. I had thought about going back to Groesbeck a couple of times. I had been asked to consider it before. But I held off for a while. If I went back, how would I top winning a state title there earlier? Well, in the spring of 2019, the Groesbeck job opened up, and I looked into it. The superintendent said if I wanted the job, it was mine. I kind of got drawn into it. My wife finally told me that she thought I should go for it—that I should do it. I ended up taking the job. It's a great place to live. And it turns out my wife, who's also in education, took the principal's job at Groesbeck High School. Coming back to Groesbeck is a new challenge for both of us."

Jerry Bomar was the last head coach profiled in this book to remain active. In his first year at Groesbeck back in 2019, the Goats compiled a 2–8 record. Bomar continued to revamp the football program. In early 2020, Bomar said about the task ahead of him, "It's worse here than I thought. We're in total rebuilding mode. But with that being said, we will get this turned around *soon*." Bomar's comments came to fruition. The Goats returned to the playoffs in 2020, 2021, and 2023, losing first-round games in all three seasons. Groesbeck regressed in 2024, fashioning a 4–6 record. At the end of the season, and after 43 years and 280 plus wins in the Texas public and private school ranks, Jerry Bomar decided to retire at the end of the 2024–25 school year. Although he didn't return Groesbeck to their glory days of 1991, he did return the Goats to respectability.

Rockport-Fulton

Coach Autry's Texas Football Debut and the 2000 4A Pirates

WHEN MOST PEOPLE think of the Rockport-Fulton area in Aransas County on State Highway 35 (about thirty miles north of Corpus Christi), they likely recall the devastation incurred when Hurricane Harvey slammed into the Texas Gulf Coast in August 2017. The area endured $800 million in damages from Harvey, a blow from which the communities in Aransas County are still recovering.

If asked about the Rockport-Fulton area, football fans might not have much to say about the hometown high school team, the Pirates, and their generally lackluster record on the field. Rockport-Fulton started playing football in 1929, and through 1996, their overall record was 231–362–24. The Pirates had made seven playoff appearances through the years but had only one playoff win, in 1992, to show for it.

That fabled playoff win came while the best player in Pirates history, Dat Nguyen, was a junior. After Nguyen left Rockport in 1994, he went on to All-America status as linebacker at Texas A&M University, capping off his Aggie career by winning the coveted Lombardi Trophy in 1998. From there, Nguyen went on to play for seven seasons with the Dallas Cowboys, from 1999 to 2005.

It was the start of the new millennium, and the players on the 2000 Rockport-Fulton Pirates squad watched their hometown hero Nguyen on the NFL field, drawing inspiration and the drive to make their own name in football history. In interviews, several players on the 2000 squad recalled Nguyen's influence, some even claiming that he was the main reason they played football for the Pirates in the first place. Receiver Jacob Setterbo noted, "We followed Dat Nguyen as kids. He inspired a lot of us to play football for Rockport. I even wore number seven, which was Dat's number when he played for the Pirates."

Randy Key, who became the Pirates quarterback in 1999 and 2000, said, "Dat Nguyen played for Rockport back when we were 3A. We got to see him play when we were younger. I remember watching him in basketball and dunking during warm-ups when he was only about 5'9". He inspired us to play football. We looked up to him. He used to come around in the summertime, back when he was playing for the Aggies and then the Cowboys."

Rockport-Fulton moved up to Class 4A from Class 3A in 1994, the year after Dat Nguyen's senior year at Rockport. Nguyen had done it all at Rockport-Fulton, playing running back and linebacker, and punting and placekicking. The combination of losing the best player in school history and moving up in classification was a recipe for disaster for the Pirates. They were 0–10 and found themselves outscored on the season 358–24. Two more winless seasons followed in 1995 and 1996, and the Pirates stood at 0–29–1 from 1994 to 1996.

Into the mix to try and save the Pirates' football fortunes came Gary Autry. A native of Van Buren, Arkansas, Autry had just won a state title as coach of Van Buren when he took the plunge into one of the most challenging jobs in Texas football.

Autry described how he ended up in Rockport: "I left Van Buren, my hometown, after twenty years, because I had always wanted to coach in Texas. I was the finalist at Abilene High School in 1996, which was a 5A school and a really good place to coach. My interview went great. I was one of the three finalists for the job. Well, I didn't get it. I called the athletic director and told him, 'I'm not mad. I need help. I want to get a job in Texas.' He said, 'If you had been a Texas coach, you would have had the job. We hired a Class 3A coach. I recommend that you get a job in Texas somewhere, anywhere.' Well, the next year, I ended up in Rockport. They had gone 0–29–1 the past three years.

"I never questioned myself, nor was I ever afraid about changing jobs. When I left Van Buren, people thought I was crazy. We had just won a state title in Arkansas, and I was going to a job where they hadn't won a game in three years! I remember one of the newspapers close to us there in Arkansas had a headline about me leaving Van Buren that said, 'From the Penthouse to the Outhouse.' Well, I got the job, and I went down to Rockport that spring. First, I worked on getting a weight room. Most importantly, I had a great superintendent because he gave me what I needed and let me be in charge. And I answered to him. If there was a problem, he would come over to my house and get things straightened out. They let me do what it took to win."

Something Autry brought with him from Van Buren that helped resurrect the Pirates' fortunes was an offense that most thought to be antiquated by 1997—the Wishbone. Autry learned the intricacies of the offense when he traveled to Westfield High School in the Houston area from Van Buren in the early 1990s to learn it from its originator, Emory Bellard. Ironically, Bellard had started his coaching career down the road from Rockport as an assistant coach at Alice High School. It was there he learned the original principles of the offense from the head coach there in the late 1940s, Gover "Ox" Emerson.

Coach Autry recalled, "We ran the Wishbone offense. The Wishbone was the great equalizer for us at Rockport. Opposing teams just didn't see it much anymore. Spread offenses and the passing game had mostly replaced it by the late '90s. We had just average talent. I don't think any of the guys played in college. Randy Key, our quarterback, could have, but he decided not to. He was a good passer. It worked very well for me through the years. When we ran it right, it was hard to stop us.

"I actually got to learn the Wishbone from the master himself, Emory Bellard. Pat Wozniak, who eventually became one of my assistants at Rockport, knew Emory. Wozniak had been a position coach for Bellard at Westfield High School in Houston. I knew Coach Wozniak from my early days of coaching in Missouri. It was a unique situation. I would come down from Arkansas to visit with him. It was like getting a PhD in the Wishbone. Coach Wozniak originally told me how to approach Bellard. He said, 'Coach Bellard doesn't give a damn about what you're doing. Go about it by asking him, 'Whatever you're willing to share with me, I would appreciate.' Coach Wozniak also said to bring Coach Bellard a half gallon of Chivas Regal. Coach Bellard loved it. And, for whatever reason, Coach Bellard liked me. He wouldn't talk about his offense with just anyone. He said, 'What do you want to know?' He showed me what he put in at Texas, how to attack an eight-man front, where the reads were. He taught me that there were four basic defensive fronts to stop the Wishbone. We practiced against those four defensive fronts so our players could recognize the defense they were up against. It was great. Another thing I learned from

Wishbone Offense architect Emory Bellard at his first coaching job in 1951 as an assistant at Alice High School. Courtesy of Robert D. Jacobus

watching him was that he was also the best practice organizer I've ever been around."

Bubba Scott is a Rockport native and played for the Pirates from 1978 to 1980. He later returned to Rockport to join the coaching staff in 2000. He spoke about what football was like in Rockport before the arrival of Coach Autry: "I grew up in Rockport, and we had no football tradition. The three years I played, we weren't very good. I graduated in 1981. I coached in Sinton before I came back to Rockport. Sinton had made it to the area round in 1992, and the coach left after the season. I came over to Rockport-Fulton and got here when things were pretty bad. We went 0–29–1 from 1994 to 1996. I was at the junior high and scouted games for the varsity. I went to *all* of the games. Our goal back then was not to win but just to keep the score down. It was a horrible situation.

"That all changed when Coach Autry came. He brought a whole different culture. It was all good; it was something we needed. It was his way or the highway. The kids and the community bought into it. It turned out to be a good situation for Coach Autry, too. My son Jake played with a really good group of players in seventh and eighth grade. They didn't lose a game in junior high. They even beat Gregory-Portland and Calallen. They ended up starting out with Coach Autry as freshmen, and they were seniors for the season we had in 2000. It was all good. He brought the Wishbone with him. Sometimes when we ran it, you just couldn't stop it. We had a great backfield. Randy Key was a great quarterback, very good on the option. He could fly. He could also throw the ball if he needed to. Alan Soriano was our fullback; David Moss, our leading rusher, was the left halfback; and Brett Baer was the right halfback. He was a helluva lead blocker."

Gene Walkoviak joined Gary Autry's staff in 1998 after a twenty-year stint as head coach at Jasper High School, where he compiled a 169–52–7 record. He said the following about Coach Autry: "I met Gary at a coaches' clinic in Hot Springs. He's a heckuva coach. He always told you where he stood on things. He stood for discipline. The players may not have always liked what he did, but they respected him. I was with those seniors on the 2000 team from their sophomore year until their senior year. A lot of them were three-year starters. What I remember the most about that year is how much we improved. Even with the playoffs, we got a little better every week. When Gary got there, they had been 0–29–1. I ended up coming to Rockport through Pat Wozniak, who Gary had known for years. He had been the coach at Little Cypress–Mauriceville, and I had been at Jasper."

Jacob Scott, Bubba's son, was Mr. Everything for the 2000 Pirates. Scott played receiver and defensive back, returned punts and kickoffs, and was even the deep snapper on the punt team. He described what it was like to play for Autry: "It was tough to play for him. Sometimes I questioned why he did the things he did. At times, he was not the nicest of people. He could be a brute. You know what, though? We needed it. It was the spring of my eighth-grade year, and the varsity had just gone 0–29–1. Then Coach Autry came in, and he was the saving grace of Rockport football. He would set expectations, and he didn't waver. In the end, though, we won—so it was worth it. Autry demanded perfection and discipline. He knew what it took to win. He taught us to stay the course. Teams knew we were going to run the ball. We had to execute. We would only throw the ball five or six times a game, although we did throw a little more during the playoffs."

Jacob Setterbo added, "I remember at the end of our eighth-grade year, Coach Autry got us all together and said things were going to change. We barely had a weight room. There was a junior high weight room inside their locker room. Within a year, we had a brand-new weight room by the stadium. Strength and conditioning were key for Coach Autry. We even added new stands by my senior year to accommodate all the new fans—nice aluminum bleachers.

"Coach Autry had very high expectations. He was very demanding and disciplined. He was tough on us, especially during two-a-days. I remember during two-a-days, there were some rumblings about quitting, but we didn't. Coach Autry used to say, 'All right, get on the line!'—which meant we were running gassers. He would punish us if things weren't going well in practice. He did treat us first-class, though. He would surprise us sometimes, too. We would always have steak dinners on game day. I remember one time on a Thursday, he got all of us out of class and we had nap time. Before the Port Lavaca game, he gave us the Monday off, no practice. I swear I didn't hear him speak until my junior year when I got on varsity. Coach Wozniak was his right-hand man. He was more of a leader. We would lift weights three times a week, and he would always gather us together at the end of the workout and tell us a story. Coach Autry would just stand off to the side, cross his arms, and scowl."

Randy Key recalled, "I was on varsity as a sophomore. I was the backup quarterback and the free safety. It got me experience as far as game speed and slowing down the game. My junior year, I was the starter at quarterback. Things got intense. We ran the Wishbone. You had to have intelligent players to execute it, and you had to understand how the offense was designed. Everybody had to do their job for it to work. If they didn't, it would break down. By our senior year, we had the offense down pat. Everybody knew their jobs. Coach Autry ramped it up for me. Being a quarterback for Autry, you had to learn how to be a leader. I was a different type—I led by example. I wasn't so much a vocal leader. I had to be a role model on and off the field. Once I got the system down part of the way through my junior year, we started to dominate. We started killing people. We lost our first playoff game in 1999, though. I got hurt early in the game. But that experience of losing inspired us to do better in our senior season."

In 1997, Autry's first year at the helm, the Pirates finished 2–8 but followed that up in 1998 and 1999 with back-to-back 7–3 seasons, good for third place in their district both seasons and a playoff spot. The Pirates lost their bi-district playoff games both years. Because of the team's steady improvement under Autry and the school's large senior class, the 2000 Pirates were expected to contend for a playoff spot. The District 30–4A race appeared to be a toss-up between Rockport-Fulton and perennial South Texas powerhouse Gregory-Portland, about thirty miles southwest of Rockport.

"By my third season, we were starting to taste success," Gary Autry recounted. "We made the playoffs but lost our quarterback on the third play of the game, and we lost a close one to Mercedes. We were better than Mercedes. I felt bad about not going farther. We had a lot of juniors on that team, and I knew we could be pretty good in 2000. We also had some really good coaches. I kept very few coaches from before I got there. I did keep Bubba Scott, Jacob's dad. He was a good coach.

"We had five guys on our staff that had been head coaches elsewhere—guys like Pat Wozniak or Gene Walkoviak, who had been at Jasper. He packed up and came down here. Johnny Mac Hollinger was another good one. He had been at UTEP [University of Texas at El Paso] and knew the option. I know coaches, and I don't know of a better coach than Johnny. He was our offensive coordinator, and he was able to dial up some good plays. We were on the same page. We called plays together. I was lucky to have good coaches, but I was also not afraid of their strengths. Too many coaches are afraid of hiring someone that knows as much as they do. They feel threatened. I would hire the best guy possible."

Jacob Scott added, "We figured we had the chance to have a good senior year. We did lose our center, Luke Roquette, and his brother Cody before the season because they moved. Luke was our anchor in the Wishbone. Ace Nava stepped in at center and did a great job, though. I think it helped that we were in a new district. Most of the district teams we would be playing hadn't seen the Wishbone. We had a good core group coming back, about thirty-five or forty seniors. Randy Key had been the starting quarterback his junior year, so that helped. He was good at reading defenses. We had high expectations for ourselves, and we were gym rats, too. We lifted weights and worked out together."

Gary Autry concluded, "For the first time, the kids expected to win, and the community expected us to win. We had high expectations."

The opening game of the 2000 season for the Rockport-Fulton Pirates was a September 8 away contest against the Aransas Pass Panthers, a Class 3A school just ten miles away. Aransas Pass had won the previous two meetings between the schools after Autry took over for the Pirates, including a 10–7 victory in 1999. In a tight contest, Rockport-Fulton prevailed over the Panthers 40–33. The game was not clinched until Roston Pash returned an interception thirty-five yards for a score, with the Pirates clinging to a slim one-point lead with fifty-six seconds to go. The Pirates started the 2000 season off on the wrong foot, falling behind the Panthers 14–0. After Rockport-Fulton tied the score at 14, Aransas Pass took the lead at the half, 21–14 and extended the lead to 27–14 early in the third quarter. Randy Key hit David Moss with a sixty-five-yard scoring pass just moments later to narrow the Panthers' lead to 27–21, and after a fifteen-yard Jacob Scott touchdown on a reverse and a missed extra point, the score was knotted at 27–27 with 4:45 left in the third quarter. Early in the fourth quarter, the Pirates took their first lead at 34–27 on Alan Soriano's six-yard run. Aransas Pass scored later in the quarter and failed on a two-point conversion attempt that would have given them the lead. The Panthers got the ball back one more time, but Pash dashed their hopes with his game-clinching interception.

Randy Key recalled, "We went through two-a-days, and we had a couple of scrimmages. The first one, we dominated. We added a few wrinkles to the Wishbone, and we dominated our second scrimmage, too. We were looking good. When we played our opening game against Aransas Pass, though, we were kind of flat. Coach Autry laid into us after the game. He told us, 'You're better than that!'"

Week two was a September 15 home contest against the Class 5A Corpus Christi Miller Bucs, a team the Pirates beat 35–12 in 1999. Rockport-Fulton improved to 2–0 on the season with a 34–6 win over Miller.

The Pirates scored on their first play from scrimmage, as Randy Key threw a fifty-six-yard touchdown pass. Key followed that up with a twenty-one-yard touchdown run in the second quarter to go up 14–0. After Miller struck back with a score of their own to make it 14–6, the Pirates added two more touchdowns before halftime to raise their lead 27–6. The Pirates then dominated the contest on their first possession of the second half, as they went sixty-one yards in five plays, with Alan Soriano going the last thirteen yards for a touchdown.

Next up for the 2–0 Pirates was a neutral-site game on September 22 in the Alamodome in San Antonio against the Class 5A San Antonio Jay Mustangs. The Pirates jumped on the Mustangs from the opening kickoff, as Cavon Finnels went fifty-four yards with his kick return. Moments later, Randy Key hit Cody Revel with a perfectly thrown ball for a twenty-three-yard touchdown with 9:18 to go in the opening quarter. Jay tied the score on their first possession with a seventy-five-yard scoring bomb just a minute after the Pirates' score. Later in the first quarter, Rockport-Fulton capitalized on a Mustangs fumble when David Moss scored from twenty yards out with 1:11 to play in the first quarter. The Pirates made it 21–7 when Alan Soriano scored from a yard away just before halftime. Jay closed the gap to 21–13 when they scored on their opening drive of the third quarter, but the Pirates extended their lead to 27–13 when Key connected on a thirty-three-yard touchdown pass. Jay struck back with a touchdown with 1:56 left in the third quarter to close within 27–20. The Pirates countered as Key hooked up with Jacob Scott for a sixteen-yard touchdown pass, and the Pirates' lead grew to 34–20 with 10:35 remaining in the contest. Scott then followed up his touchdown on offense with a key interception on defense. Jay climbed to within a touchdown with 3:54 remaining, but the Pirates defense stopped Jay on their final possession at midfield on a fourth and two play with just seconds to go. The Pirates were now 3–0 for the first time in recent memory.

Jacob Scott recalled, "We went to the Alamodome to play San Antonio Jay. Coach Autry knew we would be playing on turf there. He was preparing us for the playoffs. He figured at some point we would be playing on turf. It was preparation for our potential playoff run. He knew it would be a playoff-type atmosphere in the Alamodome. He paid attention to detail. He knew this could be our year. He chartered buses to San Antonio; we did everything first-class. He didn't miss a thing. The one negative was, I did give up a touchdown in the Jay game. I read the coverage wrong and gave up a long pass. I got burned. Coach Wozniak gave me the business when I came off the field. I made up for it, though. I ended up catching a touchdown pass later, and I also intercepted a pass."

A September 29 away date with the 3–0 Kingsville Brahmas was in store for Rockport-Fulton in week four. The Pirates came away with a hard-fought 41–25 win. The team got off to a quick start when they scored on their opening possession. Kingsville tied the score at seven with 5:46 left in the first quarter and on their next possession went ninety-nine yards for a score to take a 13–7 lead with 7:22 left in the second quarter. Rockport-Fulton struck right back as they went sixty-seven yards in six plays, with Brian Solis going the final five yards for the score with 5:45 remaining in the first half. After a Brahmas punt, David Moss ripped off a sixty-yard run down to the Kingsville five. From there, Solis scored again, giving the Pirates a 21–13 advantage. Kingsville pulled to within 21–19 right before the half, going fifty-nine yards in seven plays. But the third quarter belonged to the Pirates. Two plays after the second-half kickoff, Key raced fifty-eight yards down the left sideline for a score to put Rockport-Fulton up 28–19. On their next possession, the Pirates went ninety yards in fifteen plays with Moss, who rushed for 123 yards on the evening, scoring from two yards out. In the fourth quarter, Rockport-Fulton extended their lead to 41–19 on a twenty-two-yard reverse by receiver Jacob Scott, the third game in a row the Pirates and Scott had pulled off that trick play. Kingsville added a late touchdown to account for the final score.

"Kingsville was good," Jacob Scott noted. "Their coach was Richard Whitaker, who was just getting started as a head coach. He ran the Flexbone, which is a variation of the Wishbone. He eventually moved on to Port Lavaca, and he's had some really good teams there over the years."

The 4–0 Pirates now had an October 6 homecoming matchup with the Flour Bluff Hornets from District 31–4A. Rockport-Fulton made the night a good one for the homecoming crowd, jumping to a 24–0 halftime lead and cruising to a 30–6 win over the Hornets. Ernie Surrell, who was filling in for an injured Alan Soriano, rushed for a game-high 127 yards. The Pirates opened the game with a fifteen-play, eighty-yard drive for a touchdown. Randy Key covered the last four yards into the end zone. Rockport-Fulton took advantage of a three-yard Hornets punt early in the second quarter as they took over on the Flour Bluff forty-three. Brett Baer scored from two yards away to make it 14–0 Pirates with 7:53 remaining in the half. The Pirates then went sixty-eight yards in eleven plays on their next possession, with Key scoring again, this time from three yards away, and the Pirates led 21–0 with 1:35 remaining until halftime. The Hornets promptly fumbled on their next possession, and Rockport-Fulton hit a thirty-seven-yard field goal just before halftime to go up 24–0. After a scoreless third quarter, Key hit David Moss with a fifty-five-yard scoring pass to put the Pirates up 30–0. Flour Bluff avoided the shutout when they scored with 2:06 remaining. Rockport-Fulton was now finished with their nondistrict schedule and boasted a 5–0 record for the first time in school history.

The Pirates opened District 30–4A play with a big game right off the bat against the Beeville Jones Trojans. The week-six home game on October 13 looked to be a challenge, as Beeville stood at 4–1 on the season. Rockport-Fulton overcame a 16–14 halftime deficit to take a 37–23 win over Beeville. Beeville jumped out to a 7–0 lead with 2:32 left in the opening quarter before Rockport-Fulton came back to tie the score at seven before the end of the quarter; then the Pirates took a 14–7 lead on a Randy Key three-yard run with 8:43 left before halftime. Beeville pulled within 14–13 but missed an extra point with 6:03 left in the quarter. After a fourteen-yard Rockport-Fulton punt, Beeville kicked a forty-two-yard field goal as time expired in the first half to go up 16–14. The second half started as badly as the first half ended, as Beeville recovered the second-half kickoff at the Pirates thirty-seven before the Rockport-Fulton players could get to the ball. Two plays later, with just fifty-three seconds elapsed in the second half, the Trojans scored again and were up 23–14.

Jacob Setterbo reminisced about the miscue on the second-half kickoff: "I made a mistake, which didn't make Coach Autry very happy. Beeville kicked off to start the second half, and their kick went just over my head. Well, I didn't go for the ball. I had been taught by the coaching staff to never go backward to get the ball. I was a rule follower. Beeville recovered the ball and scored a few plays later. When I came off the field, Coach Autry said to me, 'You're the dumbest smart kid I know.' One of the other coaches pulled me aside and said, 'Don't worry about it. You were just doing what you were taught.' I'm sure glad we came back to win."

The Pirates responded to the Beeville touchdown with a seventy-five-yard drive, which culminated with Key hitting David Moss in the flat, and he ran it in for a twenty-three-yard touchdown to make it 23–21 Beeville. Seven plays after a Trojans' punt, Ernie Surrell scored from five yards out, and the Pirates added a two-point conversion to put Rockport-Fulton up 29–23 with 1:42 left in the third quarter. The Pirates added an insurance touchdown in the fourth quarter when Key hit Jacob Scott on a thirty-three-yard scoring strike. Another two-point conversion by Rockport-Fulton made the final count 37–23. With the win, the Pirates were 1–0 in District 30–4A play.

Week seven was a battle of the undefeated, with the 6–0 Pirates on the road against the 6–0 Gregory-Portland Wildcats in an October 20 matchup. Gregory-Portland was likewise 1–0 in District 30–4A play, having beaten Port Lavaca Calhoun 48–12 in their district opener. After losing to Gregory-Portland for twenty-five straight years, the Pirates under Autry had beaten the Wildcats the previous two seasons, including a 42–0 home win in 1999. Bubba Scott said, "Gregory-Portland was always a big game. We played them there and they watered down our sideline before the game. It hadn't rained. They were trying to slow us down. We had some speed on our team."

Watering down the Pirates' sideline didn't help Gregory-Portland, as Rockport-Fulton made it three in a row over the Wildcats, with a tense 17–10 overtime win. The night ended better than it started for Rockport-Fulton, as Gregory-Portland scored on their first possession to take a 7–0 lead with 6:52 left in the opening quarter. The rest of the first half was scoreless, with both defenses dominating. The defenses continued to be at the forefront in the third quarter before the Pirates finally got a break when Jacob Scott returned a punt off a fake reverse to the Wildcats twenty-three. Five plays later, Rockport-Fulton booted a twenty-two-yard field goal with 6:18 remaining in the third quarter to narrow the Wildcats' lead to 7–3. At the end of the third quarter, Rockport-Fulton launched their only touchdown drive of the game. Fifty-seven seconds into the fourth quarter, Alan Soriano bulled in from four yards out, and the Pirates led 10–7. Gregory-Portland was held at bay until the final six seconds of regulation, when the Wildcats kicked a game-tying field goal to send things into overtime. Gregory-Portland had held Rockport-Fulton's Wishbone attack and quarterback Randy Key in check for most of the regulation play, but Key finally broke loose when it mattered most, though, as he ran for a twenty-four-yard touchdown on the second play of overtime to give the Pirates a 17–10 lead. Once they were on defense in overtime, the Pirates gave up a five-yard run on first down, but then three straight incomplete passes by the Wildcats ended the game. The clutch win left the Pirates at 7–0 overall and 2–0 in District 30–4A play.

Jacob Scott recalled, "My junior year, we beat Gregory-Portland badly at our place 42–0. We returned two interceptions for touchdowns. We knew it was going to be a tough game down there. They had a big group of seniors coming back, too. The song 'Who Let the Dogs Out?' was very popular our senior year, and Gregory-Portland had their own version that they would play, but it was 'Who Let the Cats Out?' Well, our booster club had this traveling sound system that they would bring to away games. Our team had adopted 'Who Let the Dogs Out?' and 'Bad to the Bone' as kind of our unofficial team songs. When Gregory-Portland came on the field, they tried playing their 'Who Let the Cats Out?,' but our sound system and our 'Who Let the Dogs Out?' drowned them out. They were not happy."

The Pirates returned home for an October 27 contest with the Port Lavaca Sandcrabs, who were in the midst of a dismal 1–9 season. The Pirates made short work of the Sandcrabs as they trounced them 54–0. The onslaught started on the opening kickoff, as Brian Solis grabbed the ball from the Sandcrabs return man and raced ten yards for the score, with only twelve seconds elapsed. From there, David Moss went thirty-three yards for a score with 8:01 left in the first quarter to make it 14–0. At the end of the quarter, Randy Key hit Jacob Setterbo with a thirty-six-yard scoring pass to make it 21–0 after one period. Setterbo added another touchdown on a six-yard reception thirty-nine seconds before halftime to go up 28–0. The Pirates then recovered a surprise onside kick and converted that into a David Moss two-yard touchdown run with just one second remaining until halftime. Ernie Surrell started the second half scoring for the Pirates when he ran for a four-yard touchdown to make it 40–0 with 10:04 remaining in the third, and after Jacob Scott intercepted a Sandcrabs pass at their own twenty-two, David Moss scored one play later to make it 48–0. Cavon Finnels capped off the scoring on the night for the now 8–0 Pirates with a seventy-yard run to make the final 54–0.

Jacob Scott returns an interception twenty-two yards in a 54-0 rout of Port Lavaca. Courtesy of Jacob Scott

Jacob Setterbo recalled his team's big night against the Sandcrabs: "I was mostly a blocking receiver, and I wasn't catching many passes.

I actually thought about asking to be switched to running back. Against Port Lavaca, though, I had a really big game. I was able to catch a couple of touchdown passes, so it all worked out."

November 3 brought another home game, this time against the 7–1 Pleasanton Eagles. The Eagles entered the district contest with only one loss on the season—to Floresville in District 30–4A play. The Pirates rolled to a 37–6 halftime lead and coasted to a 50–26 win. David Moss started the scoring with an eleven-yard touchdown run in the first quarter. Randy Key followed with a fifteen-yard touchdown run of his own to go up 14–0 with 4:19 left in the quarter. After a Pirates' twenty-two-yard field goal to make it 17–0, Pleasanton came back to score their only touchdown of the half to make it 17–6. However, Jacob Scott returned the ensuing kickoff ninety-five yards to the Pleasanton three-yard line to deflate the Eagles' hopes. Alan Soriano added a one-yard touchdown plunge with 3:46 to go in the half to make it 30–6. The Pirates then drove 67 yards for another score just before halftime as David Moss scored from nine yards out. The Eagles outscored the Pirates 18–13 in the second half, but it was of little consolation to Pleasanton. With one game left in the regular season, Rockport-Fulton stood at 9–0 overall and 4–0 in District 30–4A play, just one game away from the first perfect regular season in school history.

The Pirates' week-ten away contest against the Floresville Tigers on November 10 was a key game. Floresville stood at 7–2 overall and 3–1 in district play, having lost to Gregory-Portland 7–6 in week eight. The Tigers, with a victory over Rockport-Fulton, had a chance to force a three-way tie for the District 30–4A title along with Gregory-Portland. But the Pirates left no doubt as they wrapped up a perfect regular season with a 33–18 victory. Floresville came out swinging as they went eighty-two yards in thirteen plays on their opening possession to take a 6–0 lead. The Eagles added another score with six seconds left in the first quarter to go up 12–0. The Pirates came right back early in the second quarter as they went sixty-three yards in seven plays, with David Moss taking the ball in from sixteen yards out. Floresville punched in another score with 2:11 remaining until halftime to make it 18–7. The Pirates came right back, and just before halftime, David Key hit Jacob Scott down the middle with a ten-yard scoring pass.

Rockport-Fulton took their first lead of the night in the third quarter when they took the ball eighty-two yards in fourteen plays, taking almost eight minutes off the clock on their opening possession. Key went the final seven yards for the score. After a failed two-point conversion, the Pirates were up by 19–18. The Pirates added to their lead when Jacob Scott scored on a seventeen-yard reverse with 8:36 left in the game, which was becoming his bread-and-butter play on the season. Key added an eighteen-yard scoring run with thirty-five seconds left to account for the final 33–18 margin. With the regular season complete, Floresville ended up as the third-place team in District 30–4A, while Gregory-Portland took second. The Rockport-Fulton Pirates were district champions.

"I contributed in the Floresville game," Jacob Setterbo recalled. "I caught a couple of passes. Conditioning was a big factor in this game. It was something we prided ourselves on. Floresville jumped on us in the first half, but we wore them down in the second half. During the season, we usually took over during the second half of our games."

The Pirates headed to the Class 4A Division II playoffs, slated to face the San Antonio Alamo Heights Mules, the third-place team in District 27–4A, at Pirate Field on November 17. The Mules were 7–3 overall and 5–2 in district play. Alamo Heights boasted a strong passing attack, as they had thrown for more than two thousand yards during the regular season. The Mules' passing attack, however, was no match for the Pirates' Wishbone offense, as Rockport-Fulton rolled to a 42–18 win on a wet and cold night in Rockport.

The Pirates scored on their opening possession as Randy Key took the ball in from six yards to put the Pirates up 7–0. Rockport-Fulton added another first-quarter score, this time on special teams, as David Moss handed the ball to Jacob Scott on a reverse on a punt return, the bread-and-butter play for Scott, and he took it in from his own forty-five to pay dirt. The Pirates made it 21–0 when Ernie Surrell scored from four yards away, just four seconds into the second quarter. The lead grew to 27–0 the next time the Pirates had the ball, when Jacob Scott took a reverse handoff from David Moss and raced to the Mules' six-yard line after a seventy-yard run. Key scored from the three a couple of plays later to make it 27–0. With 2:52 to go before halftime, Alamo Heights finally got on the scoreboard to make it 27–6 at the half. The Pirates received the second-half kickoff and scored on their first possession as Jacob Scott continued his stellar evening by hauling in a fifty-yard pass from Randy Key to put the Pirates up 34–6. After Alamo Heights scored the next two times they had the ball, narrowing the gap to 34–18, the Pirates put the final nail in the Mules' coffin when Key scored on a four-yard run with 7:18 to play. Scott closed out his big evening with an interception to seal the win.

Jacob Scott summed up the big game: "Alamo Heights was one of the early teams to run the spread offense. They had an Astroturf field, which was good for the spread. They wanted to play at home. Well, they lost the coin flip and had to play us at our place. It turned out to be a nasty night. It was thirty-seven degrees, muddy, and wet. They couldn't handle it. I had a punt return on a reverse for a touchdown. I had a couple of other big plays on offense, plus I had an interception. Going into the game, we were wondering if Coach Autry was going to let us wear warm-weather gear on the sideline to stay warm. He said, 'You're wearing your uniform and that's it.' Alamo Heights came out in all kinds of stuff to keep warm. Coach Autry had instilled it in us to be tough."

For their second playoff game, the Pirates won the coin flip again, allowing them to host a playoff game for the second week in a row. Their opponent was a familiar one, the Flour Bluff Hornets, which the Pirates had beaten 30–6 in their homecoming game on October 6. Jacob Scott and his teammates realized the importance of the game and how they couldn't take Flour Bluff lightly. "We had played Flour Bluff once already at our homecoming, and we beat them pretty handily," Scott said. "I guarantee we didn't take them lightly, though. I remember we had a very serious week at practice. Even though we were playing at home again and had beaten them before, we were serious. We had come this far, and we weren't going to screw things up now."

Although the playoff contest was much closer than the teams' regular-season matchup, Rockport-Fulton got a turnover on Flour Bluff's first possession, scored, and never looked back in a 42–21 win. After an interception during the Hornets' first play from scrimmage, the Pirates' David Moss scored, and the Pirates led 7–0 with just twenty-seven ticks elapsed off the clock. Flour Bluff tied the score with 4:13 to go in the first when Rockport-Fulton fumbled the ball in their own end zone and the Hornets recovered for a touchdown. The Pirates came right back from their miscue with a Cavon Finnels seventy-three-yard kickoff return to the Flour Bluff seventeen. Moss took the ball from there and scored his second touchdown of the night to put the Pirates ahead 14–7. Then, on the last play of the first quarter, Randy Key scampered sixty yards for Rockport-Fulton's third touchdown of the period. The Pirates increased their lead to 28–7 when Moss scored his third touchdown, this time from eighty yards out with 5:37 left before halftime. With seven seconds left in the half, Flour Bluff tried to climb back into the game when they scored a touchdown to make it 28–14. After a scoreless third quarter, Rockport-Fulton scored two touchdowns in the fourth quarter, one by Alan Soriano and the other by Randy Key, to put the Pirates up 42–14. Flour Bluff added a late tally to account for the final score.

Now 12–0 for the first time in school history and having won two playoff games for the first time in a season, the Pirates turned their attention to the winner of the New Braunfels–Lake Travis game, with Rockport-Fulton taking on the winner. New Braunfels ended up with a heart-stopping 28–25 win, scoring a winning touchdown via a thirty-five-yard touchdown pass with just five seconds left in the contest.

The Pirates were slated to take on the 8–4 Unicorns on December 1 at Blossom Stadium in San Antonio. Randy Key had his finest game as a Pirate, with twenty-three rushes for 181 yards and three touchdowns and also throwing for 207 yards and two second-half scores, including a thirty-yard game-winner to Jacob Scott with just nineteen seconds to play. Rockport-Fulton overcame a 21–7 halftime deficit to gain a last-minute 35–28 win over the New Braunfels Unicorns, propelling the Pirates into the state quarterfinals with an impressive 13–0 record. New Braunfels came out firing, scoring a touchdown but missing the extra point on their first possession; they took the lead at 6–0. Randy Key's first-quarter touchdown run did put the Pirates up briefly 7–6 with 6:26 left in the quarter. In the second quarter, however, the Unicorns took a two-touchdown lead on thirty-three- and one-yard runs to go up 21–7 at halftime.

The Pirates started mounting their comeback midway through the third quarter when Ryan Picarazzi partially blocked a Unicorn punt and the Pirates took over on the New Braunfels forty-three-yard line. Three plays later, Key scored from twenty-six yards out to narrow the gap to 21–14. In the fourth quarter, Rockport-Fulton tied the game when Key hit David Moss coming out of the backfield with a pass and Moss took it ninety yards to pay dirt to tie the score at 21–21 with 8:52 to play. Not to be outdone, the Unicorns immediately responded with a sixty-six-yard touchdown pass to go up 28–21. With their backs to the wall and their perfect season on the line, the Pirates went to work with 7:42 left. Rockport-Fulton went on a sixty-seven-yard, twelve-play drive that ate up almost five minutes of the clock to tie the score at 28–28. Key scored the game-tying touchdown from two yards out, also racking up runs of fourteen and fifteen yards during the drive.

New Braunfels got the ball back, picked up one first down, and was forced to punt. Moss caught the Unicorns' punt at his own forty-three, and the Pirates went to work on their final drive. Key was sacked on the first play for a six-yard loss back to the thirty-seven. From their own thirty-seven with fifty-five seconds left, Key hit Scott with an eighteen-yard gain to the Unicorns' forty-five. New Braunfels was called for a personal foul at the end of the play, which brought the ball to the Unicorns' thirty. That set up the game-winning play, as described by Jacob Scott: "Against New Braunfels, we were down by fourteen. We started throwing the ball more after halftime. I ended up having six or seven catches. If the cornerback was within five yards or less from me, I would run a fade route. If he played seven yards or more off of me, I would run a stop route. The New Braunfels kid was playing me in between. We got the signal from Coach Autry on the sideline that said, 'Take 'em'—that we were going deep. I was on the left hash mark, and I went right down the sideline. It was a perfect throw. Randy hit me in the middle of the end zone. We had been setting them up with the stop routes. Coach Autry showed what a good play caller he was on that play."

Gary Autry added, "New Braunfels was tough. The New Braunfels game was a little bit out of character for me. We ended up having to throw the ball more than we usually did. On our ninety-yard touchdown pass, we caught them cheating, and we used a throwback pass to score on that play. We usually didn't do too many trick plays, besides our reverses and fake reverses on punts and kickoffs, but we did on the ninety-yarder."

When the Pirates got to the quarterfinals, they faced none other than their old nemesis and former district foe the Calallen Wildcats, traditionally the top high school football program in South Texas. The Wildcats were led by Coach Phil Danaher, the winningest coach in Texas high school football history. When he retired after the 2021 season,

The Pirates celebrate as time expires in Rockport-Fulton's dramatic 35–28 last-second comeback win over New Braunfels. Courtesy of Jacob Scott

Danaher's record stood at 490–118–4 overall, which is the Texas record for high school coaching victories, and 423–81–2 in thirty-eight seasons at Calallen. Gary Autry won the coin flip and decided to play the December 8 game at Memorial Stadium in Victoria, which had Astroturf and would aid his Wishbone attack. The only loss of the season the 12–1 Calallen suffered was in a nondistrict contest against Gregory-Portland, who Rockport-Fulton had beaten in district play.

Jacob Scott recalled feeling hopeful going into the game: "We had beaten Gregory-Portland, and Gregory-Portland had beaten Calallen earlier in the season. We thought we had an advantage. We felt like they were the only team that could possibly stop us. They ran the fifty defense and were very good up front. They were good. We had played them close the previous couple of years when they were in our district. We thought we had a shot."

Unfortunately for Scott and the Pirates, they really had no shot at taking down the Wildcats. With Jessie Pavelka for Calallen rushing for five touchdowns, the Wildcats pounded the Pirates 39–16. Calallen scored on their second possession as Pavelka ran thirty-two yards for a score to make it 7–0 with 6:56 left in the first. The Pirates gave their fans a glimmer of hope as they struck back for a score of their own when Randy Key capped off a seventy-yard scoring drive with a four-yard run with 1:35 left in the opening quarter. The Wildcats answered back with a seventy-three-yard drive of their own when Pavelka scored his second touchdown of the afternoon, this time from seventeen yards away. The Wildcats tacked on two more scores before halftime, the second one a forty-nine-yard Pavelka score, and went to the locker room with a 26–7 advantage.

The Pirates fared a little better at the start of the third quarter, capitalizing on a Calallen fumble and turning it into a thirty-four-yard field goal to make it 26–10. The Wildcats then took the ball eighty yards in thirteen plays over six minutes, and Pavelka scored from twenty-nine yards out at the 3:14 mark to make the score 32–10. Rockport-Fulton then came back to score on the last play of the third quarter when Key hit Brian Solis with a forty-six-yard scoring pass down the middle of the field, making it 32–16. Any hopes for a Pirates comeback were dashed early in the fourth quarter when Pavelka raced for his fifth score of the afternoon, this time from forty-nine yards away. Calallen improved to 13–1 on the season and advanced to the Class 4A Division II semifinals, while the Pirates' historic season ended with the same 13–1 mark.

Years later, in hindsight, Randy Key said, "In the playoffs, we opened up the offense a little more and we threw the ball a bit more. We should have been throwing more throughout the season. This got us when we played Calallen. Calallen was prepared. They were setting up in defenses we recognized, but then they shifted. They knew what we were going to run. I wish we would have passed more. Calallen was our roadblock. Every team has that one opponent who has their number, and we just couldn't get over the hump against Calallen."

Jacob Scott also reflected on the loss: "We played in Victoria on field turf, and it was at 2:00 p.m. We weren't used to that. Calallen also used a couple of trick plays against us that they hadn't used since the preseason. They broke them out against us. One of them was a double option where they tossed the ball to the tailback and he pitched it to the receiver. Coupled with the fact that Coach Danaher's kids at Calallen play hard for him and are hard-nosed, it was not a good day. I really felt that if we could have gotten past them, we could have won it all. Our next opponent would have been West Orange–Stark, and we had seen film on them. We could have beaten them. We met the one team that knew how to stop us, and they did."

After his memorable 2000 season with the Pirates, Gary Autry abruptly left Rockport-Fulton. He explained, "My mom was sick back in Arkansas, so I took a head coaching job in Greenville, Texas, which is only about 200 miles from Van Buren. Rockport was about 650 miles away from her. Greenville was much closer to her." Autry stayed for one season in Greenville, installing his Wishbone offense and making the playoffs. He continued coaching in Texas and Oklahoma until his retirement after the 2010 season.

Since Gary Autry left after the 2000 season, the Pirates have compiled a pedestrian 129–126–0 record from 2001 to 2023. Rockport-Fulton has secured ten playoff wins since 2013 but has yet to advance to the state quarterfinals like their 2000 team under Autry.

Years later, the Rockport-Fulton players reflected on their memorable season. Jacob Scott recalled, "We had a great coaching staff. Coach Hollinger was a great offensive line coach. Coach LeGrand was a great receivers coach. The coaches trusted me. I lived football. I was like Coach Wozniak's coach on the field on defense. I lived at the field house. I watched film there; I was up there all of the time. On defense, I would call the coverages in the secondary for Coach Wozniak. Our coaches were older, for the most part, and I wondered sometimes why they came to Rockport. It is a retirement community, and I think it was a good place for them to wrap up their careers. They were impressive, though. They all brought to the table that you had to be tough. You can't have a weak mind to play this game. Coach LeGrand was a gambler. Autry was systematic. Coach Wozniak was very good at getting his message across. My dad brought his calm demeanor to the table. We needed all of these coaches and their minds to make it work. That core staff stuck together for four years, from the time we were freshmen. They showed that they believed in us and that they were going to stick it out with us, and so we in turn gave them everything we had. We weren't always the most athletic team around, but we were always in our best condition and we had been taught to be physically and mentally tough."

"We did have a special team," Randy Key added. "We bought into what Coach Autry was selling. Rockport was a different place before Coach Autry showed up. He came in as we were coming into our freshman year. He practiced tough love on us. If you didn't have thick skin, you didn't last very long. I do know we went from very little success as a 4A program to him taking us to a whole other level. He used to preach to us, 'Bigger, faster, stronger, every day.' He got us a thirty-thousand-square-foot weight room. We needed it to compete. Once we moved up to 4A, we had to be stronger to compete with Gregory-Portland and Calallen. We had no strength training program. After my sophomore year, they tore down the bleachers and press box so they could put new ones in and then redid our field. Autry pissed some people off, but he got results. By my junior and senior year, we were selling out. It was special for the whole community."

Jacob Setterbo concluded with, "It does hurt that Calallen beat us. It was bad to lose to them and have our careers end. After the Calallen game, I was upset, but I have this lingering memory of one of our linemen, Ernest Kerlick, and how upset he was. Like me, he was a senior and couldn't play football anymore. He was crying in the shower by himself. And he was a pretty tough guy. I wouldn't trade what we went through for anything. It was tough—the two-a-days, the heat, the talk of tyranny, having the town behind us. There was some strife, sometimes between the offense and defense, and we almost got into some fights. We got through it, though. Coach Scott used to tell us, 'You guys are special.' And he was right. It was a special season thanks to my teammates and our coaching staff."

Fort Worth

"The Most Unlikely State Champions in Texas History"— The 2003 4A Division I North Crowley Panthers

IN TEXAS HIGH SCHOOL FOOTBALL, the Fort Worth area of the Dallas–Fort Worth Metroplex has never been known for its football prowess, suffering the same run of bad luck as El Paso to its west. The Masonic Home in Fort Worth, a charitable foundation providing housing to widows and orphans alike, fielded powerhouse high school football teams in the area in the 1930s and 1940s. But beyond this, Fort Worth's only other claim to glory on the gridiron was in the 1948 now-defunct City Conference state championship game featuring Arlington Heights High School. The City Conference was a four-team playoff that took place after the 1948 through 1950 seasons, between the city champions of Texas's four major cities at that time: Houston, Dallas, Fort Worth, and San Antonio. Arlington Heights defeated Houston Lamar 20–0 in the 1948 title game. Then came the great drought. No other Fort Worth school played for a state title for nearly fifty years. No Fort Worth teams even appeared in the semifinals from 1959 onward—until 2003, when, out of this sea of mediocrity, came the most unlikely Cinderella story of all.

In 1998, North Crowley High School was a relatively new school within the Fort Worth city limits and became the second high school in Crowley ISD. Following in the tradition of Fort Worth schools, the Panthers had a dismal start to their football program, going 13–37 in their first five seasons. But all that would soon change.

The Panthers' first coach was Mike Papas. Originally from the Kansas City area, Papas played college football at Austin College in Sherman. After graduation in 1981, Papas took a coaching job at the local high school in Sherman, and from there, he was an assistant at Crowley High School from 1982 to 1985. In 1986, Papas moved on to Corsicana High School, where he served under head coaches Donnie Denbow and Tom Wilson. Papas moved up to offensive coordinator under Wilson and was instrumental in helping the Tigers reach the state finals in 1997 in the Class 5A Division II, where they lost to Texas City 37–34.

Papas described how he became the first head coach in North Crowley football history: "I had made some connections when I had coached at Crowley back in the early 1980s. The principal at North Crowley was an assistant principal at Crowley when I was there. The head coach who was at Crowley was now the athletic director. The job at North Crowley was far from big time. Only three people applied for it. We had a tough first year and went 1–9. It seemed like there was a black cloud hanging over us. A big problem was that we played varsity ball that first year. Most of the time in Texas, new schools play a couple of years of junior varsity football to help prepare for their first varsity season. We ended up going into one of the toughest Class 3A districts in the state. We were in the same district as Aledo, who were the 3A state champs, and Alvarado, who had moved down from Class 4A. Then, after a couple of years in 3A, we moved up to Class 4A and were thrown into a district with Brownwood and Stephenville—plus Aledo moved up with us. We were screwed at first. To top it off, during my first spring training in 1998, we only had five kids come out for practice. Our superintendent, Sidney Poynter, was great, though. He just told us to stay the course and be patient. I thought we could be a good program. I had seen the attendance zones for us and Crowley High School, and I felt like we had a good mix of kids to be competitive."

Papas then discussed how he attempted to instill a winning attitude in the North Crowley football program by ensuring the school's success in other sports: "One key for us was when I hired Eugene Rogers to be my defensive coordinator. Eugene had been with me at Corsicana, but he had never been a coordinator before. He drove over to Crowley from Corsicana every day in the spring of 1998 to help establish our offseason program. We also tried to build up other successful programs at North Crowley. The two programs we mainly focused on were powerlifting and track and field—we put a lot of effort into those. Eugene had been the track and field coach at Corsicana. Well, our work paid off, because we won state in powerlifting in 2002 and 2003, and we won our region in track and field in 2002 and 2004. Both of those sports obviously correlate to football. We thought their success would have a carryover effect on our football program, and eventually they did. The kids got a taste of victory."

Lance Moss, who took over as the Panthers' starting quarterback midway through the 2003 season, recalled his time with Coach Papas and Coach Rogers: "Coach Papas was a great coach. He was a leader. He made it feel like a family atmosphere in the football program. He used to do things like have movie nights up at the field house the night before our games. Our saying was that we were like a 'Band of Brothers,' like the HBO series about World War II that came out around that time. Coach Papas wasn't too aggressive. He was more of a players' coach. He was more offensive-minded. Our defensive coordinator was Eugene Rogers. He was kind of the opposite of Coach Papas. Coach Rogers was a players' coach, too, but he was a little more in your face. He was very detail-oriented. He designed our defense to shut down teams like Texarkana."

Matt Panfil, who played safety and receiver, while also handling the placekicking and punting for North Crowley, added, "Coach Papas is a good man. He worked hard to make men out of us. He could get emotional sometimes. He was like a dad to us. There was and still is a lot of love and respect between Coach Rogers and his players. He got us to play to our full potential. He was a little more fiery than Coach Papas. He was a motivator. His techniques were different. I would run through a wall for him. Coach Rogers didn't give out too many compliments to us, so when I got a 'good job' from him, it *really* meant something. He used to start our film sessions every week with highlights of the best hits from the previous week. We started developing an attitude on our defensive line. Things started to really sink in. We eventually got in the mindset that the other team was not going to get another inch."

As the Panthers prepared for that fateful 2003 season, it was almost a foregone conclusion that the three playoff representatives from District 8–4A would be perennial powers Stephenville, Brownwood, and Aledo. Many considered the district to be the toughest Class 4A district in the state. Brownwood had won seven state titles under Gordon Wood in the 1960s, '70s, and early '80s, Stephenville won four state titles under Art Briles in the 1990s, and Aledo won their first state title in 1998.

However, Matt Panfil and his fellow Panthers had high hopes for a successful season. Panfil recalled, "We had a good senior class. We were tight. At the start of the season, we thought we could be pretty good, even though we hadn't had any real success as a program and had gone 3–7 the year before."

Unfortunately, the 2003 season started like previous seasons for the Panthers. They lost to two teams that finished 5–5 on the regular season—27–21 to the Midlothian Panthers on September 5 and 10–7 to the Azle Hornets on September 12.

Mike Papas was disappointed with what looked like another losing season on the horizon. "I felt we started to turn the corner a little bit when we played at Stephenville in 2002. We only lost by a touchdown, and we had a chance to win it in the end. It gave the kids some hope and confidence. We started 2003 slowly, though. We lost our first two games, but we should have won them both. We played poorly and sloppily. It was embarrassing."

The 2003 season sunk even lower the next week when the Panthers lost 48–28 on September 19 to a mediocre Alvarado Indians team that ended up going 4–6 on the season. Papas recalled what eventually came to be the turning point of the season: "After the Alvarado game, we had a team meeting. We had played awful once again—sloppy, too many turnovers, you name it. It was the Saturday morning after our loss to them. The players came out, and we went out on the field and ran to loosen up their legs. In all of the coaches' minds, a meeting was needed. They had mentioned it to me. On the field, after we finished running, we had one. We talked about accountability. We weren't holding ourselves to a high enough standard. We had to stop our selfishness. Some good players got called out. The kids called other kids out, the coaches called some kids out. It wouldn't have surprised me if the kids had called out some of the coaches! We had some strong personalities on that team. They had mature minds, though. They weren't vindictive or petty. The meeting was led mostly by the players. We ended up making some changes because of that meeting. Afterward, we had more accountability, trust, more people buying into what we were trying to do—and we tried to eliminate selfishness."

Matt Panfil also recalled that fateful meeting, which proved to be a turning point for the struggling team: "The Alvarado game was a low point. We turned the ball over six times and had two interceptions run back for touchdowns against us. We handed the game to them. After Alvarado, we had our 'Come to Jesus' meeting. It was the Saturday morning after we lost. Everyone laid it out there and spoke their piece. I didn't realize it at the time, but if we didn't turn it around, the coaches may have been let go. As a high school kid, it didn't register that this was their livelihood. We knew we had to turn things around. What the meeting did was make people emotionally commit. It got intense. One of the coaches—not Coach Papas—slammed his fist down on a table and broke it."

Panfil added, "Even in the locker room after we started 0–3, before the team meeting with the coaches, the players were still talking about going to the playoffs. We met with no coaches around and talked about how we could still be pretty good. Some of the guys thought we were crazy. What helped our team too was that we started getting rid of some of the players who weren't good for the team. They were like a cancer in the locker room. I was a captain, and I would tell them that they couldn't play for North Crowley anymore. I wasn't afraid to be a jerk. I wanted my teammates' respect, but I was not always their friend."

Apparently, the meeting worked because the Panthers proceeded to turn their season around. On September 26, they picked up their first win of the 2003 season in their District 8–4A opener with a 34–0 whitewashing of their school district rival the Crowley High School Eagles. North Crowley limited the Eagles to just forty-eight yards rushing on twenty-five carries and only eight yards passing. Crowley never crossed midfield in the contest. Lance Moss got the scoring started when he caught a five-yard touchdown pass from quarterback Casey Stuhlman in the second quarter that gave the Panthers a 7–0 halftime lead. In the second half, Stuhlman and tailback Brandon Martin each ran for two touchdowns. Martin led all the rushers, with 124 yards on twenty-seven attempts.

Mike Papas recalled, "The Crowley game was a turning point. They weren't a bad team. We played a good first half, though. We then backtracked a bit and got beat at Brownwood because of a couple of big plays."

On October 3, North Crowley dropped a home game to the Brownwood Lions 30–7. The loss dropped the Panthers to 1–4 overall and 1–1 in District 8–4A play. Lance Moss said, "About the only highlight was our only touchdown. I scored on a ninety-nine-yard run. We were just trying to move the ball from the goal line so we could have a little more room to punt, but I ended up breaking it."

Matt Panfil also had the misfortune of becoming injured during the contest: "Against Brownwood, I separated my shoulder. I had intercepted a pass and came down wrong. When I hit the ground, I hurt it badly. I missed over half the game. I went to the hospital, and they found there wasn't any structural damage, so I couldn't really hurt it any worse by playing, I just had to manage the pain. I came back from the hospital and went straight to the stadium. I wanted to go back in, but Coach Papas wouldn't let me. I had to miss the next game against Brownwood, too. I was disappointed because I really wanted to beat them!"

After the Panthers lost to Brownwood, things didn't get any easier, as they had to face two District 8–4A favorites, Stephenville and Aledo, in back-to-back road games. On October 10, however, the Panthers pulled off a huge upset, defeating the Stephenville Yellow Jackets in a 13–7 upset. The Yellow Jackets entered the game 4–1 and 2–0 in District 8–4A play.

North Crowley sacked Stephenville quarterback Conner Elms eight times and limited the Yellow Jackets' ground attack to minus-seventeen yards on the night. The Panthers scored with just twenty-nine seconds left in the first half when, after returning a punt of thirty-eight yards, Lance Moss threw a five-yard touchdown pass to David Nickle. North Crowley added a third-quarter touchdown by Brandon Martin on a nine-yard run to make it 13–0. On the night, Martin ran for eighty-one grueling yards on twenty-five carries. Stephenville finally scored with 5:50 left to play to make the score 13–7. On the Panthers' next possession, the play of the night and possibly of the 2003 North Crowley season belonged to Panthers punter Tyson Reich. Late in the game, nursing a slim six-point lead and punting from deep in his own territory, Reich decided to fake the punt and ran twelve yards for a first down on a fourth and six play. The Panthers ran out the clock from there, and they were now 2–3 overall and 2–1 in District 8–4A play.

Mike Papas recalled Tyson Reich's key play: "Ken Kershaw coached our punters. He had taught them to read the play before they kicked the ball. If there was no rush, they could try a fake punt to make a first down. That's what happened with Stephenville. Our regular punter was out, and we had our middle linebacker, Tyson Reich, filling in. Well, there was no rush—so he takes off and gets the first down. I remember saying, 'You better make it, you SOB!' Thankfully, he did, and we ran out the clock."

Matt Panfil added, "I really wanted to play against Stephenville, but my shoulder was hurt. It was their homecoming. We used to play a lot of teams' homecoming games. Tyson Reich, who lived down the street from me, was our backup punter that night. He was pretty good. I had been taught to look around before I punted and, if I saw an opening, run for it. I did that a few times. Well, Tyson faked that punt at the end of the game to help us beat Stephenville. I told him later, 'If you hadn't have made it, you would have had to go to the Stephenville sideline—not ours.'"

Mike Papas also talked about an auspicious series of circumstances surrounding the Stephenville contest, which he believed impacted the Panthers' entire season: "Before the Stephenville game, God gave me a vision. The Fort Worth paper ran an article about a game that had happened eighty years prior, on the very same day: Notre Dame played Army, and they were both powerhouses. The great sportswriter Grantland Rice wrote the article, which talked about Notre Dame and their famous starting backfield, the 'Four Horsemen.' Well, one of the Four Horsemen was named Jim Crowley, the same last name as our school. Notre Dame pulled off the upset that

Lance Moss and Matt Panfil meet at midfield for the coin toss for a key district game against state powerhouse Stephenville. North Crowley pulled off a 13-7 upset win. Courtesy of Matt Panfil

year against Army 13–7, with Jim Crowley leading the way. Rice even talked about the blue-gray October sky on the day the game was played—basically our school colors. I told our kids about my vision before the game. And what's really crazy is that our 13–7 score matched Notre Dame's win over Army. It felt like destiny. It was the turning point for us."

Next up for the Panthers on October 17 was a matchup at Aledo. The Bearcats were 5–1 overall and 3–0 in district. Aledo had developed into a state powerhouse under head coach Tim Buchanan. The Bearcats were in the midst of a streak where they made the playoffs every year from 1996 to 2023, winning twelve state titles. But on this night, the North Crowley Panthers would not be denied, as they pulled their second improbable road win in a row—this time by a 10–6 count. North Crowley's defense dominated the night, giving up only nine first downs and fifty-six yards rushing. The Panthers' defense also had three interceptions and two fumble recoveries. Just as important, North Crowley was turnover-free on the evening. The Panthers struck first on the night early in the second quarter, when Casey Stuhlman hooked up with Deon Finley on a forty-seven-yard scoring pass. North Crowley added to their lead with 8:04 left in the first half when Matt Panfil connected on a thirty-six-yard field goal to make it 10–0. In the third quarter, North Crowley played keep-away from Aledo, with two time-consuming drives that ended up with no points for the Panthers. Aledo finally got on the scoreboard with 9:41 left to play on a sixty-three-yard-pass play. North Crowley, as they had done with frequency all season, blocked the crucial extra-point attempt to keep the margin at four, and the Panthers held on from there for the win.

The District 8–4A schedule now favored the Panthers. With wins over perennial powers Stephenville and Aledo, North Crowley held the tiebreaker over those two schools for a playoff spot. The remaining district schedule was set up favorably for the Panthers. They faced Granbury, Joshua, and Fort Worth Brewer—teams with a combined 3–9 in district play.

On October 24, North Crowley faced up against Granbury in an away game. Granbury was 2–5 overall and 2–2 in district. The Panthers pummeled the Pirates 30–0 with another dominating defensive performance. They held Granbury to four first downs and 110 total yards on the night. Meanwhile, North Crowley ran for 259 yards and passed for 121 more. The night was not without hardship, though, as North Crowley lost quarterback Casey Stuhlman to a season-ending broken leg on a keeper play late in the second quarter. Lance Moss filled in for the rest of the game and the season. Before Stuhlman's injury, he had hit Deon Finley with a thirty-five-yard scoring play in the first quarter to open the scoring on the night. Brandon Martin ran for 154 yards on twenty-six carries, and Moss filled in capably in the second half for the Panthers as he ran for one touchdown and threw for two more.

The loss of Stuhlman left North Crowley with yet another challenge to overcome. The Pirates did the best they could to regroup and now had to rally around the somewhat untested Lance Moss, who had been starting at safety on defense.

"Casey Stuhlman was a great kid," Mike Papas recalled. "Lance Moss took over at quarterback for us. I feel that he was one of the best athletes in the state in Class 4A. He was a great hurdler in track. He was a starter on defense at defensive back. Sometimes late in games, we would get him some snaps at quarterback to give him some experience—just in case we needed him. He was one of the first real dual-threat quarterbacks in the state of Texas. It was lights out once he took over at quarterback. He took our offense to a new level. Casey was a good quarterback, but I don't know if we could have won state without Lance taking over."

Matt Panfil added, "We were pretty much a running team. We gave the ball to Brandon Martin, who we knew by the nickname Peanut, and let him run with it. Casey Stuhlman, our quarterback, broke his leg against Granbury, and I was on the field when it happened. He broke his leg, and I remember his foot was hanging down by his butt. They had to put a rod in his leg, and he was in the hospital for over a week. I love Casey Stuhlman. He was big and strong, but he wasn't a great athlete. Lance Moss took over for him. Lance was a weird X factor. In high school football, you have to put the ball in the hands of your best athletes. And Lance was an incredible athlete. We would tell him something like, 'Lance, do a front flip,' and even though he had never done one before, he would do it. He was by and far the fastest athlete in the state. He could break off a run for eighty yards at any time."

Tim Buchanan, the Aledo coach, said this about North Crowley: "The other kid North Crowley had at quarterback was a good quarterback. He wasn't going to turn the ball over. Lance Moss, though, was an athlete. The game after they beat us, their quarterback broke his leg, and Moss took over full time. North Crowley was great defensively, with players like Matt Panfil. Once Moss took over, their offense could score more points to help out their defense."

Lance Moss gave his assessment on taking over at quarterback: "Casey Stuhlman broke his leg in the Granbury game and was done for the season. He's a great guy. We had rotated some at quarterback, but once he got hurt, I was taking snaps full time. My taking over changed the team. I was lucky—the team rallied around me. I admit I felt a little pressure now that the team had turned to me. My backup was a freshman, so it was pretty much on my shoulders. I guess I was one of the early dual-threat quarterbacks. When I took over at quarterback, we were heavy on the option. Passing was not my strong suit. I was an athlete, so I used my legs. Not too many people could keep up with me. I ended up winning state in the 110-meter hurdles in the spring."

Halloween brought a home contest against the Joshua Owls. Joshua was 4–4 overall but was only 1–4 in district play. With Lance Moss under center for the first time, the Panthers beat the Owls 30–17. Joshua jumped on North Crowley early, scoring a touchdown on their first possession. The Panthers tied it at seven, when Lance Moss threw a twenty-yard touchdown pass to Andre Dixon. Moss added a seventeen-yard touchdown run in the second quarter, and Matt Panfil kicked a forty-seven-yard field goal late in the second quarter to put North Crowley up 17–7 just before the half. Joshua came out in the third quarter like they did in the first, as they scored ten points to tie the game at seventeen. With just over two minutes left in the third quarter, Moss and Dixon hooked up again, this time on a fifty-yard scoring play. In the fourth quarter, the Panthers added an insurance touchdown, this time on a thirty-eight-yard run by Moss. In his first night as the Panthers' starting quarterback, Moss led all rushers with 146 yards on twenty-one carries and passed for another 133 yards on seven completions. North Crowley was now over .500 overall for the first time all season, at 5–4, and their District 8–4A mark stood at 4–1, with one more district game to play.

The Panthers' final regular-season game was on November 7 against the Fort Worth Brewer Bears, 4–5 overall and 2–4 in District 8–4A play. North Crowley hung on for a close 14–10 victory over the Bears, clinching a playoff spot in the Class 4A Division I playoffs. Stephenville, who ended the regular season undefeated, and Aledo, who came in third, would represent District 8–4A in the Division II playoffs.

Trailing Brewer 10–7, Mike Papas made a crucial decision with two seconds to go in the third quarter. Papas called a timeout to force Brewer, who faced a fourth and twenty from their own five-yard line, to punt into a strong wind. The punt traveled into the wind only thirty-two yards, and Lance Moss picked up the ball for the Panthers and returned it down to the Bears' five-yard line. Three plays later, Moss scored from the one with 10:25 to play. With the score now 14–10 North Crowley, the Panthers' defense took over, limiting Brewer to forty-two yards total offense on their last three possessions. The Panthers limited the Bears to eighteen yards rushing on eighteen second-half carries.

The Panthers' two-game streak got Lance Moss and the team ready for the playoffs, as Mike Papas recalled: "Lance Moss got his feet wet and got ready for the playoffs during our last two games against Joshua and Brewer. In our last game against Brewer, we overlooked them a little bit, I think because we had already qualified for the playoffs."

Mike Papas was taking no chances and wanted his team as prepared as possible for a potential playoff run. He said, "Since this was our first time in the playoffs, I turned to Steve Freeman of Brownwood for some help and advice. He did some nice things for me. One thing he shared with me that we used with our players was a playoff book. Steve sent me a copy of his. It was a well-guarded secret, but he let me use it as an example. The playoff book was a reference point for the players that we would use in meetings. It had everything in there, like messages from the senior players and coaches, the opposing teams' records and what their uniforms looked like, what the stadiums we were playing at were like, the state 4A playoff brackets, and more. These were details that we felt would make our kids more comfortable and at ease."

The Panthers were preparing for their first playoff game in school history. Their opponent was 10–0 Fort Worth Arlington Heights at Birdville ISD's stadium on November 14.

Mike Papas said, "Our first-ever playoff game in the history of our school was against Arlington Heights. We knew the first game would be tough because we had never been there before. I was concerned about getting that first win under our belt."

"We were told how bad we were going to get beat all week," Matt Panfil added. "People forget we came out of the toughest district in the state, so we had been tested. We knew they were 10–0 and were pretty good, but when we got together the Sunday before the game at our usual spaghetti dinner, we would say things to each other like, 'You mean to tell me you can't block this guy?' We had a new sense of confidence that didn't even exist in years past."

The North Crowley Pirates took their first playoff game in school history, beating the Arlington Heights Yellow Jackets 28–14, as Brandon Martin rushed for 172 yards and four touchdowns for the Panthers. North Crowley capitalized on three miscues early in the game that did in the Yellow Jackets. In the first quarter, Arlington Heights' punter was tackled at his own two after a low snap, setting up Martin's first score. Later in the quarter, the Yellow Jackets muffed a punt at their own forty-three, setting up another Martin score. The next time Arlington Heights had the ball, they threw an interception, and the Panthers returned it to their opponent's seven. Martin scored from the five-yard line two plays later, and North Crowley went into halftime with a 21–7 lead. The Panthers added to that lead in the third quarter when they blocked a Yellow Jackets' punt at their two-yard line. From there, Martin went in for his fourth touchdown of the night, and the Panthers led 28–7. Arlington Heights added a third-quarter touchdown to make the 28–14 final.

With the victory, the Panthers moved on to face the 7–4 Wichita Falls Rider Raiders on November 21 in Wichita Falls. Although the Panthers got off to a slow start, giving up a seventy-three-yard touchdown run on the first play of the game, the Panthers took a 30–16 victory. The opportunistic defense once again helped lead the Panthers to victory. After the opening touchdown by Rider, the Panthers' defense settled down, allowing only forty-seven yards the rest of the way. North Crowley linebackers Deante Jones and Terryn Taylor each forced fumbles in the second half that were converted into touchdowns. The Panthers also had three sacks and two interceptions. Senior tackle Rahmmad Jones returned a fumble twelve yards for a touchdown to give North Crowley a 21–10 third-quarter lead, and senior offensive lineman Rubin Beckner recovered a fumble in the end zone in the fourth quarter for another score. North Crowley also had a special team's touchdown when Lance Moss, who also ran for 110 yards in the victory, returned a Raiders punt seventy-one yards for a score in the second quarter to put North Crowley up at halftime 14–10.

Lance Moss talked about his big punt return: "I loved returning punts. I loved being back there by myself, knowing I could change the game with just one return. That's what happened against Rider. Coach Kerbow had taught us how to build a wall to the left or right to block for me. The return against Rider was to the left, and I eventually cut back across the grain. The only player to beat ended up being the punter, and I easily outran him to the end zone."

Matt Panfil recalled, "Rider was much better than Arlington Heights. It took a big team effort to beat them. Some guys made some really big plays. I remember hearing that their wide receiver and utility back committed to Notre Dame—I don't know if he ended up there or not. Their quarterback ended up at Baylor. We fell behind on the first play as their guy took it to the house. I missed a tackle on the play, so it was partially my fault. We had to battle back after that."

"To show you how much our players' confidence had grown and how resilient they were," Mike Papas added, "Rider scored on the opening play of the game, a seventy-three-yard run. After that, one of our assistant coaches on offense, who had a son on the team, told his boy, 'Just go out and have a good time.' His son came back with, 'Dad, we got this. We're better than they are.' It was the strongest case of a complete buy-in by the players that I had ever seen."

North Crowley now advanced to the Region I finals against another surprise team, the El Paso Riverside Rangers, to be played on November 29 at historic Ratliff Stadium in Odessa. The 10–2 Rangers were trying to make history. By beating El Paso Irvin in their bi-district playoff game and then upsetting Amarillo Palo Duro High School 20–7, Riverside became the first 4A team from El Paso to make it to the quarterfinals since 1964.

Mike Papas recalled, "Riverside had a very capable program inside the city of El Paso. They were well respected. They had beaten Amarillo Palo Duro, and that got our attention. We took the bus to Ratliff Stadium in Odessa. Playing there was probably a bigger deal for our coaches than our players, since the coaches knew all about Odessa Permian and *Friday Night Lights*. Ken Kershaw, our special teams coach, was kind of our staff history buff. He was a big Texas high school football historian, so going to Odessa and Ratliff Stadium was a big deal to him. For a lot of the players, especially some of our kids whose families didn't have that much money, this was their first overnight stay out of town somewhere, along with taking a chartered bus and having meals in restaurants. I was a little worried that our kids would get distracted by all the special treatment, but that wasn't the case."

When the bright lights of Ratliff Stadium came on, it was the North Crowley defense that capitalized on four Riverside turnovers, and those miscues helped propel North Crowley to a 35–8 win over the El Paso Riverside Rangers. The Panthers forced four Riverside turnovers, with William McLaughlin returning a third-quarter Riverside fumble for a forty-four-yard touchdown. For the second straight game, a Panthers offensive lineman recovered a North Crowley fumble for a touchdown. Curtis Bridges recovered a Lance Moss fumble in the end zone in the second quarter to give North Crowley a 14–0 halftime lead. The Panthers' defense limited Riverside to just 179 total yards, with fifty-six of those yards coming on the Rangers' lone scoring drive late in the fourth quarter. North Crowley themselves had only 225 total yards, including just fifteen passing, but one of Lance Moss's three completions did go for a six-yard touchdown pass in the fourth quarter to put North Crowley up 35–0. Moss added a thirty-nine-yard touchdown run in the third quarter. Brandon Martin led all rushers with 156 yards on twenty carries, including a one-yard touchdown run for the Panthers to open the scoring in the first quarter.

Matt Panfil reflected on his team's newfound confidence: "We knew that if we took care of business, we would take Riverside. They just couldn't match up with us. They played hard, but we were just better."

The North Crowley Panthers advanced to the Class 4A Division I semifinals, where the foe that awaited them was slated to be much more formidable than El Paso Riverside. Waiting in the wings for the Panthers on December 5 at nearby Texas Stadium in Irving was the number-one-ranked Class 4A team in the state, the defending state champion, and the owners of a twenty-two-game winning streak: the 13–0 Texarkana Texas High School Tigers. The Tigers had outscored their opposition 387–106 on the season and had recorded four shutouts. However, since star senior quarterback Chris Marshall was out for the game for disciplinary reasons, the Tigers were led in this contest by freshman Ryan Mallett, who as a senior in 2006 became the top quarterback in the state of Texas. Mallett went on to play at Michigan, Arkansas, and in the NFL.

Mike Papas reminisced about the matchup: "Nobody gave us a chance against Texarkana. They were the defending state champs and had won twenty-two in a row. One sportswriter said that we were a seven-touchdown underdog. He said it would be the most lopsided playoff game in state history. They were good, with ten starters back on offense. Both of their wide receivers ended up playing at the University of Texas. Freshman Ryan Mallett was filling in at quarterback. They were loaded."

"There was a local sportswriter and journalist by the name of Matt Diggs, and he said we were forty-nine-point underdogs," Matt Panfil mused. "People weren't giving us a chance. Texarkana had won twenty-two games in a row. Their offensive line averaged three hundred pounds per man. You didn't see that back in 2003. They had several players go to the University of Texas. I went to a Nike summer camp with some of their players, and they were something else—very talented. Ryan Mallett was the best true freshman I'd ever seen. Me and Tyson Reich were watching film of Texarkana on the way back from Odessa, and I admit I was nervous watching it. I just didn't want to be embarrassed."

Mike Papas discussed how the two schools agreed on where and when the game was going to be played: "Texarkana had played their game on Friday night. We played on Saturday. Barry Norton, the Texarkana coach, flew to Odessa, and after our game we met to decide our playoff site for the semifinal. Back then, coaches had total control over which site they would play at. We ended up playing at Texas Stadium, which was very close for us, just being in Irving. Texarkana had to travel a few hundred miles. But we had to play on December 5—a Friday night instead of Saturday—which meant we had one less day to prepare for the game than Texarkana did. I had to get it across to the kids that none of that mattered. Let's get ready to play the game."

Matt Panfil described a key moment right before kickoff: "As Tyson Reich and I are walking out to midfield, getting ready to do our captain thing, I said to him, 'I just hope it's close.' Tyson said, 'Yeah, me too.' When we got out there, the Texarkana captains refused to shake our hands and were saying things like, 'You're effin' sorry' and 'You don't deserve to be here'—stuff like that. I looked at the referee, and he just kind of shrugged his shoulders like, 'What can I do?' We went back to the sidelines and told the team what Texarkana had done to us, and that really got us fired up."

And indeed, Panfil's strategy must have worked, because that night, the North Crowley Panthers pulled off one of the biggest upsets in Texas high school football history as they shocked the number-one-ranked Texarkana High School Tigers 17–13 at Texas Stadium. The Panthers' defense rose to the occasion once again, limiting the Tigers to just eighty-one yards rushing on the night. Ryan Mallett did pass for 213 yards but was just thirteen for thirty-seven throwing. Mallett also suffered two interceptions—the last one on a Matt Panfil pick in the end zone with just fifty-four seconds to play. North Crowley's Brandon Martin had his fourth straight playoff game, with more than one hundred yards with 104 yards on twenty-two carries. Martin also scored both of the Panthers' touchdowns.

North Crowley opened the scoring in the game on a twenty-six-yard field goal in the first quarter by Matt Panfil. Texas High responded with a ten-play, eighty-seven-yard drive of their own for a score. The Tigers used a trick play as receiver Nathan Jones received a lateral and pulled up and threw a six-yard touchdown pass to Quinton Hope. Martin scored his first touchdown on a four-yard run with forty-four seconds left to go until halftime, to give the Panthers a 10–6 halftime edge. The touchdown was set up by North Crowley's second blocked punt of the game, this one by Matt Panfil—something they had specialized in all season.

Mike Papas explained, "Blocked punts were the key against Texarkana. We blocked at least one punt in every playoff game. Against Texarkana, we blocked two and got a hand on a third. I believe we led the state in blocked punts for the season. We worked on it a lot. In fact, it was hard to work on punt returns in practice because they would block so many punts."

Matt Panfil blocks a Texarkana punt, helping lead the North Crowley Panthers to a 17–13 state semifinal win, breaking Texarkana's twenty-two-game winning streak. Courtesy of Matt Panfil

Texarkana forged back ahead 13–10 at the end of the third quarter, thanks to a seventy-one-yard-pass play from Mallett to Quentin Hope. North Crowley immediately struck back with Martin's five-yard touchdown run, with 11:27 remaining in the game. Martin's touchdown was set up after Lance Moss connected with Andre Dixon on a fifty-four-yard-pass play down to the Tigers' five.

Papas remarked on the Moss-to-Dixon completion that set up the winning touchdown: "We also completed our longest pass play of the season against them. Lance hit Andre Dixon with that long pass in the fourth quarter to set up our go-ahead touchdown. I knew at some point in the season our passing game would come through when we needed it—and it did."

Lance Moss gave his assessment of the big pass play: "I'll be honest with you—I was usually afraid to pass the ball because I wasn't so good at it, and I was scared it was going to be intercepted. On the pass to Andre Dixon, though, I threw it perfectly. I faked the throw to our outside receiver, Matt Panfil, and I threw it to Andre, our inside receiver. Andre was not the fastest guy in the world, and he was caught before he scored. Brandon Martin ran it in, though. He was a beast. Our nickname was 'Thunder and Lightning.' He was thunder; I was lightning."

The game was still in doubt when Panfil came up with his game-clinching interception. Mike Papas recalled, "With just a few seconds left with us up 17–13, they were inside our forty and tried a deep pass down the sideline. They threw it into double coverage, and Matt Panfil came up with the interception in the end zone on his back. What a win. It was a total team effort: offense, defense, and special teams. After the game, we knew we had accomplished something big. We were ecstatic, but we were not satisfied. We had one more game to go."

Matt Panfil recalled a satisfying moment at the end of the contest: "After the game, some guy came up to interview me. He was a short, squatty guy with long hair, and he said he wanted to do a live webcast. He said his name was Matt Diggs with Texas PrepXtra. I said, 'Hey, you're the guy who said we were going to lose by seven touchdowns! I don't want to do an interview with you!' So I left him hanging."

The Panthers were now set to play for the Class 4A Division I state title. Their opponent would be another traditional Texas high school football powerhouse, the Bay City Black Cats. Before anything could happen, though, the two teams had to decide on a site and date for the championship game. Mike Papas said, "Since we played on a Friday night, we drove to San Antonio to the Alamodome to watch the other semifinal, Bay City against Corpus Christi Calallen. It was a good game, and Bay City pulled it out. I felt Calallen had a sounder football team, but Bay City was very athletic—almost as much as we were. Coach Cherry and I sat down after the game to make plans for our game. I didn't want them to play two games in a row at the Alamodome, and it was only about an hour and a half away for them as opposed to four and a half hours for us. We decided on Kyle Field at Texas A&M. It was about the same distance for both of us. Bay City was a coastal school, a lot farther south than we were, and we wanted to play them outside—not indoors like the Alamodome. At game time, it was about thirty-eight degrees, which was an advantage for us. We were a little more accustomed to the colder weather."

Bay City was indeed a powerhouse. They had won the state Class 4A title in 2000 and were runner-up in 2001 under Chad Morris, who went on to win two more state titles at Austin Westlake in 2008 and 2009 and later became the head coach at SMU and Arkansas. Morris left after the 2002 season, and Alan Cherry was in his first season with the Black Cats. He had successful stops at Hart, Hamlin, and Crane, recording ten-plus wins in ten of his thirteen seasons as a head coach. The 13–1 Black Cats had won a series of close games to reach the finals, beating Friendswood 21–17, Dayton 22–16, Beaumont Central 13–3, and Corpus Christi Calallen 23–21.

As usual, the Panthers were decided underdogs and got little respect from the prognosticators. Six out of seven sportswriters with the *Fort Worth Star-Telegram*, the hometown newspaper for North Crowley, chose Bay City to bring home the crown. The day before North Crowley played Bay City for the championship, sports editor Jeff Blackmon of the *Hood County News* summed up the sentiments of most high school football fans in the state: "If you would have told me before the start of the 2003 football season that North Crowley would be playing for a state title and would have gone further than Aledo and Brownwood—I would have gone to the looney bin. Goes to show that in sports, you never know what may happen."

Mike Papas recalled, "Once again, we didn't get much love from the sportswriters before this game. I can't say I blamed them, though. Bay City was very talented. They had several Division I players on their roster, and they had a lot of tradition. They had been there before."

Matt Panfil also commented on the Panthers' lack of respect: "Our pep rallies were pretty pathetic. I've been to other schools' pep rallies, so I know what a good one looks like. I remember our pep rally before we played Bay City for state. They said, 'Stand up if you believe we can win!' Only about a third of the students stood up. Even our own classmates didn't think we could win. We were the redheaded stepchild of the area. Crowley didn't claim us, but Fort Worth didn't either—even though our school and a lot of the students had Fort Worth addresses. Before our senior year, everybody would come to the games to watch the band. After they finished their halftime show, most of the fans would go home. For away games, the band would charter buses while we were stuck riding the old yellow school buses. I remember my junior year, we would always have announcements on the TV before class. I always remember on Mondays, the announcers would come on and say sarcastically, 'Well, the football team lost again.'"

Despite (once again) getting little respect from the media or fans, on December 13 in College Station, the North Crowley Panthers upset the Bay City Black Cats for the Class 4A Division I state title. Although North Crowley had fewer total yards than Bay City, 264 to 319, the Panthers capitalized on five Black Cats turnovers to pull off another upset, this time by a count of 20–6. Bay City seemingly controlled the first half everywhere except for the scoreboard, as they outgained North Crowley 140 yards to just 65 but turned the ball over three times and trailed 7–0 at the break. North Crowley capitalized on a Bay City fumble at their own forty-three and drove fifty-seven yards in eight plays to score with 4:50 to go in the second quarter. Lance Moss rang up the score for the Panthers with a keeper from the one-yard line.

After the Panthers' touchdown, Bay City drove the ball all the way to the North Crowley eight just before halftime but suffered an interception to kill the drive. The Panthers then took the second-half kickoff and proceeded to drive eighty yards to go up 13–0, the last yard coming on a Moss pass to tight end David Nickle. Bay City immediately came right back with a three-play, eighty-three-yard drive, the last play being a seventy-yard scoring strike from the Black Cats' Scott Elliot to Shaun Green. After a missed extra point, North Crowley led 13–6 with 7:50 to go in the third quarter.

Matt Panfil mentioned his thoughts on the Black Cats' score: "In the third quarter, I made a tackle on the Bay City sideline. Someone caught me with their cleat in my groin. Not only did it hurt like the devil; it broke the skin. They had to take me to the locker room at Kyle Field to get checked out. As I was going up the runway to the locker room, I turned around and watched the very next play, and they scored on a long touchdown pass. We were in a Cover 2, and it was on my side of the field. If I had been in the game, I probably would have stopped it. I ended up getting back out on the field just in time to kick the extra point after Lance scored his touchdown on our next possession. My pants weren't even buttoned. After I came back, I ended up picking off two passes."

On the Panthers' next possession after Bay City's touchdown, Moss retaliated with a fifty-six-yard sprint to the end zone, which put North Crowley up 20–6. Bay City could never mount a serious threat after that, as two more interceptions gave the Black Cats five turnovers on the evening.

Lance Moss recalled, "On my touchdown run, I faked the ball to Brandon Martin. Our guard, Rubin Beckner, pulled and helped provide my blocking. I used to love running behind Rubin. He would always open up big holes for me. Well, he did this time, too. As I was heading down the sidelines, I thought I was all by myself. Nobody had ever caught me from behind. But a Bay City defensive back caught up with me because he had the angle on me. He tried to bring me down short of the goal line, but I dove over him and barely scored."

Years later, Mike Papas summed up what was a typical North Crowley victory: "To be honest with you, it was a boring game. We were not going to let them light up the scoreboard. We knew if we played good special teams, played ball control, and kept good field position, we would play to our strengths. We knew what we were good at, and we tried to maximize it. The fans in the stands may have

Mike Papas and Matt Panfil hold the Class 4A, Division 1 state championship trophy after a 20-6 victory over Bay City. Courtesy of Matt Panfil

thought it was boring, but we didn't care. We were used to winning ugly. We had done it all season."

Papas then recalled how he felt in the moments after the win: "It's funny—you're as happy as you can be, but there's emptiness. We loved each other. This was the last time I would see this team together. It was over. It felt like a punch in the nose. It was fun to be around this group of kids. The coaches and kids were good for each other."

Aledo coach Tim Buchanan said about the Panthers' miracle run to the state title: "I remember telling Mike Papas before the playoffs, 'Y'all are gonna win state. You're going Division I, and the only school in your way is Texas High in Texarkana. They'll find a way to screw it up.' Sure enough, they did. Their star quarterback was busted as he was getting on the bus to go to Texas Stadium. Now Texas High had to play a freshman."

Matt Panfil gave his impressions also: "They had a parade after we won the title, and it wasn't that well attended. That was okay, though—we still had each other, and in the end, that's what really mattered. After that 'Come to Jesus' meeting earlier in the season, we started believing in something that was bigger than us individually. We learned what we could accomplish if we all worked together. What we did was so unique."

Lance Moss concluded, "Our team was very disciplined. We were not the fastest or the biggest team out there, but we got it done. We played field position football and limited our turnovers. We really didn't have any blowout wins. We kind of won ugly and played totally as a team. We truly were the 'Band of Brothers.'"

After their improbable run to the state title, North Crowley under Papas made two more trips to the playoffs, going 7–4 in 2004 and 9–2 in 2005, losing both first-round playoff games. Four more losing seasons under Papas followed, and he left North Crowley after the 2009 season to take a college coaching job at East Texas Baptist University in Marshall. Papas's overall record in twelve seasons for the Panthers stood at 51–77–0. After Papas left, North Crowley's record from 2010 through 2021 stood at 38–83–0. The five wins the Panthers rang up on their road to the 2003 Class 4A Division I state title remain the only playoff wins in school history until the 2021 team secured a first-round win.

When all was said and done, the 2003 Class 4A Division I state championship by North Crowley topped them all. Greg Tepper, managing editor of *Dave Campbell's Texas Football* magazine, wrote an article that ranked the most surprising state champions in Texas high school football history.

North Crowley topped the list. Tepper said, "When we talk about unsuspecting state champions, this is the gold standard, and we may never see anything quite like it again. For one, North Crowley was basically a nobody in Texas high school football. Over its previous five seasons, the Panthers had won a grand total of thirteen games . . . and when the Panthers made the playoffs, it was their first appearance ever. Secondly, North Crowley found itself in a district of heavyweights, like Brownwood and Aledo and Stephenville. Thirdly, North Crowley wasn't particularly amazing at anything. What North Crowley could do, though, was make the big play at the big time . . . and became the most unlikely state champions in Texas history."

Sources

INTERVIEWS

Alborn, Ray: October 30, 2019
Arnold, Louis: July 2, 2019
Autry, Gary: July 12, 2019
Barbee, Larry: November 22, 2019
Bennett, Brandon: March 31, 2020
Bomar, Jerry: August 16, 2019
Braley, Larry: October 11, 2019
Briles, Art: December 2, 2019
Brnovak, Gaylon: September 18, 2019
Buchanan, Tim: August 16, 2020
Burchers, Jack: June 27, 2019
Burnett, Phillip: March 18, 2020
Bussey, Ray: November 12, 2019
Dyer, John: January 28, 2020
Gilder, Gordon: January 7, 2020
Guilbeaux, Mark: April 7 and 22, 2020
Harvey, Doug: July 9, 2019
Hobrecht, Fred: July 8, 2019
Hodges, Randy: January 25, 2020
Hunter, Bill: July 8, 2019
Jennings, David: July 10, 2019
Jones, Lenoy: April 14, 2020
Keil, Robert: April 7, 2020
Key, Randy: November 24, 2019
Kittley, Rob: October 9, 2019
Kloss, Alan: July 9, 2019
Lamb, John: October 6, 2019
Lisle, Mike: November 22, 2019
Mauldin, Tony: August 12, 2019
McCain, Vic: April 1, 2020

McMillan, Harrison: December 16, 2019
Morrison, Barry: November 18, 2019
Moss, Lance: March 16, 2020
Oliver, Barney: November 13, 2019
Panfil, Matt: March 22, 2020
Papas, Mike: July 24, 2019
Peterson, Ike: August 2, 2019
Pittcock, Nolan: November 21, 2019
Prestridge, Mark: December 23, 2019
Reagan, Richard: August 11, 2019
Rueda, David: January 14, 2020
Russell, Charlie: July 10, 2019
Scott, Bubba: October 24, 2019
Scott, Jacob: November 16, 2019
Setterbo, Jacob: November 19, 2019
Shaver, Steve, Jr.: June 30, 2019 and October 6, 2020
Shaver, Dee Dee: November 21, 2019
Slape, Roy: January 20, 2020
Smith, Dave: November 28, 2019
Snyder, Bobby: March 11, 2020
Stewart, Mike: November 15, 2019
Thompson, Sherwood: May 16, 2015
Turner, Cole: October 7, 2019
Vanover, Finis: July 1, 2019
Walkoviak, Gene: April 17, 2020
Williams, Doug: July 6, 2019
Williams, Wilbur: November 18, 2019
Wilson, Jasper: October 27, 2019

NEWSPAPERS

Abilene Reporter-News
Archer County News
Austin American Statesman
Baxter Bulletin
Baytown Sun
Beaumont Enterprise
Big Lake Wildcat
Brownsville Herald
Brownwood Bulletin

Cameron Herald
Childress Index
Clifton Record
Corpus Christi Caller-Times
Corsicana Daily Sun
Del Rio News
El Paso Times
Fort Worth Star-Telegram
Galveston Daily News
Gatesville Messenger
Groesbeck Journal
Hood County News
Kerrville Mountain-Sun
Kountze News
Liberty Vindicator
Llano News
Longview News-Journal
Lubbock Avalanche-Journal
Marshall News-Messenger
McAllen Monitor-Sun
Odessa American
Paris News
Port Arthur News
Rockport Pilot
San Antonio Express
Silsbee Bee
Tyler Courier Times
Valley Morning Star
Vernon Daily Record
Victoria Advocate
Waco News Herald
Waco News Tribune
Wise County Messenger

Index

Page numbers in italics refer to figures.

Akins, Eddie, 125, 127, 134
Alamo Stadium, 12, 105–106
Aledo Bearcats, 178, 182
Alice Coyotes, 7, 8
Alpine Bucs, 88
Alvarado Indians, 179–80
Anders, Steve, 67
Anderson, Charles, 41, 44, 46–47, 51
Anderson, Greg, 112
Anderson, Roger, 50
Aransas Pass Panthers, 162
Archer City Wildcats, 18, *19*; *vs.* Big Lake Reagan County Owls, 30–32; Bussey's role, 19, 20, 22, 25, 26, 30, 31, 35; *vs.* Clifton Cubs, 28–30; *vs.* Crowell, 24; *vs.* Electra, 21–22; Gary Tepfer's role, 20, 21, 23, 24–25, 27–31, 33–35; *vs.* Goldthwaite Eagles, 27–28; Graves's role, 19–21, 22, 26, 35–36; *vs.* Henrietta Bearcats, 23; Holder's role, 21, 23, 24, 27; *vs.* Holliday, 23; *vs.* Ingleside Mustangs, 32–35; *vs.* Keller Indians, 26–27; *vs.* Knox City Greyhounds, 24–25; Morrison's role, 20–21, 22, 24, 25, 27, 32, 34; *vs.* Munday Moguls, 25; *vs.* Nocona, 21; Oliver's role, 20, 23, 29, 31, 33; *vs.* Olney Cubs, 22; Robert Tepfer's role, 31, 34; Stewart's role, 19, 20, 21–22, 24, 27, 29–31, 33–34; *vs.* Throckmorton Greyhounds, 24; winning Class A state title, 35
Arnold, Louis, 41, 45, 46, 48
Austin-Bergstrom International Airport, 37
Austin High School, El Paso, 78
Autry, Gary, 157–58, 161–62, 165, 172–74

Baer, Brett, 164
Bailey, Charles, 131
Balderrama, David, 82
Barbee, Larry, 62–63, 65, 66–68, 70–71
Bass, Dean, 7, 11, 14, 17
Bay City Black Cats, 191–94
Beaumont French Buffaloes "Buffs," 96–97; *vs.* Aldine Mustangs, 105–106; Cedric Jones's role, 106; *vs.* Charlton-Pollard Cougars, 105; *vs.* Dickinson Gators, 99; District 22-5A season, 97–88; *vs.* Forest Brook Jaguars, 99–100; *vs.* Galveston Ball Tornadoes, 109–10; Guilbeaux's role, 98, 99–103, *103*, 105–108, 113; *vs.* Houston Sterling Raiders, 107–108; Keil's role, 98–104, 107–108, *108*, 110–14; *vs.* LaPorte Bulldogs, 106–107; *vs.* Nederland Bulldogs, 101–102; *vs.* Odessa Permian Panthers, 111–15; Paul Jones's role, 99, 101, 102, 104, 108–10; *vs.* Port Arthur Jefferson Yellow Jackets, 100–101; *vs.* Port Arthur

Lincoln Bumblebees, 99; *vs.* Port Neches–Groves Indians, 100; *vs.* San Antonio Madison Mavericks, 110–11; Shaver's role, 97–98, *98*, *103*, 103, *115*, 115–16; Shaver Jr.'s role, 104–106, *108*, 109, 111–12, *115*, 115–16; Turner's role, 98, 101, 105–106, 108, 109; Vanover's role, 108–109, 111, 114; *vs.* Vidor Pirates, 102; *vs.* West Brook Bruins, 102–104; *vs.* West Orange–Stark, 104, 105; Williams's role, 102–107; Wycoff's role, 99, 100, 113
Beckner, Rubin, 186–87
Beeville Jones Trojans, 10, 165–66
Bellard, Emory, 14–16, 158, *158*
Bellville Brahmas, 145–46
Bennett, Brandon, 137–39, *140*, 142–49, 151–52, 154
Big Lake Reagan County Owls, 30–32
Big Sandy Wildcats, 72; Harper's role, 72; Mitchell's role, 72, 73–74; Overstreet's role, 72; Smith's role, 72–73
Big Thicket National Forest of East Texas, 37
Bissinger, H. G. "Buzz," 117, 129
Blackmon, Jeff, 192
Blue Ridge Tigers, 124
Bobb, Norris, 103
Bomar, Jerry, 136–37, 142–45, 149–51, *150*, 153–55
Boyd, Larry, 126
Brackens, Tony, 143
Brahmas: *vs.* Alice Coyotes, 7–8; *vs.* Beeville Trojans, 10; *vs.* Breckenridge Buckaroos, 14–17; *vs.* Cleburne Yellow Jackets, 13–14; *vs.* Corpus Christi College Academy Cavaliers, 9; *vs.* Cuero High School, 7–8, 10; *vs.* Edinburg High School, 7, 8; *vs.* Falfurrias Bulls, 11; Harvey's role, 2, 4; Hobrecht's role, 2–3; Holland's role, 1–2, *2*, 7, 17; *vs.* McAllen Bulldogs, 8; Pilot's role, 4–7; *vs.* Port Lavaca Calhoun Sandcrabs, 10; *vs.* Robstown Cotton Pickers, 7, 10–11; *vs.* San Antonio Sam Houston, 11–13; *vs.* San Antonio Tech Buffaloes, 8; Thompson's role, 3–4; *vs.* Tivy Antlers, 9
Braley, Larry, 118–21
Breckenridge Buckaroos, 14–17
Bremond Tigers, 129–32
Bridges, Curtis, 188
Briles, Art, 60–61, *61*, 63–64, 66–71, 75–76
Briles, Dennis, 59–60, 61, *63*, 70, 75, 77
Briles, Wanda, 75
Brown, Joshua, 41
Brown, Tyrone, 140, 141, 145
Brown v. Board of Education, 3
Brownwood Lions, 178, 180
Bryant, Malcom, 86
Buchanan, Tim, 182, 184, 195
Buna Cougars, 45
Burchers, Jack, 2, 10, 13; about game against Breckenridge Buckaroos, 15; about Houston, 6; about Kerrville's trip, 9; about match against McAllen Bulldogs, 8; about Pilot, 5
Burnet Bulldogs, 45–47, 150–53
Burnett, Philip, 119, 121, 124, 126–28, 130, 133
Bussey, Ray, 19, 22, 25, 26, 30, 31, 35

Calallen Wildcats, 172–74
Cameron Yeomen, 50–51
Canutillo Eagles, 89–90
Cash, Norm, 78
Cathedral Irish, 82
Celeste Blue Devils, 125
Charlton-Pollard Cougars, 105
Cherokees, 11, 12
Cherry, Alan, 192

Childress Bobcats, 92–95
Childress, Jim, 27
Childs, Don, 30–31, 32
Chillicothe, 63–64, 67, 69
Chisum Mustangs, 122
Cleburne Yellow Jackets, 13–14
Clifton Cubs, 28–30
Clint, 84–85
Coastal Bend area of Texas, 3
Collins, Edwin, 41, 51–52, 54
Colts, 83
Comer, Chris, 123
Cooke, Shannon, 85
Cooper, Dwrain, 152
Copperas Cove, 47–48
Corpus Christi College Academy Cavaliers, 9
Corpus Christi Miller Bucs, 162–63
Cougars, 75–76
Crockett Bulldogs, 52–53, 139, 142–43, 151
Crowell, 24
Crowley High School Eagles, 180
Crowley, Judy, 25
Cuero High School, 7–8, 10
Culpepper, Pat, 13

Dallas Carter High School, 129–30, 132
Danaher, Phil, 172–74
Danbury, 74
Daniels, Tommy, 9
Dave Campbell's Texas Football magazine, 118–19, 121, 195–96
Del Valle Cardinals, 37–38; Anderson's role, 41, 44, 46–47, 51; Arnold's role, 41, 45, 46, 48; Brown's role, 41; *vs.* Burnet Bulldogs, 45–47; *vs.* Cameron Yeomen, 50–51; Collins's role, 41; *vs.* Copperas Cove, 47–48; *vs.* Elgin, 44–45; expectations for 1967 season, 43; fall of, 55–56; *vs.* Georgetown, 47; Hilgers's role, 41, 47; *vs.* Kenedy Lions, 47; *vs.* Kountze Lions, 53–55; Lamb's role, 39, 44, 46, 47, 50–51, 53, 55; *vs.* Llano Yellowjackets, 46; *vs.* Longhorns, 50; Moreland's role, 44–45, 46, 50–51; *vs.* Round Rock, 47; *vs.* Schulenberg Shorthorns, 44; Shaver's role, 38–39, 55; Smith's role, 38–39, 41, 43–44, 55; *vs.* Smithville Tigers, 46; *vs.* Tomball Cougars, 51–52; Williams's role, 39, 41, 45, 46, 50
Del Valle High School, 37
Detroit Eagles, 124–25
Dickinson Gators, 99
Dixon, Andre, 184, 191
Doaks, Henry, 52
Dungy, Tony, 73
Dyer, John "Rocky," 79, 80, 83, 84, 86, 89–90, 94–95

East Chambers Buccaneers, 48
Edinburg High School, 7, 8
Edna Cowboys, 148–50
Electra, 21–22
Elgin, 44–45
Elms, Conner, 181
El Paso Riverside Rangers, 187–88
El Paso Socorro Bulldogs, 82–83
Emerson, Gover "Ox," 158

Fabens Wildcats, 78; *vs.* Alpine Bucs, 88; Balderrama's role, 82; *vs.* Canutillo Eagles, 89–90; *vs.* Cathedral Irish, 82; *vs.* Childress Bobcats, 92–95; *vs.* Clint, 84–85; *vs.* Colts, 83; Dyer's role, 79, 80, 83, 84, 86, 89–90, 94–95; *vs.* El Paso Socorro Bulldogs, 82–83; *vs.* Gadsden Panthers, 82; Gallo's role, 80; Genaro Rodriguez's role, 82; Harvey

Gonzalez's role, 82; Joe "Burger" Rodriguez's role, *85*, 85–86; Jose Rodriguez's role, 80; *vs.* Kermit Yellow Jackets, 85–87, 90; *vs.* Marfa Shorthorns, 83; Maurice Hodges's role, 78–79, *79*, 81, 95; Ortega's role, 80; Ortiz's role, 80, 88, 92; Randy Hodges's role, 79, 81–85, 87–88, 90, 92–94; Rivera's role, 80, 82, 83, 86, 88–89, 92, 93; Rueda's role, 80, 81, 83–84, 86, 88–89, 91–92, 94, 95; Sims's role, 94; Slape's role, 80, 81–83, 87–92, 94; Sonny Rodriguez's role, 83, 88; *vs.* Stamford Bulldogs, 91–92; *vs.* Van Horn Eagles, 87–88; Zavalas's role, 84
Fairfield Eagles, 143–44, 147–48
Falfurrias Bulls, 11
Fannindel Falcons, 118; Akins's role, 125, 127, 134; *vs.* Blue Ridge Tigers, 124; Boyd's role, 126; Braley's role, 118–21; *vs.* Bremond Tigers, 129–32; Burnett's role, 119, 121, 124, 126–28, 130, 133; *vs.* Celeste Blue Devils, 125; *vs.* Chisum Mustangs, 122; *vs.* Detroit Eagles, 124–25; Fields's role, 133–34; *vs.* Flatonia, 132–33; Gaffney's role, 133; *vs.* Gunter Tigers, 127–28; *vs.* Honey Grove Warriors, 122; Jones's role, 122, 124–27, 131–32, 133; *vs.* Maud Cardinals, 121, 125; McCain's role, 119, 120–21, 124–27, 131, 133, 134; *vs.* Mount Enterprise Wildcats, 126–27; Nichols's role, 128; *vs.* Prairieland Patriots, 122; *vs.* Union Hill Bulldogs, 121, 125–26; Wilburn's role, 122, 124, 125, 127, 131; Williams's role, 119–26, 129–32, 134–35; Woods's role, *119*, 119, 122, 133, 134; *vs.* Wortham Bulldogs, 128–29
Fannindel High School, 117, 118
Fields, Glenn, 121, 132–34
Finley, Deon, 182, 183
Flatonia, 130, 132–33
Flores, Arturo, 7
Floresville Tigers, 168–69
Flour Bluff Hornets, 164–65, 170–71
Forest Brook Jaguars, 99–100
Fort Worth Arlington Heights, 176, 185–86
Fort Worth Brewer Bears, 183, 185
Fort Worth Metroplex, 176
Frederick Douglass High School, Kingsville, 3, 5
Friday Night Lights (Bissinger), 74, 111, 117, 119, 135; about Class 5A semifinal playoff site controversy, 129–30; racial discrimination against Miles, 123
Fulbright, David, 85, 86, 90

Gadsden Panthers, 82
Gaffney, Steve, 133, 134
Gallo, Jesus, 80, 88
Galveston Ball Tornadoes, 109–10
Garcia, John, 33
Georgetown, 47
Gibson, Charles, 145, 148
Gilder, Gordon, 39, *41*, 41–43, 45, 48–51, 53–58
Goldthwaite Eagles, 27–28
Gomez, Fernie, 89
Gonzalez, Harvey, 82
Granbury, 183–84
Grant, Vernon, 101
Graves, Grady, 19–21, 22, 26, 35–36
Gregory-Portland Wildcats, 161, 162, 166–67
Groesbeck, Abram, 136
Groesbeck Goats, 136; *vs.* Bellville Brahmas, 145–46; Bennett's role, 137–39, *140*, 142–49, 151–52, 154;

Bomar's role, 136–37, 142–45, 149–51, *150*, 153–55; Brown's role, 140, 141, 145; *vs.* Burnet Bulldogs, 152–53; *vs.* Crockett Bulldogs, 139, 142–43; *vs.* Edna Cowboys, 148–50; *vs.* Fairfield Eagles, 143–44, 147–48; Gibson's role, 145, 148; *vs.* Hamshire-Fannett Longhorns, 146–47; *vs.* Hardin-Jefferson, 153–54; Jones's role, *138*, 138–41, 144, 146, 148–50, 152–53; LeNoir's role, 142; *vs.* Mart Panthers, 140–41; *vs.* Mexia Black Cats, 139, 141–42; Morgan's role, 141; *vs.* Palestine Westwood Panthers, 142; *vs.* Robinson Rockets, 141; Sherrod's role, 146; Smith's role, 142, 143; *vs.* St. Pius Panthers, 141; Tatum's role, 141; *vs.* Teague Lions, 143; *vs.* Waco Robinson Rockets, 144–45
Guffey, Steve, 126
Guilbeaux, Mark, 98, 99–103, *103*, 105–108, 113
Gunter Tigers, 127–28

Hamshire-Fannett Longhorns, 50, 146–47
Hardin-Jefferson Rebels, 48, 153–54
Harper, Lawrence, 72
Harvey, Doug, 2, 4, 9–12; 1958 season memories, 8; about game against Cleburne Yellow Jackets, 14; about Houston, 6–7; about Kerrville's trip, 9; match against Breckenridge Buckaroos, 16; about Pilot, 5
Hayward, Nicky, 131
Haywood, James, 28, 29
Henrietta Bearcats, 23
Hentschel, Jerry, 115
Hilgers, Bill, 41
Hilgers, John, 41, 47
Hobrecht, Fred, 2–3, 9; about match against McAllen Bulldogs, 16–17; about Pilot, 7
Hodges, Maurice "Moe," 78–79, *79*, 81, 95
Hodges, Randy, 79, 81–84, 87–88, 90, 92–94
Holder, Billy, 21, 23, 24, 27
Holland, Russ, 1–2, *2*, 7, 17
Hollinger, Johnny Mac, 161
Honey Grove Warriors, 122
Hope, Quinton, 190
Horton, Walter, 32
Houston Lamar, 176
Houston Sterling Raiders, 107–108
Houston, Woody, 6
Howard, Johnny, 30, 32
Huddleston, Charles, 16
Hughes, Detrick, 101
Hull-Daisetta Bobcats, 33, 51
Hunt, Bud, 66, 71
Hurricane Harvey, 156

Ingleside Mustangs, 32–35

Javelinas, 1
Jay, Donald, 2, 3
Jayton Jaybirds, 66
Johnson, Robert, 49
Johnson, Ronnie, 8, 14, 17
Johnston, Charlie, 92, 94
Jones, Bobby, 33, 34
Jones, Bruce, 122, 124–27, 131–32
Jones, Cedric, 106
Jones, Deante, 186
Jones, Lenoy, *138*, 138–41, 144, 146, 148–52
Jones, Nathan, 190
Jones, Paul, 99, 101, 102, 104, 108–10
Jones, Rahmmad, 186
Jones, Willie, 7
Joshua Owls, 183, 184–85

Keil, Robert, 98–104, 107–108, *108*, 110–14
Keller Indians, 26–27
Kenedy Lions, 47
Kerbel, Joe, 14–15
Kermit Yellow Jackets, 85–87, 90
Key, Randy, 156–57, 160–63, 166, 167, 169, 171, 173–75
Kirbyville Wildcats, 45
Kittley, Elsie, 75
Kittley, Rob, 62, *64*, 64, 66, 67, 69–71, 73, 76
Knox City Greyhounds, 24–25, 65–66
Kountze Lions, 37–38; *vs.* Buna Cougars, 45; *vs.* Crockett Bulldogs, 52–53; *vs.* Del Valle Cardinals, 53–55; *vs.* East Chambers Buccaneers, 48; expectations for 1967 season, 43–44; Gilder's role, 39, *41*, 41–43, 45, 48–51, 53–58; *vs.* Hamshire-Fannett Longhorns, 50; *vs.* Hardin-Jefferson Rebels, 48; *vs.* Kirbyville Wildcats, 45; *vs.* Hull-Daisetta Bobcats, 51; McMillan's role, 40, 42, 53; Moody's role, 51–54; *vs.* Newton Eagles, 45; *vs.* Port Acres Austin Eagles, 48–50; *vs.* San Antonio Randolph Ro-Hawks, 56; Sims's role, 41, 53, 57–58; Snyder's role 39–40, 43–44, 49, 56; *vs.* St. Mary's Hornets, 45; Tate's role, 39–41, *44*, 55, 58; *vs.* West Hardin, 45; Williams's role, *40*, 40, 42, 43, 57; Wilson's role, 40; *vs.* Woodville, 45

Lamb, John, 39, 44, 46, 47, 50–51, 53, 55
The Last Picture Show (McMurtry), 18
Lemmons, Jerrod, 128
LeNoir, Marty, 142
Lisle, Jimmy, 60
Lisle, Mike, 60, 61, 62, 64, 66–68
Looney, Lee, 24
Loraine Bulldogs, 67
Luker, James, 9

Macias, Jimmy, 66, 71
Mallett, Ryan, 188–90
Marfa Shorthorns, 83
Marshall, Chris, 188
Martin, Brandon, 181, 183, 190
Martinez, Sergio, 88
Mart Panthers, 140–41
Matador Matadors, 70–71
Maud Cardinals, 121, 125
Maxwell, Mitchell, 152
McAllen Bulldogs, 7, 8
McCain, Vic, 119, 120–21, 124–27, 131, 134
McKone, Jim, 11–13
McLaughlin, William, 188
McLemore, Jim, 13–14
McMillan, Harrison, 40, 42, 53
McMurtry, Judy, 26
McMurtry, Larry, 18, 35–36
McReavy, Richard, 30
McWilliams, David, 13
Merket, Eddie, 67
Mexia Black Cats, 139, 141–42
Miles, James "Boobie," 119, 122–23, 134
Mitchell, Bobby, 73–74
Mitchell, Mike, 115
Moody, Larry, 51–54
Moreland, Bobby, 44–45, *46*, 50–51
Morgan, Derrick, 141
Morren, Perry, 93
Morris, Chad, 192
Morrison, Barry, 20–21, *22*, 24, 25, 27, 32, 34
Moss, David, 162, 163–65, 167–70
Moss, Lance, 177–78, 180–81, *182*, 183–85, 187, 191–95
Mount Enterprise Wildcats, 126–27

Munday Moguls, 25, 66
Murray, Jeffrey, 108

Nava, Ace, 162
Nederland Bulldogs, 101–102
New Braunfels, 171–72
Newton Eagles, 45
Nguyen, Dat, 156, 157
Nichols, Gary, 128
Nickle, David, 181, 193
Nocona, 21, 23
Nolan, Leo, 115
No Pass No Play policy, 118
North Crowley High School, 176
North Crowley Panthers, 176; *vs.* Aledo Bearcats, 178, 182; *vs.* Alvarado Indians, 179–80; *vs.* Bay City Black Cats, 191–94; *vs.* Brownwood Lions, 178, 180; Class 4A Division I state championship, 195–96; *vs.* Crowley High School Eagles, 180; *vs.* El Paso Riverside Rangers, 187–88; *vs.* Fort Worth Arlington Heights, 185–86; *vs.* Fort Worth Brewer Bears, 183, 185; *vs.* Granbury, 183–84; *vs.* Joshua Owls, 183, 184–85; Martin's role, 181, 183; Moss's role, 177–78, 180–81, *182*, 183–85, 187, 191–95; Panfil's role, 178, 179–80, 183, 184, 186–90, *190*, 193–95, *194*; Papas's role, 176–80, 183, 185–87, 189–92, *194*, 194–95; Reich's role, 181, 189; *vs.* Stephenville Yellow Jackets, 178, 180–81; *vs.* Texarkana Texas High School Tigers, 188–91; *vs.* Wichita Falls Rider Raiders, 186–87
North Crowley Pirates, 186

Odessa Permian Panthers, 111–15, 117–18; Class 5A semifinal playoff site selection, 129–30; Comer's role, 123; *vs.* Dallas Carter, 132; Miles's role, 119, 122–23, 134
Odessa, Texas, 117–18
Oliver, Barney, 20, 23, 29, 31, 33
Olney Cubs, 22
Ortega, Ramon, 80
Ortiz, Jerry, 80, 88, 92
Overstreet, David, 72

Panfil, Matt, 178, 179–80, 183, 184, 186–90, *190*, 193–95, *194*
Papas, Mike, 176–80, 183, 185–87, 189–92, *194*, 194–95
Pavelka, Jessie, 173
Pesch, Joe Ed, 16
Phillips, "Bum," 97
Phillips, Chuck, 153
Phillips, Marcus, 124
Pilot, James "Preacher," 4–5, 12, 17; 1958 season memories, 8; Kerrville's trip memories, 9; match against Breckenridge Buckaroos, 16; praise from teammates, 5–7
Pittcock, Nolan, 61, 63, 70, 74
Pitts, Billy, 34
Pleasanton Eagles, 168
Port Acres Austin Eagles, 48–50
Port Arthur Jefferson Yellow Jackets, 100–101
Port Arthur Lincoln Bumblebees, 99
Port Lavaca Calhoun Sandcrabs, 10, 167–68
Port Neches–Groves Indians, 100
Prairieland Patriots, 122
Prosper Eagles, 70

Reagan, Richard, 153
Reich, Tyson, 181, 189
Revel, Cody, 163
Rhoads, Leonard, 66, 69
Rhoden, Alton, 9

Richard King High School Brahmas. *See* Brahmas
Rising Star Wildcats, 69–70
Rivera, Ernie, 80, 82, 83, 86, 88–89, 92, 93
Robinson, Adrian, 148, 149
Robinson, Bo, 129, 131
Robinson, Floyd, 3
Robinson Rockets, 141
Robinson, Wendell, 129
Robstown Cotton Pickers, 7, 10–11
Rochester, 67–68
Rockport–Fulton Pirates, 156; *vs.* Aransas Pass Panthers, 162; Autry's role, 157–58, 161–62, 165, 172–74; *vs.* Beeville Jones Trojans, 165–67; Bubba Scott's role, 159, 166; *vs.* Calallen Wildcats, 172–74; *vs.* Corpus Christi Miller Bucs, 162–63; *vs.* Floresville Tigers, 168–69; *vs.* Flour Bluff Hornets, 164–65, 170–71; *vs.* Gregory-Portland Wildcats, 161, 162, 166–67; Jacob Scott's role, 160–64, 166–74, *167*; Key's role, 156–57, 160–63, 166, 167, 169, 171, 173–75; Moss's role, 162, 163–65, 167–70; *vs.* New Braunfels, 171–72; Nguyen's role, 156, 157; *vs.* Pleasanton Eagles, 168; *vs.* Port Lavaca Calhoun Sandcrabs, 167–68; *vs.* San Antonio Alamo Heights Mules, 169–70; *vs.* San Antonio Jay Mustangs, 163–64; Setterbo's role, 160, 165, 167–68, 175; Soriano's role, 162, 163, 166, 168, 171; Surrell's role, 164, 165, 167; Walkoviak's role, 159; *vs.* West Orange–Stark, 174; winning celebration against New Braunfels, *172*
Rodriguez, Genaro, 82
Rodriguez, Joe "Burger," 80, *85*, 85–86
Rodriguez, Sonny, 83, 88
Roquette, Cody, 161–62
Roquette, Luke, 161–62
Round Rock, 47
Rueda, David, 80, 81, 83–84, 86, 88–89, 91–92, 94, 95
Rule Bobcats, 59; Art Briles's role, 60–61, *61*, 63–64, 66–71, 74; *vs.* Aspermont Hornets, 65; Barbee's role, 62–63, 65, 66–68, 70–71; *vs.* Big Sandy Wildcats, 72–75; *vs.* Chillicothe, 63–64, 69; Dennis Briles's role, 59–60, 61, *63*, 70, 75, 77; Hunt's role, 66, 71; *vs.* Jayton Jaybirds, 66; Jimmy Lisle's role, 60; Kittley's role, 62, 64, *64*, 66, 67, 69–71, 73; *vs.* Knox City Greyhounds, 65–66; *vs.* Loraine Bulldogs, 67; Macias's role, 66, 71; *vs.* Matador Matadors, 70–71; Merket's role, 67; Mike Lisle's role, 60, 61, 62, 64, 66–68; *vs.* Munday Moguls, 66; *vs.* Newcastle Bobcats, 68; Pittcock's role, 61–62, 63, 70, 74; *vs.* Prosper Eagles, 70; Rhoads's role, 66, 69; *vs.* Rising Star Wildcats, 69–70; *vs.* Rochester, 67–68; *vs.* Santa Anna, 66–67; *vs.* Throckmorton Greyhounds, 64–65, 68; Turner's role, 62, 63; Wilson's role, 60, 61, 73, 74–77; Wood's role, 59

San Antonio Alamo Heights Mules, 169–70
San Antonio Jay Mustangs, 163–64
San Antonio Madison Mavericks, 110–11
San Antonio Sam Houston, 11–13
San Antonio Tech Buffaloes, 8
Sandefer, Carrie Lynn, 15
Sandefer, Jake, 15
Santa Anna, 66–67
Schott, Marty, 154

Schulenberg Shorthorns, 44
Scott, Bubba, 159, 166
Scott, Darrol, 131
Scott, Jacob, 160–64, 166–74, *167*
Sedberry, Marvin, 115
Setterbo, Jacob, 160, 165, 167–69, 175
Shaver, Dee Dee, 38, 97, 106, 114–15
Shaver, Steve: role as Beaumont French Buffaloes' coach, 97–98, *98*, 103, *103*, 114–16, *115*; role as Del Valle Cardinals' coach, 38–39, 46, 55
Shaver, Steve, Jr., 104–106, *108*, 109–12, *115*, 115–16
Sherrod, Keith, 146
Shotwell, Pete, 14
Sims, Donald, 94
Sims, James, 41, 53, 57–58
Slape, Roy, 80, 81–83, 87–92, 94
Smith, Bill, 106
Smith, Dave, 38–39, 41, 55; about expectations for 1967 season, 43; about match against Schulenberg Shorthorns, 44
Smith, Lovie, 72–73
Smith, Rock, 142, 143
Smithville Tigers, 46
SMU, 58
SMU Mustangs, 75
Snyder, Bobby, 39–40, 43–44, 49, 56
Solis, Brian, 173
Soriano, Alan, 162, 163, 166, 168, 171
Southern Methodist University (SMU), 58; SMU Mustangs, 75
Southlake Carroll, 150–51
Spencer, Alvin, 69
Stamford Bulldogs, 91–92
Stephenville Yellow Jackets, 178, 180–81
Stevens, Steve, 71
Stewart, Mike, 19, 20, 21–22, 24, 27, 29–31, 33–34
St. Mary's Hornets, 45
St. Pius Panthers, 141
Stuhlman, Casey, 182, 183
Surrell, Ernie, 164, 165, 167

Tate, Ted, 39, 55, 58; leading Kountze Lions in practice, *44*; praise from teammates, 39–41
Tatum, Elgrick, 141
Taylor Ducks, 38
Taylor, Terryn, 186
Tepfer, Gary, 20, 21, 23, 24–25, 27–31, 33–35
Tepfer, Robert, 31, 34
Tepper, Greg, 195–96
Texarkana Texas High School Tigers, 188–91
Texas A&I. *See* Texas A&M University
Texas A&M University, 1–2, 72, 92, 156
Texas Football magazine, 118–19, 121, 195–96
Thompson, Sherwood, 3–4; about Pilot, 5
Throckmorton Greyhounds, 24, 64–65, 68
Tilson, Tom, 71
Tivy Antlers, 9
Tomball Cougars, 51–52
Traylor, Tommy, 30
Turner, Cole, 62, 63
Turner, Melvin, 98, 101, 105–106, 108, 109

Union Hill Bulldogs, 121, 125–26

Van Horn Eagles, 87–88
Vanover, Finis, 108, 111, 114
Vidor Pirates, 102

Waco Robinson Rockets, 144–45
Walkoviak, Gene, 159, 161

Walshe, Jean, 9
Ware, Andre, 99
West Brook Bruins, 102–104
West Hardin, 45
West Orange–Stark, 104, 105
Whitaker, Bill, 8
Whitaker, Richard, 164
Whitely, Buzzy, 148
Wichita Falls Rider Raiders, 14, 186–87
Wilburn, Steve, 122, 124, 125, 127, 131
Wildcats. *See* Archer City Wildcats
Williams, Doug, 119–26, 129–32, 134–35
Williams, Fred, *40*, 40, 42, 43, 57
Williams, Wilbur, 39, 41, 46, 50–52
Williams, Willie, 102–107
Wilson, Derrick, 107
Wilson, Jasper, 60, 61, 73, 74–77
Wilson, William, 40
Winger, Rickey, 54
Wood, Gordon, 59, 178
Woods, Fred, *119*, 119, 122, 133, 134
Woodville, 45
Wortham Bulldogs, 128–29
Wozniak, Pat, 158, 161, 174
Wycoff, Keith, 99, 100, 113

Ysleta High School, El Paso, 78

Zavala, Harvey, 84